Al-Khoei Fo...
Wishes you ...
Eid Al-Ga...
& Eid Al-Mubahala
14th January 2007

GW01090266

مؤسسة الإ

DATION

4

THE SHI'AH
ORIGIN AND FAITH

Allama Muhammad Husayn Kashif al-Ghita
Najaf al-Ashraf-Iraq

Published by
Cultural and Guidance Section
AL-KHOEI FOUNDATION

THE SHI'AH — ORIGIN AND FAITH
Original Title: *Aslush Shi'ah Wa Usuloha*

First Published in Pakistan in 1980 by
ISLAMIC SEMINARY PUBLICATIONS
A Publishing Division of
ISLAMIC SEMINARY PAKISTAN
P.O. Box 5425, KARACHI-74000
This impression 2002

Copyright © Islamic Seminary Pakistan
All rights reserved

ISBN 0-941724-23-9

Mailing Address
The General Secretary,
Al-Khoei Foundation,
Chevening Road,
London NW 6,
ENGLAND

Conditions for Sale
This book or any part thereof is sold subject to the condition that it shall not by way of any trade or otherwise be lent or resold, hired out or otherwise circulated in any form of binding or cover other than what it is published in, without a similar condition including this condition being imposed on the subsequent purchaser or donee, except with prior written permission of the copyright owner.

The Commander of the Faithful
Imam Ali(P) wrote to his followers:

وَهُوَ اسْمٌ شَرَّفَهُ اللّٰهُ فِى الكِتَابِ فَإِنَّهُ يَقُولُ: " وَاِنَّ مِنْ شِيْعَتِهِ لَا بْرَاهِيْمَ "
وَاَنْتُمْ شِيْعَةُ نَبِيِّ مُحَمَّدٍ ...اِسْمٌ غَيْرُ مُخْتَصٍّ وَاَمْرٌ غَيْرُ مُبْتَدَعٍ

"Allah has favoured the word SHI'AH by using it in the Holy Qur'an. He says: *Verily Ibrahim was one of the Shi'ah of Nuh*, and you are amongst the Shi'ah of Muhammad (Peace be on him and his progeny). This name is neither restricted to a particular group nor is it a newly adopted religion".

What the Holy Imam really meant is that since he himself is the vicegerent of the Holy Prophet his Shi'ah are in fact the Shi'ah of the Holy Prophet.

(Mustadrak Nahjul Balaghah, part II, Page 29

Ayatullah Kashif al_Ghita

بِسْمِ اللهِ الرَّحْمٰنِ الرَّحِيمِ

اَلْحَمْدُ لِلهِ الَّذِى عَلَّمَ بِالْقَلَمِ
عَلَّمَ الْإِنْسَانَ مَا لَمْ يَعْلَمْ
وَصَلَّى اللهُ عَلَى مُحَمَّدٍ وَآلِهِ وَسَلَّمْ

Contents

Foreword

The history of the Shi'ah Faith of Islam has been the history of blood and tears. Scattered through its pages are events replete with persecution and sufferings. On the intellectual level, the Shi'ah Faith has been misunderstood and, therefore, misconstrued. A minor prejudice at the top assumes alarming proportions by the time it reaches the masses. A minor difference among the scholars becomes the bone of contention. It is, therefore, not surprising that there should be a terrible misrepresentation of our faith and our beliefs. Since the Shi'ah happen to be in minority it is easy for their opponents to use their venomous efforts to defame them. Their image is disfigured, their views are distorted, their beliefs are misrepresented. The Shi'ah Faith is presented, both in form and contents, in a manner which is totally opposed to its reality. This is really a source of grave injustice which must be nipped in the bud.

When we examine the causes of this pathetic plight of the Shi'ah Faith, we come to the painful realization that partly we ourselves have also been responsible for it. If our opponents misconstrue our intentions and misrepresent our cause, it is something we can easily understand. However, when we take stock of what we ourselves have done in this respect, we find that we have miserably failed to counteract the prejudiced statements of the narrow-minded opponents.

This fact will become crystal clear when we look at our publicity media. Everyone knows that in modern times

9

publicity is the very tongue we speak with. Without publicity, we are no more than dumb fellows. One can imagine how a dumb man can plead his case. The question is: Do we have this tongue? Do we make our voice heard? What publicity channels do we have in foreign lands? How is our cause presented to others? What literature is there to project the Shi'ah Faith? If the answers to these questions are in the negative, are we not justified to be called tongue-less and dumb. If in such a state of affairs we are misunder-stood, the fault is no doubt ours.

It is true that books and treatises have been published. They are good in a way but the question here is whether they meet the requirements of the situation as it stands, not only among the Muslims but also among the non-Muslims. We stand all the more handicapped when our beliefs have to be interpreted and explained in the light of new developments in the field of science and technology.

The truth is that we are like silkworms weaving round ourselves a big cocoon of superstitions and imaginary supports, not knowing that we are making ourselves captives of our own superstitions. It is good to have a fort for self-defence but the fort should not turn into a prison for ourselves. Once we lose contact with the outside world and once we get sidetracked from the latest developments in life around us, we become backbenchers to begin with, ultimately to sink into oblivion in due course of time.

The Christians have their missions all over the world. They have powerful publicity media. There is an influx of their literature. There is a flood of their propaganda. How do we stand as compared to them? The question of our being eloquent and logical does not at all arise. It is thus evident that our cause goes by default. It is thus apparent that Islam gets misunderstood even among the Muslims themselves, much less to be said about the non-Muslims.

It is our own faults which make ourselves misunder-stood by our Sunni brethren as well as the non-Muslims. This is the plight of our social life! When we look within ourselves, we find that our superstitious and vague customs are the biggest weapons in the hands of our adversaries.

These irrational usages provide material for anti-Shi'ah propaganda in the hands of others.

There are certain rites and rituals being followed by the credulous and ignorant people. Unfortunately they are attributed to Shi'ah beliefs and practices. Lighting candles before the oven; fastening materials to the drinking fountains; reciting of the tragedies of Karbala near a pot containing Samnu (a dish with juice of germinating wheat or malt mixed with flour), cooking soup ascribed to the name of Imam Zaynul Abidin with well-known formalities and ceremonies, dried fruit associated with the name of Imam Ali Mushkil Kusha, dramatization of the events of Karbala, providing water and broom to welcome Khizr and a host of other rituals are the stock in this trade. What wonder if they recoil on our own discredit!

If we study the hostile propaganda against the Shi'ah we still find at its root superstitions and meaningless rituals. So far as the basic articles of our faith are concerned they stand resplendent in all their purity and sublimity and not a shadow of doubt has been cast upon them.

The gist of the whole thing lies in the doublefold action of clearing the deck and putting the house in order. The first is the need to cleanse our house of these superstitions and the second is to establish powerful publicity media with two specific objectives in mind. One is to present the Shi'ah Faith in its pristine purity and glory and the other is to counteract the hostile propaganda in the most effective manner possible.

Kāshiful Ghita, the great Shi'ah saint and research scholar has very rightly enunciated the Faith in the Ja'farite Jurisprudence by publishing his renowned book **Aslush Shi'ah wa Usuloha** in Arabic. By dint of the might of his powerful pen and by his analytical approach, he tore asunder the screen of superstitions that had over shadowed the true complexion of Shi'ah Beliefs and presented to the Mulims in general the Shi'ah Faith in its original purity. His brilliant exposition of the Shi'ah case was aimed at proving the fact that the Shi'ah neither were a sect of idolaters nor were they a sect outside the pale of Islam.

11

The book was aimed at convincing all the ranks of the Muslims that the Shi'ah never considered Imam Ali to be an incarnate of Allah or to be more suited and more entitled to the Prophethood than the Holy Prophet himself! It was further to prove that the Shi'ah were not at all guilty of introducing innovations in Islam or of tampering with the text of the Holy Qur'an.

On the contrary it was intended to show that in the matter of basic principles and fundamental beliefs as well as in the subsidiary issues, the Shi'ah Faith has derived profusely from the Holy Qur'an and Hadith (traditions) and from the teachings of Ahlul Bayt (the Holy Progeny) being closest to the Holy Prophet Muhammad, peace be on him and his progeny, and on account of their being fully conversant with his traditions and being duly imbued with the spirit of those traditions.

It was in this setting that this book has been published. It fulfilled the purpose of its publication so admirably that it had to be reprinted more than 18 times and it ran short of stock every time. Demand for it came from most of the Muslim countries and it had to be translated into numerous languages. In order to make oneself truly acquainted with the truth about the Shi'ah Faith, this book is a must for every Muslim, Shi'ah or Sunni.

This book is a source of guidance even for the followers of Ahlul Bayt. Through it, they can learn the truth about themselves and their faith. As regards the Muslims in general it will serve as a powerful medium of understanding and conciliation between the two great sects of Islam. With true understanding, there will be opened for all of us the gateways of unity, friendship and amity so that the Muslims should constitute a single and integrated echelon to combat the enemies of Islam, about whom the Holy Qur'an says: *Allah loves those who fight for His cause in ranks firm as an unbreakable concrete wall.* (Surah al-Saff, 61:4)

In view of the great service this book has rendered to the Muslim cause, we pray for the soul of the revered Allama to rest in eternal peace.

Publishers.

About the Book

VIEWS OF THE ORIENTALISTS AND SCHOLARS

The publication of the book, Aslush Shi'ah wa Usuloha occasioned an extraordinary response in the East and West and the Publisher received a larger number of letters about it. Although all these letters are not available with us, we can lay our hands on some of them published in the magazine A'tidāl. We reproduce them below in token of appreciation of this book by great scholars.

A Russian scholar Gratsh Kafiscy from Leningrad writes: "The book **Aslush Shi'ah wa Usuloha**" is a valuable and authentic book. Every scholar would like to read it. I am studying this book along with the book **Fajarul Islam** which I received last year.

A German scholar Zusfashthat from Koniskosiy writes: "Some days ago when I came back from a journey I happened to see the book **Aslush Shi'ah wa Usuloha** I sincerely thank you and Allama Kashiful Ghita for that. I went through it and found myself greatly enlightened by it. I would recommend all seekers of knowledge to benefit themselves from it. Is there anyone better suited to teach the people than the scholar and the learned?

The famous Turkish scholar Dr Hadi Terfi from Istanbul writes: "I have gone through the book **Aslush Shi'ah wa Usuloha** which you have been kind enough to send me. I found it to be a priceless gift. I thank the learned scholar who has compiled this book. I should like to draw the attention of all the orientalists, as soon as I can, towards this book which they should study".

13

Sālim Karankavi, a Professor in the Bonn University (Germany) wrote to the Publisher: "I studied the book **Aslush Shi'ah wa Usuloha** carefully and found it to be a treatise which satiates completely those who are thirsty of correct information about the Shi'ah Beliefs. While confirming the discourse of the learned author of this book, I am of the view that he has furnished such detailed information about the Shi'ah Faith and that too in such a concise manner that it could not have been possible except through a recourse to voluminous writing.

However, is it possible to safeguard all the old beliefs in the advanced society of modern times? I feel that if the Holy Prophet were still alive, he would have declared permissible certain things which were prohibited previously. For example, we find that the esteemed author of the book has personally permitted a photograph of his to be taken, although according to some sects it is not permissible. In any case, I am not qualified enough to discuss this and other similar matters. As the object of the learned author has been to explain the Shi'ah Faith as it existed in the early days of Islam has well acquitted himself of this responsibility. I would recommend to the orientalists of this country to obtain this book so that they may be able to make a considerable addition to their knowledge of the subject".

The magazine A'tidāl made the following comments after reproducing this letter: We communicated to Allama al-Ghita the views of Mr. Sālim Karankavi and the opinion which he has offered with regard to photography in the light of Islamic laws is appended below. The Allama remarked as under:

"The pictures which are not permissible in Islam are only those which fall under the catergory of sculpture. Even in that case also they are confined only to the statues of living creatures made by hand. However, religious arguments advanced for porhibiting the making of pictures, do not cover photography by usual or extraordinary means and those arguments do not take these matters into consideration. Hence, these matters are covered by the original permission. However, Islam and its laws are so wide and extensive in character that they become compatible and harmonious with every proper and genuine culture, without creating any difference between the past and the present".

The renowned scholar Ahmad Zaki Pasha wrote from Cairo: "I am highly obliged for the present book (written by the learned scholar Kashiful Ghita). There is no denying the fact that this book has been written in a very beautiful and attractive manner and the author has removed the veil from the face of realities and brought to light true facts about the Shi'ah Faith viz. the faith of the people who till now did not themselves say anything on the subject and did not inform us of their beliefs.

We should be thankful to Prof. Ahmad Amin for his fables about the Shi'ah which he circulated without any investigation and without quoting any references because they prompted Allama Kashiful Ghita to take up the pen and write, with perfect coolness, and to circulate facts about the Shi'ah without injuring the religious sentiments of others. I, however, feel that you have exaggerated while saying that some Egyptians, Palestinians and Syrians consider the Shi'ah to be sinners. I do not consider this among us. The person who has told you to the contrary has perhaps jested or else he must have some evil intentions. However, as regards the contents of some books written by Sunni scholars wherein unjust, contradictory and misleading things have been imputed to the Shi'ah, it may be said that in fact the Shi'ah themselves are responsible for such maligning because they have been negligent as far as acquainting others of their religious beliefs is concerned. In any case these idle talks which gained capital from the political differences of the Ottomans should be abandoned. Unfortunately, both Egypt and Iran were the victims of these inauspicious politics. Notwithstanding the fact that Egypt was a Sunni country, the expansionist and despotic politics of the Turks and non-Turks cared neither for facts nor for religious sentiments.

In short, I believe that this book is very useful for the establishment of Muslim unity which is the basic and an effective factor for all of us. I praise this great scholar who has assumed this great responsibility, the responsibility which cannot be discharged except by those who are like him and by the people whom Almighty Allah has selected for waging war against deviations and for eradication of evils, restoration of real life and rejuvenation of the past glory of Muslim Ummah. I hope that under the auspicies of such sublime activities Muslim Ummah will be in a position to advance, under the shining sun of reality, along with other developed countries of the world".[1]

[1] In a postscript, Ahmad Zaki Pasha has made some observations on the book and has requested the author to furnish a reply. Out of these observations the following two are worth mentioning.

(i) As regards *Mut'ah* (Fixed Time Marriage) he writes: "With all your sound and interesting discussion and reasoning about the Fixed Time Marriage there are still some doubts in my mind in this regard from the point of view of religious and social order. For example, what will be the position of a child who is born as a result of the Fixed Time Marriage, especially when, with the period of the Fixed Time Marriage having come to an end, the father has gone away and the child is born after his departure. Allama Kashiful Ghita has not clarified this ambiguous point in his narrative.

(ii) As regards those who do not believe in the Fixed Time Marriage, you say that they hold views contrary to the explicit contents of the Holy Qur'an. However, in the matter of succession, you yourself believe that in particular circumstances women do not inherit anything (among them being the women under the Fixed Time Marriage). Is this judgement not opposed to the text of the Holy Qur'an? If Caliph Umar has pronounced a particular verdict on the Fixed Time Marriage so have the Imams pronounced verdicts on the inheritance of such women?

As regards the first observation, Allama al-Ghita's reply to this objection is quite clear because, firstly, such an objection can also crop up in the case of a permanent marriage. A man may contract a permanent marriage with a woman in a foreign country and may subsequently divorce her and go away. Supposing then that woman gives birth to a child, what will be the position of that child? Whatever

Continued...

Shakib Arsalān, the renowned scholar and commentator in his letter sent from Geneva wrote as under:

"I received the books sent by you as a gift and made haste to study initially the book entitled **Aslush Shi'ah wa Usuloha** and benefited much from it.

In fact all your writings are very useful and are considered to be very important for the Muslims of our age. The Muslims can find out from them the points on which

decision we take about that child will also apply to the child born under the Fixed Time Marriage. Accordingly there is no doubt that the said child is connected with its father, and it is the duty of the father to support it. In this matter, there is not the least difference between the issue of a permanent marriage and that of a Fixed Time Marriage. The main point is that our Sunni brethren have formed a different picture of the Fixed Time Marriage in their minds. This is under the influence of venomous propaganda of some people. They consider it as something similar to prostitution and fornication which is accomplished simply by reciting the formula of marriage and without any further stipulation or condition. As a matter of fact, this thinking is erroneous. In reply to the second objection he says: "It is admitted by all Muslims that if a tradition is in opposition to the Holy Qur'an, it is totally unauthentic and should be discarded. It is also clear that what is implied by opposition is total opposition viz. the contents of the tradition should be totally in contrast with those of the Holy Qur'an. However, if there is a general order in the Holy Qur'an and a special order in the tradition there should be no objection if we make an exception to the generality of the Qur'anic verse by means of the special tradition. Most of the scholars of Islam, rather all of them, apparently agree regarding the permissibility of making exceptions to the general orders of the Holy Qur'an by a special tradition.

To conclude, the opposition of Umar, the second Caliph to the wording of the verse relating to the Fixed Time Marriage is total opposition and this cannot be allowed for any reason whatsoever. On the other hand the opposition to the Qur'anic verses and the tradition on succession, which prohibit inheritance in certain circumstances, is the opposition between the general and the special, and hence this interpretation is permissible".

the Shi'ah and the Sunni agree and those in which they differ. With your efforts you are reducing as far as possible the gulf between the two sects. While reasoning, you make various propositions the objects of discussion, with sufficient information and clear-cut arguments".

The former American Minister Plenipotentiary in Baghdad, Mr. Leo W. Henderson who is considered to be an Orientalist, wrote thus in his letter to Shaykh Abdul Ghani of Egypt who was a teacher in the School of Allama Kāshiful Ghita: "On my return from a recent journey I have come to know that one of our employees has undertaken the translation of your condensed pamphlet consisting of extracts from the book **Aslush Shi'ah wa Usuloha.** I have by now read the beliefs and the principles of the Shi'ah Faith and in my opinion this pamphlet is the best and the most dependable document on the subject. I am sending a copy of its text in Arabic and its English translation to Washington as I desire that the dignitaries of our government who study developments in this part of the world, like myself, should possess better and more accurate information about the sublime Shi'ah beliefs. Of the various facts which make the value of your pamphlet evident, one is that in spite of my best efforts I have not been able to find in Baghdad a copy of the original book written by Allama Kashiful Ghita".

In another letter, while expressing gratitude for having been supplied with a copy of the original book, he writes: "My friends and I are of the opinion that this book should be translated into English so that all people who know that language, including my countrymen, should become well aware of the Shi'ah School of Islam and its beliefs".

* * * * * *

A Profile of the Allama

Allama Kashiful Ghita has attained immortality as the author of **Aslush Shi'ah wa Usuloha**. With affection, spirit, and freshness, this biography tells the story of one of the most dazzling figures, the Muslim world has ever known.

Here is the intimate side of Kāshiful Ghita's life, his schooling, his working, his journeys and his speeches which have been echoed throughout the Muslim world.

He was born in 1294 A.H. in the Holy City of Najaf Ashraf, Iraq and was named as Muhammad Husayn. On this auspicious occasion a renowned poet of that city composed a beautiful couplet which means: "When his date was settled, Islam was given the good news that soon be would be chosen for the commendation of Imam Husayn".

The prophecy made by the poet, was soon fulfilled. With the passage of time he grew up to be a stalwart among Muslim scholars and one of the most eminent personalities of the Muslim world. What a true prophecy it was!

He was eminently suited for such a position because firstly, he belonged to a family which had for years spread its strong and leafy branches over the heads of the Muslims like a fruit orchard. It was a noble family whose history proceeded along with the glorious history of Najaf Ashraf, and which discharged the responsibilities of the Chief and the Guide of the great religious movement for 180 years i.e. since the time his forefather Shaykh Kizr bin Yahya migrated to Najaf Ashraf from a small town Janaha, situated in the south of Hilla. He was succeeded by

19

his son, Shaykh Ja'far Kabir, a great saint who wrote the well-known book under the caption **Kāshful Ghita**. Saints, scholars and eminent literary men appeared from amongst his brothers, sons and grandchildren each of whom had his share in rendering meritorious services to the world of knowledge and faith till the turn of Shaykh Muhammad Husayn had arrived. He completed his primary education in Najaf Ashraf. Thereafter, he ·began attending lectures of great saints of his time. He learnt *Usulul Fiqh* (Fundamentals of Jurisprudence) from alhāj Riza Hamdani and Muhammad Kazim Yazdi each of whom was a genius of his time. He also benefited from Mirza Husayn Nuri and received a certificate from him with honours. He learnt *Kalām* (Scholastic theology) and Philosophy from Shaykh Ahmad Shirazi, Mirza Muhammad Baqir Istehbanati and Shaykh Muhammad Riza Najafābādi.

On account of the fact that Allah had endowed him with extraordinary intelligence, sagacity and aptitude, he made progress in different branches of knowledge in a short span of time and while he was still young, acquired a position on account of his knowledge which was worthy of recognition so much so that he and his brother Shaykh Ahmad began to enjoy the special confidence of the scholars of the centre of learning, Najaf Ashraf, and especially, the great authority of the time Sayyid Muhammad Kazim Yazdi who entrusted to them the task of sending replies to many questions on religious matters. After the demise of that great authority, a large number of people from Iraq approached Allama Kāshiful Ghita with a view to accepting him as the religious leader. The star of his fortune continued to shine and became more luminous day by day. The people of Iraq became more and more inclined towards him and consequently his position of being a "general authority" in Iraq was accepted and confirmed.

Seminars for instructions and discussions were held by him throughout his life and religious students and seekers of instructions in different fields of Islamic learning hovered round him like moths hovering round light and drank their hearts full from the pure fountain of his knowledge and learning so much so that scores of volumes of books were compiled from his different speeches and lectures obtained through the intermediary of his pupils.

FASCINATING MANNER OF DISCOURSE

Besides his high scholastic position, Allama Kāshiful Ghita possessed an effective and fascinating manner of discourse. He spoke with forceful logic and unparalleled eloquence. His lectures used to be so sweet and enchanting that at times hours elapsed but his audience did not feel them to have been more than a few moments. It often happened that he mounted the pulpit on some special occasion and enlightened the thoughts of the hearers in such a way that they opened the doors of their hearts and surrendered themselves to his eloquence.

During his discourse he introduced the subject with great dexterity and utilized his inherent faculty to arrive at the valid conclusion. He also made his speeches interesting with special maxims. The universities and great educational centres of Najaf, Baghdad, Cairo, Quds, Tehran and Karachi have not yet forgotten his resounding addresses.

HISTORICAL JOURNEYS

He did not refuse to do anything in order to attain his sublime and sacred objects so much so that his mind was poised to mount the stars in the skies and revolve round the spacious heavens above.

Unlike many people who do not step out of their environments and small towns till the end of their lives and consequently remain ignorant of the conditions of the world, he was very keen to tour the big Islamic countries and visit different cities so as to prove the truth of his lofty thoughts and the extensive and comprehensive plans which he had in his mind. Possibly in order to achieve his object there! By these means many more people heard the voice of this noble person, the voice which is still resounding in different educational centres.

In 1350 A.H. he went to Palestine to participate in **Moātamar al-Islami** which had been set up in the city of

Quds. In Masjid al-Aqsa he was requested to deliver a lecture and most of the delegates of the Islamic countries who had come to take part in the Moātamar offered their prayers led by him.

In 1371 A.H. he came to Karachi to participate in a great Islamic Congress to which he had been formally invited by the Government of Pakistan. There he delivered very moving speeches and cooperated sincerely with the participants of the Congress for the reformation of the political and social conditions of Islamic countries. When some national circles expressed pessimism and anxiety about the future activities of the Congress, he showed his determination to put up a fierce fight against all the intrigues which colonialism might initiate against its aims and objectives.

KĀSHIFUL GHITA AND POLITICAL ACTIVITIES

This great religious-cum-social leader believed that one of the foremost and the most important duties of every competent person is to take part in politics and to understand properly the matters connected therewith. He believed the correct object and meaning of politics to be preaching and guiding, prohibiting mischief, exhorting the statesmen of Muslim countries not to fall into the trap of colonialism and asking them to break the shackles of captivity to guarantee complete independence for all countries and nations. He used to say about himself: "I am drowned in politics from head to foot and it is one of my essential duties to take part in it. If I don't take part in politics, I would not consider myself upright before Allah and my conscience". He usually repeated these historic words of Imam Ali: "Allah has obtained a promise from the learned people that they will not observe silence in the face of gluttony of the tyrants and the hunger of the oppressed".

Hence, he took part in most of the national movements of Iraq in particular and national movements of all Muslim countries in genral and played an effective role in furthering the noble cause of these movements.

When the First World War broke out, he immediately

reached the city of Koth to take part in the freedom campaign of the Iraqi national against the British Occupation Forces. Similarly, he took part in the gallant fight of the people of Najaf Ashraf against the British forces and the colonialism of Ghazi. He always pursued this policy in opposition to the aggressors and the tyrants and fought fiercely against the colonialists and their supporters. He expressed his views with extraoridnary bravery and made use of all means to disgrace the British oppressors and to frustrate their nefarious activities.

INCOMPARABLE FRANKNESS

Allama Kāshiful Ghita had an incomparable frankness. When the British Ambassador came to see him at Najaf Ashraf and met him on 20th of Jumadi—I, 1371 A.H., he criticized the crude and inhuman activities of the British Government in different parts of the world. He especially objected in very strong terms and in a very effective and penetrating manner to the loss of Palestine and the plans of the British Government in this behalf, the usurpation of the Holy land of Palestine by Colonial Powers and rendering hundreds of innocent people homeless.

Similarly, in an interview which he had with the American Ambassador, he objected with the same frankness to the Connivance of the United States of America with Zionists and its support in the occupation of Palestine. He particularly told the Ambassador: "Our hearts are wounded by the blow of you, Americans. You have struck us in such a dastardly manner that we are unable to bear this injury silently". He added, "The public opinion of our nation has been mobilized completely against you. Our hearts are bleeding owing to the blow given by you at the back of the Arab nation which has broken its back-bone".

Especially in the later part of his life, he bedecked a new jewel in the crown of his life-history through his outstanding national activities. He rejected in clear terms the invitation for participation in the Bihamdun[1] Congress

[1]Bihamdun is a country town in Lebanon which was selected as a venue of the said Congress.

which had been convened by the supporters of American colonialism. He not only rejected the invitation but also published the reply thereto in a book entitled, **al-Muthul al-Ulya fil Islam la fi Bihamdun.** This book is a living example of his national heroism and defence of public interest and the part played by him in awakening the minds of his countrymen and warning them against the threat of colonialism. The boom of this book was heard in different circles like the explosion of a bomb and thus it fetched a fabulous price.

LITERARY WORKS

Notwithstanding the fact that he was awfully pre-occupied and had to give replies to various references made to him on religious matters owing to his important position as the one entitled to issue *Fatwa* (Decree), Allama was a very successful and prolific writer. He has written about thirty books on different subjects. The valuable writings left by him show that everybody is not qualified for this task which can be accomplised only by those people who possess spiritual strength, intellectual merit and moral attributes.

While in Lebanon, he supervised the publication of many literary books and added very useful notes to them.

AUTUMN OF HIS AGE

Allama's delicate and sensitive nature, coupled with the prevailing conditions of social life and environment round him as well as his activities pertaining to learning and knowledge had an adverse effect on his health and consequently he developed various ailments which had a profound effect on his body, though not on his mind.

In the last year of his life, he suffered much on account of prostrate glands. He had also suffered from this ailment previously but had been cured after treatment. This time, however, the treatment did not prove efficacious. He was first admitted into a hospital at Karkh and later arrived in Karand, for the change of climate. During the last nights of his life, his penetrating and dignified eyes were fixed on the stray sky of Karand, as if he were having a discourse with the stars and his great and angelic soul was roaming about even beyond them.

His stay in that town had not exceeded three days when thousands of eyes in Iraq began waiting for his return and for the continuance of his valuable academic and social activities. However, notwithstanding all this waiting, he breathed his last on Monday, the 18th of Zil Qa'dah 1373 A.H. and his soul departed to attain eternal bliss.

His dead body was brought from Karand to Baghdad. There was a great tumult in Baghdad. A large number of people accompanied his funeral to Najaf Ashraf. He was buried in a tomb situated at the end of Wadius Salām which he had himself got constructed two years ago and thus came under the benevolent canopy of the Commander of the Faithful Imam Ali. Meetings were arranged everywhere to pay homage to his soul. Hundreds of articles and elegies depicting his distinguished personality and meritorious services were read at these enthusiastic meetings.

Undoubtedly, Allama Kashiful Ghita will be long remembered in history as one of the most distinguished figures of Muslim Ummah.

* * * * *

How can Muslims Unite ?

During the present time there is no intelligent person, in any part of the world, who does not realize the need for unity and the harm caused by discord. Today this matter has attained a paramount importance. This reality is also felt in the same way as one feels about one's own physical conditions such as illness, health, thirst, hunger etc.

We should not forget here the indefatigable efforts and continuous struggles of the reformers as well as of the great personalities who have taken pains in this direction during recent years. They have made known this reality to the Muslims like an experienced teacher in a distinct voice, or like a proficient physician who diagnoses the ailment and prescribes the medicine and instructs the patients to take them to eradicate the serious ailment before it puts an end to their lives. These Muslim reformers have conveyed their thoughts to the Muslims who have heard them. They have said, "The dangerous malady which has today over-taken the Muslims is the discord, and the life-saving medicine for them is the same which was useful for those who are now dead. It has been and still is the call of unity and co-operation and the discarding of all the factors of enmity, jealousy and discord. Genuine efforts for achieving this sacred and lofty object have always been a part of the programme of the life of noble people whose inner eyes have been enlightened by the Grace of Almighty Allah and whose hearts have been made the centre of determination and sincerity for safeguarding the interest of their community. They have always invited people of all castes and creeds to get united. The unity of those who believe in, one Allah and the gathering of Muslims under the glorious standard of: *Lā ilāhā illallah Muhammadur Rasulul lah.* (There is no god but Allah, Muhammad is His Prophet).

They invite people to this great comprehensive plan, this firm stand and this unbreakable link insisted upon by Allah because it is not possible for the Muslim Ummah to attain salvation except through unity and in the absence of which death and everlasting destruction will overtake them. They are the missionaries of truth, the apostles of reality and the messengers of Allah sent to the people of this age. They infuse new life to the abandoned principles and teachings of Islam and once again they have brightened up the Hadith of the Holy Prophet of Islam which had been covered up by the dust of negligence.

It is under the auspices of these efforts and the continuous struggle that the vanguard of success has appeared and pure and fresh spirit has begun to move in the Muslims. Now they are gradually trying to understand one another.

The first ray of this reality appeared and the first seed of this thinking was sown at the city of Quds by the great conference **Moātamar al-Islami.** That day a number of people from various Muslim nations gathered there to study the important and basic problems of the Muslims and to exchange tokens of love and friendship disregarding the differences of geography, sect, descent, caste or language. It was a gathering which had no precedent and the eyes of all the Muslims were focussed on it. It was considered to be a shaft in the eyes of the enemies who were making misleading propaganda against it. However, in spite of the apprehensions of the enemies, the seed of unity was sown by the delegates in the minds and hearts of the common Muslims with the hope that one day the seedling would grow up into a tree and all would have a share of its sweet fruits. Yet, in spite of all the melodiousness of its tunes the Muslims, as usual, remained contented with words only and no positively practical steps were taken at all. We looked at the outward glamour of the things only but stayed away from the realities. We were content with the shell but did not care for its kernel. This attitude is exactly the reverse of what our ancestors, the very active and energetic Muslims had and who took decisions and implemented them before uttering any words. These are the attributes which others learned from us whereas we lagged behind notwithstanding the fact that we were the harbingers of this caravan. This, according to the invariable law of nature, is the result of our own doing. *This is the system of Allah which existed before, and you will never find any change in His system.* (Surah Fath, 48:23).

Our great shortcoming is that when we have said that Muslims of the world have extended the hand of friendship and unity towards one another and after having inked the pages of publications with these words we think that the object has been achieved and that with this one sentence only we have become united and have given birth to a living and dignified nation so as to obtain a worthy position among the nations of the world!

This is a gross error of our judgement.[1] Resolutions

[1] A graver mistake than this one which has cropped up recently among a number of Muslims and especially among some statesmen of Muslim countries is the significance of the question of the Arab race and the stress on the term **"Arab Nationality"**. It has assumed such dimensions that in some instances the question of religion and the law of Islam has not only been eclipsed but totally forgotten. Evidently this is a grave danger for Islam and for the Muslims.

There is no doubt about the fact that Arabs are a noble and honourable race. However, this honour can hold no comparison with the honour that Arabs as well as non-Arabs viz. Muslims in general enjoy on account of being within the fold of Islam. When the Arabs depend on Arab Nationality instead of the slogan of Islam, even if they are successful in gaining the support of 150 or 200 million Arabs, and that too with all their differences, they will be deprived of the support of 700 million of other Muslims of the world! In our opinion conversion of Islamic Internationalism into Arab Nationalism is a great mistake and which may lead to the revival of the pre-

Continued...

and words not followed by actions will be a great set-back and we will be lagging behind day by day. Such words are like a mirage that deceives us.

If the state of affairs continues to be the same, it would be impossible for the Muslims to safeguard their position and to succeed in achieving real unity and establishing their identity in the human society notwithstanding the fact that thousands of books and articles are written on the subject of **Unity** and the world is made to resound with the word **Alliance** and its synonyms and even though eloquent and beautiful speeches are delivered and mirthful verses and panegyrics are sung in its praise. These things will certainly be without any effect unless genuine effort and well-motivated campaigns coupled with the adjustment of behaviour and habits are launched.

Muslims should control their refractory passions and

Islamic Age of Ignorance and such a conception should be corrected immediately.

It is true that recently the question of Islamic Unity has been mixed up with a chain of political issues. However, transient political issues of this type which at times disappear as fast as snow is converted into water during the summer, can not ignore an important reality i.e. uniting 900 million Muslims of the world, in preference to anything else. It is because unity is based on the sacred law of Islam.

Revival of racial fanaticism, especially in the present times when the concept of racial discrimination is totally outmoded, is a strange short-sightedness, the inauspicious results of which will become evident sooner or later. We hope that our Muslim brethren will study the problems in more realistic manner, ignoring the subject of race, which is an old and a rotten topic belonging to the Middle Ages and a relic of the age of ignorance and will extend the hand of religious unity to other Muslim brethren in the East and the West and under the shadow of this great alliance (along with prevention of abuses which occasionally become necessary on this score) will struggle for the glory and grandeur of Islam and will keep in mind that the Holy Qur'an says: *If he (the Holy Prophet Muhammad) were to die or were slain, will you then turn on your heels (back to the Age of Ignorance?)* (Surah Ale Imran, 3:144) desires with the power of their wisdom and intellect and consider the welfare of their brethren-in-faith to be their own welfare. They should make efforts to guard the interests of others as they guard their own interests. They should efface enmity from their hearts and should look upon each other with the eyes of love and friendship and not with the eyes of hatred and grudge. They should clearly realize this reality that the dignity of everyone is related with the dignity of his brethren and all are friends and helpers of one another. Can anyone withhold assistance from his friends and helpers?

It may, however, be said with great regret that it is not easy to acquire these sublime objectives. Who would be prepared to observe with his Muslim brethren real equality, render them assistance in all matters, desire for them what he desires for himself, and consider his gain, dignity and success as of others? In the present conditions we, too do not expect that such equality and assistance would be forthcoming. However, we should at least uphold justice with regard to our mutual rights, should co-operate with one another and should not ignore their interests. Nevertheless, even this object will not be achieved unless the baser instincts of greed, envy, egoism and seeking supremacy over others are uprooted from the hearts of the people. These evil propensities are the source of all misfortunes. They make a chain of adversities and arrest the progress of man. The nation which is captivated by base desires is pulled down into the lowest regions of decadence and destruction and it eventually perishes.

The seed of wickedness is the very evil tendency of seeking supremacy over others. That is why it has been said that love for supremacy is the source of envy, envy generates enmity, enmity breeds discord, discord gives birth to dispersion, dispersion brings about weakness and weakness is the cause of disgrace and abjectness and which in turn brings about the decline of powers, the disappearance of blessings and annihilation of nations!

History bears testimony to this fact and we also observe that every nation that cultivates these base characteristics marches towards annihilation. The ambitions of its people fade away and their determination cools down. Discord and dispersion take the place of unity and sincerity. The blood-thirsty clutches of colonialism and exploitation squeeze their necks and their enemies overpower them easily.

However, those people whose thoughts are uniform and whose hearts are united, who lend a helping hand to one another and make haste for mutual assistance in the event of difficulties, who have no enmity in their hearts for one another, who do not avoid helping each other and who do not desist from extending sincere help in moments of emergency are such people who remain honoured, stable, safe, blessed, strong, victorious, rich and powerful during their lifetime. Allah helps them in times of adversity, relieves them from the cultches of difficulties, favours them with honour and makes them the guides and leaders of others.

REVIEW OF THE PAST

Muslims of today should carefully keep in their minds the gory past of their predecessors before the advent of Islam. They were the people who were leading a very miserable and degraded life. They had neither a leader under whose leadership they could take shelter nor the spirit of unity and alliance with which they could be comforted. Different types of misfortunes had overtaken them and ignorance had cast its dark shadow on their thoughts. They were burning in the fire of continuous wars and savage plundering. They tore away the strings of relationship and considered bloodshed permissible.

However, we know how, with the arrival of Islam, a new leaf was turned. Under the shelter of Islam, Almighty Allah united them and strengthened the bond of their unity through belief in His Unity. The same Grace of Allah spread over their heads and sprinkled Divine blessings on them. A dignified and strong government radiated over their heads and everything belonging to them received order under its shelter. Those who were weak the day before, became rulers of the world the next day. Those who were their rulers before became their subjects. Those who decided their fate in the past, began to carry out their orders then. Of course, they acquired this dignity by unity and brotherhood based on sincerity. They were really united. They truly accepted one another as brothers. Their interests were common and their decisions were unanimous. Every Muslim rendered maximum support and help to his brother Muslims.

However, we find that today Muslims have again reverted to the old ways and adversity has again made its appearance. The situation has taken such a turn that a Muslim gets nothing even from his nearest and dearest ones except obstruction and calumny and can expect nothing from them except sabotage so much so that the dread and terror to which he is subjected by his brother Muslims is not in any way lesser than that which he fears from the infidels and enemies. How can we hope for victory and dignity in these conditions?

It is impossible that Muslims should be favoured with prosperity without unity in their ranks, just as it is impossible that they should unite unless they help and assist one another. However, Muslims should know that they can not achieve unity and sincerity similar to that of their ancestors only by beautiful words, animating phrases, fiery speeches and articles, proclamations and banner headlines in the newpapers. If they think so, they are gravely mistaken. Unity is not a handful of empty words nor eloquent and rhetorical phrases, however excellent and impressive they may be. The essence of unity is the very honesty and sincerity which originates from a pure heart and is followed by sustained efforts. Unity is a chain of noble attributes, actions, talents and natural qualities which have their roots in the depth of the soul and which have embraced the entire being of the man. Unity is a moral bond and a sublime human sentiment. Unity means that the Muslims should be partners in the gains of one another and should observe the rules of justice and equity in their mutual dealings. For instance, if in a Muslim country there are two or more Muslim sects they should make it incumbent upon themselves to behave like two brothers who have inherited a house or property from their father and should respect one another's rights in accordance with the canons of equity and justice notwithstanding the fact that anyone of them may have intended aggression or jealousy against the other.

CUT OFF THESE FOUL HANDS

There should be no doubt about the fact that unity does not mean that one group of people should trample down the rights of other group and the latter group should sit silent. As it is opposed to justice, it should be told that it is creating discord. In such an event it is necessary for others to look into its claim. If what it says is correct, they should make haste to help it. If, however, what it says is wrong, they should inform it of its mistake and convince it of the true facts. In case it insists upon its error they should bring the reality to its notice by way of friendly advice and through contention with propriety in the same manner in which a kind friend advises another friend. The parties concerned should not abuse or impute unjust motives to each other and thus kindle up the fire of enmity between themselves, the same fire for which both the parties will serve as fuel and as a result of which others will devour them like a rich and delicious morsel or take possession of them like a convenient booty.

Today all Muslims, even those who are deaf and dumb, are aware that in every Islamic region the dragon of western colonialism is present with an open mouth to devour that region and all that is in it. Is the realization of this very situation not sufficient for establishing the unity of the Muslims and for kindling up the flames of honour and courage in their hearts? Should the intensity of all those pains not invite them to become united and banish all enmities and envies from their midst? The ancients have said: "When adversities attack, enmities are forgotten".

How is it possible that a Muslim should think of exercising despotic authority on brother Muslims or of exploiting them? Have they not been co-operating with

33

one another since the time their forefathers lived in these lands? Are all the misfortunes and adversities falling on their heads like lightening not sufficient to make them adopt the principles of equity and justice in their mutual dealings? After observing these deplorable scenes, we have nearly lost hope of achieving our sacred object and of picking the delicious fruit of unity, because we find that the words of the reformers and the well-wishers of Muslims have very little effect on their hearts.

If the speeches and addresses delivered by us in this regard (and later printed and published) are scrutinized, it will become abundantly clear that we have not lagged behind in making all possible efforts to achieve this great object. Unfortunately, however, we find that separation and estrangement between the Muslims is on the increase as if we had preached enmity and discord among them!

Why should we not be in a state of despair when we see with our own eyes that there are people who do their utmost to sow the seeds of discord among the Muslims and not only create but also widen the gulf of disunity. They are people like Nashāshebi who has published a book entitled **al-Islam al-Sahih** (The True Islam) and really how deceptive and unrealistic the names sometimes are! The summary of this book and the meaning of true Islam in the eye of Nashāshebi is nothing but humiliation and insult of the Ahlul Bayt (Progeny of the Holy Prophet) viz. Ali, Fatima, Hasan and Husayn (peace be on them) and the denial of all the virtues and praises mentioned of them in the Holy Qur'an and Hadith (tradition). For instance, according to his belief, the verse regarding *Tat-heer* (purification): *O people of the Prophet's Progeny! Allah intends but to remove all sorts of uncleanliness and blemish from you and to purify you with a thorough purification,* (Surah al-Ahzab, 33:33) relates to the wives of the Holy Prophet especially Ayesha. Not only this, for according to him there is no one entitled to be called Ahlul Bayt except Ayesha. Not only this but he goes so far as to say that he totally excludes, with full confidence, the Holy Prophet's daughter Fatima from his Household. Really, what a

sublime intelligence and an uprecedented code of justice![1]
In the same manner, according to the belief of Nashashebi,
the verses regarding *Mubahila* (Imprecation) and *Qurba*
(Kin) were also not revealed with regard to the members of

[1]Numerous traditions have been quoted through the channels of
Ahle Sunnah regarding this verse being earmarked for five persons
namely the Holy Prophet, Imam Ali, Lady Fatima, Imam Hasan and
Imam Husayn (peace be on them) and distinguished Sunni scholars
have confirmed the authenticity of these traditions. From among
them the famous Egyptian scholar, Muhammad Shiblanji, writes: "It
has been quoted through various authentic channels that the Holy
Prophet in such a condition that Ali, Fatima, Hasan and Husayn
(peace be on them) were with him, made Hasan and Husayn sit on
his knees and then put the sheet on all of them and recited this
verse: *O people of the Prophet's House! Allah intends but to remove
all sorts of uncleanliness and blemish from you and to purify you
with a through purification.* Thereafter, he said, "O Allah! These are
my Ahlul Bayt. Keep every kind of uncleanliness and pollution away
from them and purify them". Thereafter, he adds, "It is related in a
Hadith that Umme Salma (May Allah be pleased with her) expressed
a desire to have a place under the sheet but the Holy Prophet did not
allow her to do so and said, "No doubt you are one of the wives of
the Prophet and a good woman too but you are not my Ahlul Bayt"
(Nurul Absār, p. 102). Shiblanji further writes that Ahmad and
Tibrani have quoted this tradition from Abu Sa'id Khadari that the
Holy Prophet said, "This verse has been revealed for five persons:
"Myself, Ali, Fatima, Hasan and Husayn" (See Murtaza al-Askari,
A Probe into the History of Hadith, ISP 1982).

Moreover, in the same book and on the same page he quotes
from Ibn Abi Shayba, Ahmad, Tirmizy, Ibn Jarir, Ibn Manzar,
Tibrani and Hākim who quote from the Holy Prophet through Anas
that after the revelation of this verse whenever the Holy Prophet
went to the Masjid for the dawn prayer he passed by the houe of
Fatima Zahra and used to make a call: *O people of the House!
Allah intends but to remove all sorts of uncleanliness and blemish
from you and to purify you with a through purification.* (Surah
al-Ahzab, 33:33)

Continued...

35

the Holy Prophet's Progeny[1] and all the traditions quoted from the Holy Prophet regarding their attributes are false, even if they be available in the 'Sahah' of the Sunnis.[2]

(The above narrative is according to the tradition as quoted by Abu Sa'id Khudari. The same facts have been quoted by others with minor variations). We think that one of the notable points involved in these five dignitaries accommodating themselves under the sheet was this that it might become clearly known to all that this verse has been revealed particularly for these five persons and no one else (not even the wives of the Prophet) is included in it. In this manner the Holy Prophet wished to make absolutely clear to the Muslims that this verse had been revealed particularly for these five people, so much so that according to the tradition quoted above he openly stopped Umme Salma (May Allah be pleased with her) from coming under the sheet. However, in spite of all this, what a great injustice it is that it should be said that the above verse has been revealed particularly for Ayesha or for the wives of the Holy Prophet and does not at all include the sublime Lady of Paradise, Fatima. However, the fact which attracts attention is that in a tradition quoted from Ayesha herself, it is stated that the said verse has been revealed about these five sacred personages.

[1]The fact of revelation of the verse regarding *Mubahila* by the Holy Family viz. Ali, Fatima and their sons (peace be on them) has been confirmed by more than twenty topranking Sunni traditionalists, scholars, and commentators of the Holy Qur'an, some of them being: Imam Fakhruddin al-Razi (Tafsir al-Dur al-Manthur), Wahidi (Asbabun Nuzul) and Bayzawi (Tafsir al-Bayzawi).

In the same manner, the well-known founder of the Hambali School of Jurisprudence, Ahmad bin Hambal, in his book **Musnad** (vol. I, p. 185), Hakim in **Mustadrak** (vol. III, p. 150) and Ibn Hajar Asqalani in **Isaba** (vol. II, p. 503) confirmed the same; and a number of others. Regarding the verse of *Qurba* also many Sunni scholars like Zamakhshari, al-Razi, Ahmad, Baghvi, Tha'labi, Suyuti and many other traditionalists and commentators have stated clearly that it has been revealed regarding the Holy Progeny of the Holy Prophet.

[2]These remarks of Nashashebi are very truly in accordance with the well-known vulgar proverb: "Wished to set right his eyebrows but blinded his eye" because with the object of lending support to the caliphate of the three caliphs he has repudiated the attributes of the Holy Progeny of the Holy Prophet. He has not cared that by doing so he has rendered incredible the most authentic books of the Sunnis, on which most of the principles of their religion rest.

However, Nashāshebi is not alone in this field because earlier Nasuli, Hassān and others like him followed the same course. In spite of all this we hope that the present condition of the Muslims will improve and that dispersion and discord will be replaced by unity and friendship. In this state of affairs do we not have cause to despair?

Are Nashāshebi and his companions, who abuse the Shi'ah and the Holy Imams, not aware that this action of theirs can cause a Shi'ah writer also to stand up and engage himself in a similar campaign and direct the sharp edge of his attacks towards the Orthodox Caliphs and the Sunnis and repeat the well-known Arabic proverb which means: "Your cousins, too, possess spears". In this manner this will continue and each party will abuse the other. Will all this result in anything else?

The intellectuals on both sides should think over the matter carefully and see what the fate of the Muslims will be on such a dangerous precipice and what benefits they will derive from this business. But what is the crime of the Shi'ah? Are they guilty of any sin except of their love for the Holy Progeny of the Holy Prophet?

NO NEED TO DESPAIR OF

Notwithstanding the conditions mentioned above there is no need to despair in view of Allah's Grace and the special favour in which He holds His religion and law. It is possible that Allah may cause some zealous, compassionate and magnanimous people to rise out of the wise men of both the groups who may cut off the hands who are fanning the fire of differences by publishing such contaminated writings which would kill the very spirit of Islam. It is with this hope that we have consented to the printing of this book. In our publications we have forewarned all the Muslims and have requested them to make efforts for the revival of the spirit of friendship, brotherhood and unity among different sects of the Muslims.[1]

[1] It is a matter of great regret that in the short preface written for the seventh edition of this book, the late Allama Kashiful Ghita
Continued...

It should, however, be clearly understood that the achievement of this object has two basic preconditions:

The first condition is that the religious person desirous of discussing his own faith, should do so in such a way that he does not hurt the feelings of others and what he says should not savour vilification and insult.

expresses despair and loses all hope to which he has alluded thus "With the clear and explicit narrations in this book about the Shi'ah and the Shi'ah Faith I had expected that some of our Sunni brethren will desist from unjustified accusations in this regard. It may, however, be stated with regret, that they have totally ignored what I have said and are repeating exactly the same old story. There would not have been much cause for sadness if this thing had been done by the common people. Unfortunately, however, some people who consider themselves to belong to the category of scholars and men of letters have begun to indulge in the same old calumnies and in imputing ridiculous and unjustified allegations. It would, therefore, be justifiable if we lose hope totally. It is not known as to why and for what reason they should persist in this attitude".

Thereafter, he says: "The third edition of this book was printed at Cairo and all its copies were also circulated from there. (Recently also it has been printed in Cairo twice). It is, however, surprising that not the least change has appeared in the tone of Egyptian writers with regard to the Shi'ah. Once again they avail themselves of every opportunity of calumniating the Shi'ah in their writings. Once again they associate with the Shi'ah the same fables and myths which are the relics of the period of Ibn Khaldun and Ibn Hajar. Is it not proper that a little change should appear in the manner of their discussions and in the tone of their writings? Unfortunately however, they still look upon the Shi'ah as heretics so much so that this grudge mixed with extreme fanaticism has even involved the Fatimid Caliphs of Egypt who had rendered yeoman's service to this ancient land. Sometimes they are styled as irreligious. At other times their very pedigree is doubted and it is said that they were the descendents of the Jews. At times it is said that they were atheists. All this is said in spite of the fact that the meritorious services rendered by the Fatimid Caliphs to the world of Islam in general and

Continued...

38

The second condition, which should perhaps rank first in view of its importance, is that every Muslim should rear up love for all others the same thing which he desires for himself and purify his heart from the taints of envy and grudge. He should sincerely work hard for the achievement of this object and should not remain contented with empty, though fascinating, words which are usually said in order to protect personal interests.

to Egypt in particular are unforgetable. These distinguished people who have been made targets of calumnies only for the crime of being Shi'ah were the greatest propagators of Islamic learnings. It is sufficient to say that the credit of establishing the best jewel of Egypt's pride viz. al-Azhar University, which is the oldest centre of learning in the country, goes to them. It is now more than a thousand years since that University was established and it is considered to be the greatest seat of learning of the Sunni world which has produced thousands of scholars. Is the remote age and long life of this University coupled with its expansion and development not a clear proof of the sincerity of its founders who rendered such a valuable service to the world of Islam? Notwithstanding all this, the Fatimids are still heretics with a doubtful pedigree and so on and so forth!

Keeping in view all these conditions, Allama Kāshiful Ghita openly expresses despair. In his later years he gradually came to the conclusion that this type of thinking had become a second nature with some of the Sunni brethren and they could not easily be persuaded to review their attitude.

However, we believe that notwithstanding all these circumstances Allama Kashiful Ghita should not have lost hope of the unity of Muslims. He should have kept the fact in view that these habits and thoughts which they have inherited through centuries from generation to generation and which have taken roots throughout their souls cannot be changed so easily. This process too needs a comparatively longer period to accomplish. Hence, it is necessary that an advantage may be taken here of the time factor and the thoughts should be enlightened gradually by a chain of writings, congresses and logical and debating discussions the example of which has been set by Allama Kashiful Ghita himself. It is especially so

Continued...

Let us make the proposition more clear. The basis of real unity and brotherhood which was introduced by Islam, or in other words, which brought Islam into being and which has been adopted by all the developed nations of the world is that every individual should consider the welfare of the society not only at par with his own welfare

because the indications which generate hope can be seen in different nooks and corners of the world. Most important of these is the fact that one of the most distinguished personalities of the Sunni world who was the Rector of al-Azhar University and Grand Mufti of the Sunni School of thought Shaykh Mahmud Shaltoot took a prominent step recently in the direction of this sacred object by issuing his historic *Fatwa* (Decree) on the subject that the Ja'fari creed known as the Shi'ah Imamiyah can be followed just like other Sunni sects. Therefore it is necessary for the Muslims to know and free themselves from unjustified prejudice. (The magazine, **al-Islam**, issue No. III, 11th year, Cairo).

Through this decree he has filled a big gap and directed the Sunni to view the Shi'ah School of Thought in the same manner as they view their own four Schools of thought. Moreover, in certain matters he himself considered Shi'ah beliefs as superior to those of other Schools (e.g. invalidity of divorce pronounced thrice at one time). In such cases he made it clear that the beliefs of the Shi'ah are more consistent with the Islamic spirit.

Of course, when Shaykh Shaltut issued the aforesaid Fatwa with unparalleled compassion and bravery, Allama Kāshiful Ghita the author of this book was not alive. However, his noble soul, which had a big share in providing a background for this *Fatwa*, certainly would have become very happy. It is evident that a few decades earlier, the saints and intellectuals did not, with all their bravery and moral heroism, possess enough courage to issue such a *Fatwa*. In the same manner persons like Allama Kāshiful Ghita, too, did not perhaps, possess the ability to publish a book like **Aslush Shi'ah wa Usuloha** with its extraordinary soft, friendly and affectionate tone.

The extraordinary welcome accorded by Sunni scholars to the book entitled **Mukhtasarun Nāfe'** (one of the excellent texts of

Continued...

but above his personal welfare. It is easy to utter such words verbally but very difficult to put into practice and perhaps impossible for ourselves, the Muslims of the present age, especially so when persons following the teachings of different schools of Islamic thought are viewed. They look upon one another with fierce eyes like blood thirsty enemies and even if they occasionally express love and friendship it is only to deceive the other and to leave him in the lurch at the time of adversity. At times they utter hypocritical and flattering words to exploit their brethren-in-faith and unfortunately this deplorable tendency has taken such a deep root in their hearts that there is no effect of any preacher on them. They have perhaps forgotten or pretened to forget that a dangerous enemy is waiting in ambush who wishes to destroy all of them and sows seeds of dissension among them so that they may become deadly against each other. He has prepared his trap to ensnare the Muslims. The snare is so dangerous that it is not possible to get rid of it except by means of earnest and practical unity and alliance.

I believe that the first step which leads to attain this idea of sincere unity is to hold conferences every year or at

Shi'ah Jurisprudence) and the special interest, untainted by bigotry and fanaticism, which has been evinced in the study of theoretical writings of Shi'ah and in understanding the thoughts and beliefs of this sect, is another indication of the gradual preparation of the ground for better understanding between the Muslims of the world as well as of the dispersion of dark clouds of pessimism and suspicion from the horizon of their thoughts.

It is, however, worth mentioning that if necessary care is not exercised by both the parties, even this slight understanding, which can pave the way for a wider cohesion, may disappear due to the negligence of Muslims and their unjustified fanatical activities or due to the instigation of others who have always taken advantage of the mutual differences and have utilized them as a stepping stone for the achievement of their nefarious ends. It is, therefore, necessary that, as far as possible, full devotion and care should be observed in this regard.

least once in two years in which Muslim scholars from all Islamic countries should participate. They should first get familiar with one another and then exchange views and deliberate over matters relating to various Muslim societies. And more essential than this is the Islamic Summit Conference of the statesmen (in the real sense of the word) so that they may assist one another exactly like two hands of one body to wage war against the dangers which surround them from all sides.

The events which took place after the Second World War taught the Muslims significant lessons (provided there is an eye which can take the lesson). The fall of the ancient land of Ethiopia (Abbisynia) into the lap of others within a few months was sufficient for the awakening of all. The fall of this country was the danger signal for the Muslims of the world to be watchful of their future.

I feel that the extent to which I have spoken is sufficient for guidance and vigilance. Incidentally, however, for the sake of further benefit, I tried by revising the previous edition, to bring out this book in a more complete form. I added such fresh topics as were necessary for the completion of these discussions and further explained and amplified some of the chapters of the book. In addition to all this, every effort was made that the discourses should be concise and brief and every topic should be approached and tackled taking recourse to the shortest route so that all classes of people may comprehend them with ease.

Undoubtedly, during an age in which people have become accustomed to cover within hours and days longer distances than they traversed in months previously, it is necessary that everything, even magazines and books, should be published quickly and briefly.

However, it is not possible for me at the present time to claim that I have done justice to the subject-matter and there has been no shortcoming on my part. Nevertheless let it suffice for me that I have had good intentions and have made efforts to the extent they were humanly possible for me. I am thankful to Allah that it has been possible for me to take an initiative regarding a basic matter on modern lines. Learned men of our own times as well as of the future can expand the series of these discourses in the manner they consider best. So far as I am concerned I have opened the gate and shown the clear path. Fortunately this book has been written in the current language and in accordance with the principles of modern learning and in an impressive and useful manner without damaging in the least the religious feelings of others or hurting their sentiments. Wherever necessary short notes giving references to the original documents together with arguments thereof have also been added.

* * * * *

Reasons that Prompted to write this Book

THEY ARE GOOD BUT
UNFORTUNATELY THEY ARE SHI'AH

Two years ago an enthusiastic young man who was sent by the Government of Iraq with a group of scholars to pursue studies in 'Darul Ulum al-Ulya of Egypt wrote to me a detailed interim letter, wherein he said: "I have contacts with some great ulema (scholars) and learned men of al-Azhar University and every now and then matters relating to Najaf Ashraf, its scholars, the method of education in this great centre of learning come under discussion during our meetings. I have noticed that the scholars of al-Azhar admit the extraordinary importance of the scholars of Najaf Ashraf and praise their exalted opinions but usually after uttering words of praise they add: "But unfortunately they are Shi'ah". This young man adds: "These words surprised me much and I used to say: 'Is it a sin to be a Shi'ah? Are the Shi'ah not a sect of Muslims?' However, they, in reply, used to say things the crux of which is: No! Shi'ah are not Muslims and Shi'ah Faith is something separate from Islam. It is not at all fit to be recognized as a religion. It is a system invented by the Iranians. It is something related to politics which came into existence to bring about the fall of the Umayyads and to ensure the installation of the Abbasids. As such it has the least relationship with the Divine religion".

Thereafter, this young man continues to say: "As you are aware I am a young man of tender age and I do not

44

know how these sects have come into being and how they have spread. I have begun entertaining doubts on account of the statements which are made about the Shi'ah sect by these prominent persons who are considered to be great scholars among the Sunnis and the time is not far off when I may possibly repudiate the very fact that the people belonging to this sect are Muslims, not to speak of their being followers of a true faith". Thereafter, he asked me to explain in this connection the real and actual facts for him so that possibly the fire of doubt and suspicion might be extinguished by the water of certainty and assurance and he might get rid of this suspense. He writes: "If you do not deliver me from this perplexity, the responsibility for my blundering and perversion will be directly yours".

In reply I wrote to him on the subject supplying as much information as could possibly be supplied through correspondence and conformed to his thoughts. It could be hoped that matters so explained would be instrumental in removing the nightmare of doubt and suspicion from his mind. However, I began wondering more as compared to the doubt and indecision in the trap of which the young man had fallen as a victim. I could not make myself believe that all the incident was correct. I thought it over again and again as to how it could be possible that the scholars of cities considered to be in the vanguard of the Islamic seats of learning and focus the attention of not only the Arabs but also of all Muslims of the world, should be victims of ignorance in the matter of bringing facts to light and tearing the veil of falsehood which is usually born of personal interest, passions, desires and beliefs of ignorant people in fabricated propositions. No, I could not at all believe what the aforesaid young man had said till in those very days a book entitled **Fajrul Islam** written by the famous author Ahmad Amin reached my hands. While studying this book I found that in his discussion about the Shi'ah he had displayed an ignorance worse than could be imagined.

If today anyone stationed even in the remotest regions of the world writes such discourses about the Shi'ah, certainly he cannot be excused and he is sure to earn every sort of admonition. And this very subject provided me a conspicuous document to speak out the truth.

THE LAME EXCUSE

I began to ponder myself that if a well-known writer like him wanted to write a book which he wished to circulate among the members of a society whom the Holy Qur'an has introduced as brothers of one another, it was extremely essential for him to have gained knowledge about the posture of that society, and if without taking recourse to any such things he indulged in falsehood and calumny about the Shi'ah community, then it could be well understood that what could be expected from a group of people who really lack any worth? And he has done this notwithstanding his knowing the fact that every sensible person is aware today that we are in extreme need of strengthing the bonds of affection, friendship and unity! Muslims of the world cannot continue to live without acting on the principles of Islamic Brotherhood and unity.

If they ignore these principles they will neither lead a dignified life nor will they die an honourable death.

It is a fact that if the Muslims had known the real facts about Shi'ah faith and had taken just decisions about their brethren they would have destoryed such abominable and venomous publications which sow the seeds of discord and dissension among the Muslims and provide the deadliest weapon in the hands of colonialists and those who are inimical towards all religions.

Does these words of Ahmad Amin, "Shi'aism has always been a refuge for those who wished to destroy Islam" (Fajrul Islam, p. 230) not kindle up the fire of enmity and grudge in the hearts of the Shi'ah at large the world over? He has written these words knowing well that a flood of criticism is in this wake and that by doing so he has injured the sentiments of millions of Shi'ah Muslims.

It is a strange coincidence that Ahmad Amin, after publishing this very book and obtaining a good deal of information about scholars of Najaf Ashraf came to the city of learning and wisdom last year i.e. 1349 A.H. in the company of a group of 30 Egyptian scholars and had the honour of being present at the sacred threshold of the "Gate of the City of Learning", viz. Imam Ali. One night during the glorious month of Ramazan he came to me accompanied by his friends. It was a crowded meeting and they spent a part of the night with me. I rebuked him mildly. However, I did not say all that ought to have been said. On the other hand, I obtained inspiration from the Holy Qur'an: *When they come across something impious, pass by it nobly......and when addressed by the ignorant ones, their only response is, 'Wish you well".* (Surah al-Furqan, 25:63, 72) and did not mention many relevant things. His last excuse was that he did not possess sufficient information and literature about the Shi'ah. I then said to him: "The correct method is that when a person desires to write a book on a subject he should first collect all the documents and other necessary materials and study all its aspects. Without all this it would not be proper for him to deal with the subject".

I do not know why the libraries of the Shi'ah possess Sunni books and among them is our own library consisting of about 5000 books most of which have been written by Sunni scholars, although it is situated in a city like Najaf Ashraf which is considered to be a poor city though very rich from the view-point of knowledge and learning. On the other hand Cairo with all its greatness and exalted position, is void of Shi'ah books, with the exception of very few of them![1]

[1]Not only libraries like the library of Allama Kāshiful Ghita which then contained 5000 books and today their number exceeds 10,000 contain a majority of books of Sunni scholars but also private libraries maintained by Shi'ah scholars, writers and speakers in their houses and study centres, contain mostly a large number of such books. And the thing more important than this is that in the majority of their discussions (and more commonly discussions relating to principles of Jurisprudence, scholastic theology and commentary on Qur'an) our scholars also quote the remarks of Sunni Ulema and

Continued...

Yes, they don't have any information about the Shi'ah but in spite of that they write all sorts of things about them. And it is all the more strange and shocking that a number of Sunnis of Iran, too are in spite of their proximity and neighbourhood, are ignorant of the true facts about the Shi'ah!

make them the subject of their discourses and unrestricted discussion. And in fact their discussions are in the shape of "Simultaneous" and "Comparative" discussions i.e. not only in respect of Religious Jurisprudence but also with regard to all subjects of Islamic learning, they put different beliefs and views along with relevant documents and arguments opposite one another and select the correct beliefs and views out of them. This method is the most excellent and useful one and has been adopted in modern times as well and put into practice in many branches of learning including "Law". In fact "Unrestricted discussion" would be meaningless without adopting this method. But why should the Shi'ah have adopted this method in their discussions when others refuse to do so? The reason for this, we believe, is that the Shi'ah have faith in their logic and in the force of their arguments and consequently do not refuse to mention the views and arguments of others, whereas the restricted and unilateral method of discussion of others shows that they are doubtful of their ability to oppose the evidence available with the Shi'ah notwithstanding the fact that the current of anti-Shi'ah propaganda among them is so strong that it does not leave any possibility of their coming across fresh and notable views in Shi'ah books but they are totally ignorant of the existence of such books.

Whichever of the three possibilities there may be, it is a matter of great regret. Even if this method of discussion was acceptable in the past it stands rejected in the present age and is not considered reliable from the point of view of intensive scientific studies.

We hope that our Sunni brethren will adopt the same method of discussion, in accordance with which we discuss their views, with courage and without any prejudice, in a completely learned and logical atmosphere and will not be afraid of unrestricted discussion. This method will not only render effective assistance for the unity of Muslims but will also open new horizons for theoretical questions.

A PACK OF WILD BEASTS

A few months back a civilized young man belonging to a distinguished Shi'ah family of Baghdad wrote to the effect that he performed a journey to the province of Dailam (a province adjacent to the province of Baghdad) whose inhabitants are mostly Sunni and attended their meetings. They were very much impressed by his conversation, politeness and good manners and expressed their pleasure. However, as soon as they learnt that he was a Shi'ah they expressed surprise and said: "We do not think that any manners and politeness existed in this sect not to speak of knowledge and faith! We considered them to be a pack of wild beasts of the jungle!"

This young man tried to arouse my sentiments with strong reproaches and asked me time and again to write a small treatise about the Shi'ah. He wanted to circulate it among the aforesaid ignorant people so that they might at least, to a small extent, become acquainted with the beliefs and ways of the Shi'ah. Later this young man proceeded to Syria to visit the country-side and then went to Egypt. After studying the conditions of the Musims in these areas he wrote to me: "The manner of thinking of the Egyptians about the Shi'ah is the same as that of the people of Dailam and their behaviour towards them is identical". Thereafter he added: "Is the time not yet come that you should fulfil your promise and discharge your obligation, because the posture of the Shi'ah has become fixed in their minds in the worst possible shape?" He also narrated some other things which were exactly according to reality.

SILENCE NOT JUSTIFIED

We come across many such cases and incidents in the 'dailies' of Egypt and Syria in which venomous articles are published every now and then in this regard. They contain all sorts of calumnies and slanders about the Shi'ah, although the Shi'ah are like Joseph quite blameless and totally innocent of all such accusations.

Unfortunately, however, the ailment of **ignorance and fanaticism** is so irremediable that it has wearied even the physicians themselves.

49

Yes, after these incidents I thought it would be very unjust on my part to remain silent any longer. It was not on account of the fact that Shi'ah were being subjected to injustice and cruelty and I wished to defend them against this flood of calumnies. No, it was in view of the fact that our highest and most important object continues to remain the same, viz. to tear the veils of ignorance from the eyes of common Muslims of the world so that judicious persons may review their thoughts and adopt the path of moderation and also we should be absolved of the allegations with regard to the calumnies of the obstinate and hostile people so that there should be no justification left over for blaming Shi'ah Ulema and scholars that they are negligent in introducing their religion to others.

Another more important hope that may be entertained is that under the shade of such discussion the ties of love and friendship amog the Muslims may be strengthened and the signs of enmity and hatred may disappear because every person, especially in our age, is aware that unity and removal of differences is one of the most essential things of which a man stands in need for the continuance of social life. It is possible that Ahmad Amin who has been shrouded on all sides by thick clouds of prejudice and ignorance may not write again about the Shi'ah as under: "The truth is that the Shi'ah faith is a refuge wherein everyone who wishes to pull down the foundation of Islam on account of enmity or envy takes shelter. As such, persons who wish to introduce into Islam the teachings of their Jewish, Christian or Zoroastrian ancestors achieve their nefarious ends under the shelter of this faith". (Fajrul Islam, p. 23).

Then he reaches the place where he says: "Traces of Judaism manifest themselves in Shi'ite Islam in the shape of belief in the Return of the Imams. The Shi'ah says: 'Fire of Hell is prohibited for all the Shi'ah except a few'. This is exactly similar to the claim of the Jews that they will not be subjected to the Fire of Hell except for a short period. (Surah al-Baqarah, 2:75). Traces of Christinity are also found in Shi'ite Islam, for they say: "The relationship of Imam with Allah is the same as that of Christ!" They also say: "The spiritual and the physical worlds are united in the person of Imam. Moreover, the chain of prophethood is never broken and prophethood shall remain in the world for ever. Whoever is united with the spiritual world is a Prophet".

They believe in the transmigration of soul,[1] incarnation of Allah[2] as well as penetration.[3]

These were some extracts from Ahmad Amin's book

---

[1] Transmigration of Soul means that after the death of a person his soul immediately migrates into the body of another person or an animal or grass or inanimate things. The two well-known conditions of migration of soul are, however, its migration into the body of a person or an animal. Some philosophers (like Mulla Sadra Shirazi) have given separate names to the four conditions of *Tanasukh al-Arwāh* (transmigration of soul). If transmigration takes place into a human body, they call it *Naskh*. If it takes place into the body of an animal, they call it *Maskh*. If it takes place into the body of grass, it is called *Faskh*. If this action takes place into inanimate things, it is called *Raskh*.

According to the philosophers and scholars transmigration of soul is an erroneous concept and a large number of arguments have been advanced against it in the books of philosophy and scholastic theology. (al-Asfār and Sharhe Tajrid)

[2] Belief in the Incarnation of Allah (viz. Allah possesses body) is one of the most ridiculous beliefs which cropped up in a small group of Muslims in imitation of old nonsensical religions. This small group is called *Mujassamah* or *Mushabbah*. They believe that Allah has body along with ears, eyes, hands, feet etc.

[3] There have been people who believed that it is possible that Allah may penetrate into a human body. They were called *Holuliya* and a good many sects of theirs have been mentioned in books of history of nations viz. *Khitabiyah, Sabaiyah, Hallajiyah, Mughayriyah, Azafirah* etc. Fortunately their traces are not to be found any longer. Utterances of some of the sects of Sufis convey the concept of **Penetration**. In any case there is no doubt that this belief too, is a part of the ridiculous beliefs and irrefutable arguments about the attributes of Allah prove the falsity of such beliefs.

51

Fajrul Islam. Of course, if the considerations of safeguarding the unity of Muslims and fear of pollution of the clear water of the fountain of love were not taken care of and kindling of fire of grudge and enmity had not been apprehended and if the well-known proverb, "How can one who eats palm dates stop others from doing so" had not become applicable to us, we would have made known to Ahmad Amin as to who are these people who wish to pull down the foundation of Islam and unity of Muslims and destroy their superiority and grandeur by fabricating truth and realities.

DID THEY WISH TO DESTROY ISLAM?

Of course we would like to ask this writer which group of the Shi'ah wished to destroy the foundation of Islam. Did they belong to the Shi'ah who were the companions of the Holy Prophet like: Salman Muhammadi (Farsi), Abuzar Ghiffari, Miqdad bin Aswad, Ammar bin Yasir, Khuzayma Zush Shahādatayn, Abi Tayhān, Huzayfa bin al-Yamān, Zubayr, Fazl bin Abbas, Abdullah bin Abbas, Hashim bin Utba Marqāl, Abu Ayyub Ansāri, Abān bin Sa'id bin al-Ās, Khalid bin Sa'id (both of whom were Umayyads), Abi bin Ka'b (famous reciter of the Holy Qur'an), Anas bin Hārith bin Nabiyah (who had heard the Holy Prophet saying: "My son Husayn will be martyred in a land named Karbala. Anyone of you who is present, should not lag behind in helping him?") Hence, he joined Imam Husayn and met martyrdom).

For further information reference may be made to the books entitled **al-Isabah** and **Isti'āb** which are the most authentic biographies of the Companions of the Holy Prophet, written by Sunni scholars.

If we wish to count the Shi'ah who were companions of the Holy Prophet and undertake discussion for proving their Shi'ite Islam, we will need writing a voluminous book. Fortunately, however, the Shi'ah scholars have absolved us of this responsibility and have written very excellent books on the subject like **al-Darajāt al-Rafi'ah fi Tabaqāt al-Shi'ah** written by the Late Sayyid Ali Khan (author of many other valuable books like **Tarāzul Lughat** which is one of the best books written on Arabic Lexicon). Although he while mentioning the groups of the Shi'ah, has named only the famous companions of the Holy Prophet (besides those belonging to Bani Hashim like Hamzah, Ja'far, Aqil etc.) most of them are those already mentioned by us. The following are besides them: Uthman bin Hunayf, Sahl bin Hunayf, Abu Sa'id Khadari, Qays bin Sa'd bin Ubada (whose father was Chief of the Ansars), Burayd, Bara bin Malik, Khabbāb bin Aratt, Rafa'h bin Malik Ansari, Abu al-Tufayl Āmir bin Waylah, Hind bin Abi Hala, Jo'da bin Hubayra Makhzumi, Umme Hāni, Bilal bin Rabāh (Mu'azzin of the Holy Prophet). Most of them are the persons who have been mentioned by him in this book.

I recollect to have added up names of all those persons who are considered to be Shi'ah (from books on the lives of the companions like **al-Isabah, Usudul Ghabah,** **Isti'ab** etc.) and found that there were about 3000 distinguished companions of the Holy Prophet who were considered to be the supporters and devoted friends of Imam Ali.

We are not aware whether it was this group consisting of distinguished companions of the Holy Prophet who wanted to uproot the foundation of Islam or it was the Commander of the Faithful Imam Ali himself who wanted to do so and about whom all admit that but for his sacrifices and bravery in the battlefields of Badr, Uhud, Ahzab etc. the branches of the tree of Islam would not have become strong and would not have borne fruit so much so that it has been said about his sacrifices that he founded and built up the citadel of Islam and had his sword not been there this stronghold would never have been accomplished.

Yes, if his sacrifices before and after the Migration of the Holy Prophet had not been there and similarly if the support and assistance of his revered father Abu Talib had not been rendered in Makkah, the group of Quraysh and the rapacious wolves of Arabia would have devoured Islam and none of its signs would have been visible today. But how grateful the Muslims have been! They gave a strange reward to Abu Talib for all his sacrifices. They declared that Abu Talib never embraced Islam and departed from this world as an infidel.

On the other hand there was Abu Sufyan who kindled the fire of war. It was this man who was the instigator and chief organizer of enemy preparations against the Holy Prophet and Islam. And when he had to submit to the formidable strength of Islam, he embraced Islam under compulsion and with great unwillingness and even after that he never refrained from displaying his infidelity or enmity to Islam. It was he who said after the transfer of caliphate to the Umayyads (from the time of Uthman onwards), "O Bani Umayyah! Take caliphate like a ball!".

Yes, this very Abu Sufyan (with all these pros and cons) has, according to their belief, left the world as a Muslim whereas the ardent supporter of Islam Abu Talib died as a non-Muslim and an infidel! On the contrary Abu Talib had embraced Islam by saying: "I have realized it finally that the religion of Muhammad is the best religion in the world".

Is Abu Talib such a weak-minded and thoughtless person that while knowing it for certain that the religion of Prophet Muhammad is the best religion, he should not follow it and should fear the people? No. Not at all! Was he not the chief of 'Batha' and patriarch of Quraysh?[1]

Now we leave aside the story of Abu Talib and his faith and revert to the real subject, viz. the people who

[1]This fact has to be made known with deep regret that all persons who had in any way contact with Imam Ali, had to encounter the venomous propaganda of the Umayyads the signs of which are still visible in some books of the Sunnis. It was not only Abu Talib the kind and revered father of Imam Ali and the great supporter of Islam and of the Holy Prophet who became victim of this incessant vituperations. Even Abuzar, Ammar, Qambar etc. were not spared! To know the pure faith of Abu Talib, the supporter of Islam, refer to **Abu Talib Mu'min al-Quraysh** and **al-Ghadir** (vol. VII) and study a number of interesting documents of different schools of thought of Sunnis quoted therein.

wanted to pull down the foundation of Islam. Were they the distinguished companions of the Holy Prophet who wished to destroy the foundation of this religion or the group of persons who came after them (i.e. Tābi'in)[1] consisting of trusted personalities like: Ahnaf bin Qays, Suwayd bin Ghaflah, Atiya Awfi, Hakam bin Utaybah, Sālim bin Abi Ja'd, Ali bin Abi Ja'd, Hasan bin Sāleh, Sa'id bin Jubayr, Sa'id bin Musayyab, Asbagh bin Nabatah, Sulayman bin Mahrān A'mash, Yahya bin Ya'mar Udwani (contemporary of Hajjāj) and many more whose names alongwith proof of their being Shi'ah will make the statement quite lengthy.

THE FOUNDERS OF ISLAMIC LEARNINGS

Did this group of famous Tābi'in who were all Shi'ah wish to destroy the foundation of Islam or was it another group of Tābi'in or were other people who appeared after them? They were indeed the same distinguished people who were the founders of Islamic learning and who had laid the foundation of different branches of knowledge with their untiring efforts, e.g. Abul Aswad Du'ayli, founder of Syntax, Khalil bin Ahmad Farahidi, founder of Lexicon and Prosody, Abu Muslim Mu'āz bin Muslim Harā', founder of conjugation. He is the same person whose identity as a Shi'ah has been established by Suyuti in vol. II, of al-Muzhar as well as by others.

Ya'qub bin Sukayt, the master and the forerunner of Arabic Literature.

Similarly the founders of Tafsir (Exegesis) like Abdullah bin Abbas, the famous scholar of Islamic learning whose place is among the vanguard of exegetes and whose identity as Shi'ah is as evident as daylight. Jābir bin Abdullah Ansari, Abi bin Ka'b, Sa'id bin Jubayr, Sa'id bin Musayyab.

Muhammad bin Amr Wāqidi was the first scholar, according to Ibn Nadim and many others, who collected different branches of Qur'anic learning and was one of the

---

[1]Tābi'in were the people who did not see the Holy Prophet and were usually the disciples of his companions.

supporters of Imam Ali. The name of his Tafsir is **al-Raghib**.

Similarly, the founder of Hadith, Abu Rāfeʿ (the servant of the Holy Prophet) and author of the book **al-Ahkām vas Sunan al-Qazāyā** was one of the closest friends of Imam Ali and was his Treasurer in Kufa. After Abu Rāfeʿ, his sons Ali bin Abi Rāfeʿ the Special Secretary of Imam Ali and Ubaydullah bin Abi Rāfeʿ followed their father and accomplished his task. The former is the first person after his father who wrote a book on Jurisprudence and the latter on History and Islamic Monuments.

Similarly, the founder of the branch of learning called *Kalām* and *Aqāʿid* (scholastic theology and beliefs) and the first person who wrote on this subject was Abu Hashim son of Muhammad bin Hanafiyah who wrote an interesting book on the subject. Then came Isa bin Rawza Tābiʿi who was alive at the time of Imam Muhammad Baqir. Contrary to what has been assumed by Suyuti, these two Shiʿah scholars preceded Wāsil bin ʿAta and Abu Hanifa in this branch of knowledge.

After these two scholars other distinguished Shiʿah personalities also trod this field, e.g. Qays al-Māsir, Muhammad bin Ali Ahwal whom we call **Mumin Tāq** whereas the opponents given him the title of **Shaitan Tāq**.

HISHĀM BIN HAKAM

The Nawbakht family was a noble and learned progeny, which kept the lamp of knowledge and learning kindled for more than a hundred years and handed down to posterity very valuable writings like **Fasul Yāqut** etc. A number of these distinguished persons e.g. Hishām bin Hakam, Muhammad bin Ali Ahwal and Qays al-Māsir as well as their disciples like Abu Jaʿfar Baghdadi Sakkāk, Abu Mālik al-Zahhāk al-Hazrami, Hisham bin Sālim, Yunus bin Yaʿqub and many others like them created a headache for the materialists and scholars of other schools of Islamic thought with their penetrating and forceful logic and defeated and cornered them especially in the narrow lane of argument with regard to the Oneness of Allah and Imamate and made them helpless before their own strong

56

logic so much so that if the conversations and debates of each of these distinguished men (especially Hisham bin Hakam) with other scholars on different religious matters (which are unfortunately scattered in different books) are compiled, a volume worthy of attention will become available. Similarly, if we wish to collect the names of all Shi'ah philosophers[1] and ulema of scholastic theology and explain their activities in the field of learning, a number of volumes will be compiled.

Now we ask the writer of **Fajrul Islam**, did these great men want to demolish the foundation of Islam or were they the compilers of the history of Islam and who collected material about the life of the Holy Prophet, his miracles and the battles as well as the pious attributes of that great leader of the world of Islam and who portrayed an attractive and lively image of him and handed it down to the Muslims? Are you aware that the first person from among the Muslim scholars who undertook this important task, was Abān bin Uthman al-Ahmar Tābi'i (d. 140 A.H.) and who is said to be a companion of Imam Ja'far Sadiq and whose method was followed after him by Hisham bin Muhammad bin Sā'ib Kalbi, Muhammad bin Ishaq Muttalabi and Abu Makhnaf Azdi? It may generally be said that all persons after them who have written books on this subject have benefited from the reservoir of their knowledge and wisdom. It is an admitted fact that all these scholars who were the founders of the various branches of learning entitled **History of Islam** and **Attributes of the Holy Prophet,** were the Shi'ah scholars.

After them the great historians of Islam and distinguished personalities in this field who succeeded the aforesaid group were also Shi'ah like Ahmad bin Muhammad bin Khalid Barqi (author of **Mahāsin**), Nasr bin Muzāhim Manqari, Ibrahim bin Muhammad bin Sa'd Thaqafi, Abdul Aziz Jaludi Basri Imami, Ahmad bin Ya'qub alias Ya'qubi whose famous book on history has been published in Najaf

---

[1]See: **Falasafatush Shi'ah** by Allama Shaykh Abdullah Na'imah (Beirut).

Ashraf as well as in Europe; Muhammad bin Zakariya Abu Abdillah Hākim alias Ibnul Fee'; Mas'udi the renowned author of **Murujuz Zahab**. Muhammad bin Ali bin Tabatabai, the author of the book **al-Adab al-Sultaniyah**. And many others whose particulars it is not possible to recount.

THE BEST POETS OF ISLAM

Here too we find that the Shi'ah poets are more distinguished and more well-known than others and their works are considered to be the best in Islamic poetry. In fact the poets of Islam are divided into different groups:

(i) The Companions: The distinguished personalities belonging to this group were all Shi'ah. In the first category may be mentioned the name of Nābegha Ju'di who accompanied the Commander of the Faithful Imam Ali in the Battle of Siffin and has left as his memorial a number of epic verses recited by him during that battle.

Similarly Urwa bin Zayd who was with Imam Ali at Siffin.[1] Labid bin Rabi'ah Āmiri about whom a number of scholars have stated that he was a Shi'ah.

Abu Tufayl Āmir bin Wā'ila, Abul Aswad Dua'li, Ka'b bin Zuhayr, author of the well-known laudatory poem **Bi-Anta Sa'ād** and many others.

(ii) **Contemporary Poets of Tābi'in:** Like, Farazdaq, Kumayt, Kathir, Sayyid Himyari, Qays bin Zarih etc.

(iii) **Group of Later Poets:** These were the poets who lived during the 2nd century Hegira like De'bal Khuzā'i, Abu Nuvās, Abu Tamām, Bahteri, Abdus Salām (Deekul Jinn), Abu Shith, Husayn bin Zahhāk, Ibn Rumi, Mansur Nimri, Ashja' Aslami, Muhammad bin Wahib and Sari'ul Ghawāni.

In short most of the poets during the Abbasid rule in the 2nd and the 3rd centuries after Hegira except Marwan bin Abi Hafsa and his sons, were all Shi'ah.

[1]Refer Aghāni.

(iv) **The Poets Who Flourished in the 4th Century:** Mutanabbi Gharb (Ibn Hāni Andlusi); Ibn Ta'awizi, Husayn bin Hajjaj author of al-Majun, Mahyar Daylami, Amirush Shu'ra, Abu Faras Hamadani (about whom it is said that poetry commenced and ended with him), Kashājim, Nāshi Saghir, Nāshi Kabir, Abu Bakr Khawarzami, Badi' Hamadani, Tughrāi, Ja'far Shamsul Khilafa, Sara al-Rifa', Imaratul Yumna, Wadāi, Khubz Arzi, Zāhi, Ibn Busām Baghdadi, Sibt bin Ta'āwizi, Salāmi and Nāmi.

In short most of the poets whose names and works have been mentioned in the four volumes of the book entitled **Yatimatuth Tha'labi** were Shi'ah.

To such an extent is the popularity and genius of the Shi'ah poets that the question is asked among literary circles: "Is it possible to find a non-Shi'ah literary man or poet?" And when it is desired to exaggerate the elegance and beauty of a poetic verse it is said that it has been composed in accordance with the Shi'ah style[1] so much so that some scholars consider Mutanabbi and Abul A'la to have been Shi'ah and it is possible that some of their poetic verses may bear testimony to this assertion.

Besides the persons mentioned above, we observe that there are certain other Shi'ah poets who either belonged to Quraysh like Fazl bin Abbas bin Utba whose life history has been recorded in **Aghāni,** and Abu Dehbal Jamhi and Wahb bin Rabi'ah or they were Alavi like Sayyid Razi and Sayyid Murtaza who are considered to be great Shi'ah saints and as well as Sharif Abul Hasan Ali Hamāni son of Muhammad bin Ja'far bin Muhammad Sharif bin Zayd bin Ali bin Husayn whose entire family consisted of poets, for Hamāni has been quoted as saying "I am a poet. My father was a poet and my grandfather was also a poet". To the group of Alavi poets also belonged Muhammad bin Sāleh Alavi whose particulars have been given in the book **Aghāni** as an appendix to a piece of his five verses. Similarly there was Sharif bin Shajari and many other Alavi poets.

---

[1]See: **al-Muraji'āt al-Rayhāniya** which is one of the valuable works of late Allama Kāshiful Ghita.

(For details refer to **Nasmatus Sahr fi mun Tashayyu' wa She'r** compiled by Sharif Yamāni).

It also deserves notice that some Shi'ah are found among Umayyad poets as well like Abdur Rahman bin Hakam brother of Marwan bin Hakam, Khalid bin Sa'id bin Ās and Marwan bin Muhammad Sarwaji Umavi about whom I remember that Zamakhshari has mentioned him in his book **Rabi'ul Abrār** by the name of Marwan bin Muhammad Sarwaji Umavi Shi'i. A few of the poetic verses quoted from him are as under:

O Bani Hashim! I belong to you at all places and in all circumstances!

You are the chosen ones of Allah! Ja'far al-Tayyar is one of you!

The Commander of the Faithful Imam Ali and Hamzah the Lions of Allah as well as the distinguished Lady of Islam Fatima Zahra, daughter of the Holy Prophet and her two sons Imam Hasan and Imam Husayn belong to you!

Even though I am one of the Umayyads yet I hate them in the presence of Allah!

The same is the case with Abul Faraj Isfahani, author of the well-known book **Aghāni** as well as **Maqātilut Tālibiyin** and Abi Wardi Umavi, the famous poet and auhor of **Najdiyāt wa Iraqiyāt** and many others.

I remember that previously when I was conducting research on Islamic books I came across the names of a number of persons of the Umayyad family who were Shi'ah. For the present, however, it is not possible for me to mention the names of all of them here.

MUSLIM RULERS AND STATESMEN

We now cross over this stage and have a look on the statesmen, the great amirs, writers and famous ministers. Among them we find distinguished personalities who were all Shi'ah or pretended to be Shi'ah like the Fatimids of Egypt, Āle Buya, Hamadanis, Bani Mazid, Imran bin Shaheen, Amirul Batā-eh, Muqallid bin Musayyab Uqayli and Qarwāsh bin Musayyab.

Many of the big Abbasid Caliphs also pretended themselves to be Shi'ah like Mamun, Muntasar, Mo'tazid Ahmad bin Muwaffaq and similarly al-Nāsir Ahmad bin Mustaz'i who is more famous than others for posting himself as Shi'ah. His poetic verses and the good relations which he had with the famous ruler Ali bin Yusuf Salahuddin Ayyubi clearly indicate exaggerated Shi'ah belief of both of them which are well-known.

Similar is the case of al-Mustansar and Zil Qarnayn al-Taghlabi Wajihud Dowla Abi Mutā' and Tamim bin Mu'azin Bādis, Sultan of Africa and Morocco and many others, the mentioning of whose names only will make a lengthy list, not to speak of their biographies.

Again, if we make a study with regard to the great ministers of Islam we find that all or most of them were Shi'ah like Ishāq Kātib. And perhaps he was the first person in Islam before the establishment of the rule of Abbasids, who was given the title of "Minister".

Then comes Abu Salma Khalal Hafs bin Sulayman Hamadani Kufi. He was the first person whom Saffah, the first Abbasid Caliph, selected as his minister because he was a wise and efficient man. The Caliph entrusted the entire affairs to him and gave him the title of **Wazir Āle Muhammad** (Minister of the Progeny of Muhammad). However, when Saffah found that he had much inclination towards the Family of Imam Ali than towards Abbasids he sentenced him to death.

Similar was the case with Abu Abdillah Ya'qub bin Dawud, the Minister of Abbasid Caliph Mahdi. The Caliph had entrusted all his affairs to Ya'qub, so much so that some poets extolled him as under:

"O Umayyads! Let your minds rest in peace, for the Caliph is Ya'qub bin Dawud and not the Abbasid Mahdi".

However, at last Mahdi too put him in jail for his strong inclination towards the Shi'ah faith and he remained behind the bars till Harun Rashid set him free.

The famous Shi'ah families which rose to the position of Ministership were Bani Naubakht and Bani Sahal e.g. Fazl bin Sahal and Hasan bin Sahal. Similar is the case with

Bani Furat as for example Hasan bin Ali became the minister of al-Muqtadir, the Abbasid Caliph, thrice, and Abul Fazl Ja'far and Abul Fatah Fazl bin Ja'far also attained that position.

The family of Bani 'Amid also attained that position, Muhammad bin Husayn bin Amid and his son Abul Fateh Ali bin Muhammad known as *Zulki fāyatain* held the office of minister in the court of Ruknud Dawlah.

Similarly Bani Tahir Khuzā'i who were the ministers of Mamun and other Abbasid Caliph and Hasan bin Harun Mohlabi, Abu Dalaf Ajli, Sahib bin Ubad, the political genius Abul Qāsim Maghribi, the champion of the field of politics and the founder of the Government of Fatimids, Abu Abdillah Husayn bin Zikariya alias Shi'i, Ibrahim bin Abbas Sauli, the famous scribe of the court of Mutawakkil, Talāye' bin Razik who was one of the famous ministers of Fatimids, Afzal the Commander-in-Chief of Egyptian forces and his sons, Abul Hasan Ja'far bin Muhammad bin Fatir, Abul Mu'āli Hibtullah bin Muhammad bin Muttalib, Minister of al-Mustazhar and Mu'ayaduddin Muhammad bin Abdul Karim Qummi who was a descendent of Miqdad became Minister of al-Nāsir, then of al-Zāhir and thereafter of al-Mustansir, all of whom were Abbasid Caliphs. Similarly Hasan bin Sulayman (who was a great scribe of the Barāmaka and was addressed by the title of Shi'ah as stated in the book al-Awrāq), Yahya bin Salāmah Hasfaki, Ibn Nadim, (author of **al-Fahrist**,)Abu Ja'far Ahmad bin Yusuf and his brother Abu Muhammad Qasim (who wrote beautiful and exciting eulogy and elegy to pay homage to the Ahlul Bayt, which may be seen in the book **al-Awrāq** compiled by Sauli) were also Shi'ah. These two brothers were well-known scribes who had a long record of service during the period of Mamun.

Similarly Ibrahim bin Yusuf and his sons and the great scholars of Arabic literature Abu Abdillah Muhammad bin Imran Marzbāni author of the book **al-Mu'ajam** about whom Sam'āni and others have clearly stated that he was a Shi'ah and a Mu'tazili.[1]

[1]Of course, "Shi'ite Islam" in its own particular meaning is a faith
Continued...

There are many other such persons whose exact number is difficult to be counted. As a matter of fact if we wish to make a list of all statesmen, and other Shi'ah dignitaries who acquired distinction by dint of their knowledge, wisdom and writings and thus rendered a great service to the world of Islam, we will stand in need of compiling a number of books on the subject.

Incidentally, my late father (May Allah grant him peace) compiled a book entitled **al-Husoon al-Mani'ah fi Tabaqātish Shi'ah** on the lives of thirty groups out of the various groups of Shi'ah such as scholars, philosophers, statesmen, ministers, physicians, astronomers etc., and compiled ten big volumes of notes in this field. Unfortunately these notes are still in their original shape and only a small portion of this vast subject has so far been gone through.

Here we may ask Ahmad Amin, the fanatical writer of the book **Fajrul Islam**: If these distinguished Shi'ah personalities whose names have been mentioned here and these revered people who brought different branches of Islamic learning into being and founded Islamic knowledge were the very persons who wanted to destroy the foundation of Islam and you, your teachers and your friends made the foundation of Islam strong, would it not then be appropriate to consider Islam to be dead and say good-bye to it for ever? It is here that we should recite the well-known poetic verses of the Saint of Mu'arra.[1]

---

totally different from "Mu'tazila". To understand this fact it is quite sufficient to point out that Shi'ah consider "Imamate" (Leadership) and succession (Caliphate) to the Prophet of Islam to be publicly announced by the Holy Prophet and is acknowledged by authentic sources, whereas the "Mu'tazila" believe as a matter of principle that the Holy Prophet did not nominte any successor. However, as the Shi'ah and Mu'tazila faiths have many things in common, many Shi'ah in the past times acted for certain consideration as "Mu'tazila" like Yahya bin Zayd Alavi from whom Ibn Abil Hadid (famous Sunni historian and research scholar) has quoted many valuable theoretical investigations (Kāshiful Ghita).

[1] By **the Saint of Mu'arra** is meant Abul Ala Mu'arri who was born

Continued...

I hope that the contemporary writers as well as those who will follow will reflect, while writing, as to what they are saying and what they are writing and will not write down anything without proper research (they should know that critical and investigating pens are in their pursuit which will study, analyse and split whatever they have said and will examine every word of it).

What an excellent thing the Commander of the Faithful, Imam Ali, has said: "The tongue of a wise man is at the back of his heart (he reflects first and then speaks), but the heart of a fool is under his tongue (he speaks first and then thinks about the matter''.

UNJUSTIFIED CALUMNIES

Now we make another portion of the writing of Ahmad Amin, the subject of our study. He says: The Jewish faith has appeared in Shi'ite Islam by way of belief in the concept of *Raj'at* (the Return) which is one of the basic principles of Shi'ite Islam so much so that it could serve as an objection

in small town of Mu'arra in Syria (which possesses a very healthy climate and where he is also buried). The poetic verses mentioned below are part of his famous panegyric contained in **Saqt al-Zand** (p. 533) of his works as well as in other books. Hereunder we quote the verses under reference as well as some other attractive verses of the panegyric in question:

"When Mārid, the well-known miser of Arabia accuses Hātim Tā'i of miserliness.

And when Bāqil whose foolishness and dumbness are proverbial, rebukes Qays bin Sā'ida Ayādi, the saint and the great orator for ignorance and debility.

And when the small star 'Saha' on account of its smallness people test their eyesight, tells the bright sun, 'Alas! How much hidden and dark you are!'

And when the darkness of night tells the bright morning, 'How dark you are!'

O death! Trace us out at such a time, because life in such an environment is sad and wearisome: And, O soul! leave the body soon for you are now being mocked ''.

to this faith and could be said that Judaism has appeared in Shi'ah faith by way of belief in the concept of the 'Return'. Is it not proper for a person whose knowledge of a religion is so superficial, to keep quiet? In Arabic there is a proverb: "Leave the work which you cannot accomplish".

To make the point more clear, it may be said that although the concept of the **Return** is considered to be a part of belief, still belief in it is neither obligatory nor refusal to believe in it is prohibited. In other words Shi'ite Islam does not depend on it from the point of view of its existence or non-existence.[1]

In fact the concept of **Return** is like fortellings of the leaders of Islam about future happenings in the world like the Resurrection of Christ, the appearance of the Impostor *(Dajjal)*, the rising of Sufyani and other similar propositions which are well-known among all sects of Muslims. They are neither a part of our basic principles nor does denial thereof entail expulsion from the religion, just as belief in these things alone is not a proof of one's having accepted Islam.

The concept of the **Return** in Shi'ite Islam is exactly as mentioned above. Furthermore even if we suppose for argument's sake that belief in the concept of **Return** is a principle of the Shi'ah faith, does similarity of belief with Jews in only one aspect, justify our saying that Judaism has manifested itself in Shi'ah faith? This will be exactly like saying that Judaism has manifested itself in Islam, because Jews believe in monotheism and so do Muslims. Would it not be a baseless logic and an erroneous and unfounded inference?

Besides all this what a good thing it would have been if these persons who have criticized the Shi'ah in the past and continue to criticize them during the present times with reference to the concept of the **Return** had known

---

[1]Though the Shi'ah believe in the concept of Return yet it is not an integral part of their faith such as Justice, Imamate and other matters connected with the attributes of the Holy Prophet and the Holy Imams (peace be on them).

the meaning of the **Return** they would have understood as to what the Shi'ah meant about it!

Is it impossible for Almighty Allah to bring a number of persons to life after their death and once again provide them the physical shape? Can any Muslim deny such a possibility notwithstanding the fact that the Holy Qur'an has clearly quoted examples thereof? Have these critics not studied the narrative regarding a group of Israelities in the Holy Qur'an, when it says: *Have you not considered the thousands who left their homes for fear of death, who were then caused by Allah to die and brought back to life? Allah is generous to mankind but most of the people are ungrateful.* (Surah al-Baqarah, 2:243)[1]

Again have they not read the verse: *On that day We shall gather one group of persons from every nation and again bring them to life.* (Surah Naml, 27:83) Is the day referred to in the verse the Day of Judgement? Certainly not, because on that day all the people will not be gathered at one place and instead only a group from every nation will be gathered.

However, it is a matter of great regret that belief in the **Return** and criticism thereof has been used as a pretext by a group of Sunni ulema from the early days of Islam to the present day. Consequently when their writers of books on **Rijāl** (biographies of the narrators of traditions) narrate something through Shi'ah scholars and narrators and do not find any weak point in it from the point of view of its correctness they say: "But he believed in the concept of

---

[1]According to the exegetes this verse was revealed about a number of persons belonging to Bani Israel who lived in a town called Dawardān in the vicinity of Iraq. When they were ordered for jihad and their forces got ready to encounter the enemy, they scattered away on the pretext that the enemy land might be polluted with contagious disease and did not partake in the jihad. However, according to the Divine command they all perished and then again came to life after death. The exegetes have given their detailed account with reference to the said verse and this is one of the clear proofs of the concept of *Raj'at* (Return).

66

the **Return**, as if they wanted to say: "It is regrettable that he was an idolater and had accepted someone to be a partner of Allah! The story of Mu'min Tāq and Abu Hanifah in this context is well-known".

In any case it is not my intention to defend this belief (Return) here or anywhere else, because in my opinion this matter is too trifle to deserve such discussion. In my view this discussion is not worth the edge of a nail. On the other hand my desire is to acquaint Ahmad Amin with his gross error and his unjustified attack.

STRANGE CALUMNY

Another baseless thing imputed to the Shi'ah is that they believe the fire of Hell to be prohibited for the Shi'ah except to a very small number. I do not know where he has come across this assertion. Is it proper that a person who undertakes discussion and analysis of beliefs and religions, should attribute something so evil and improper to a community without any proof or documentary evidence? Can a research scholar adopt such a wrong method?

Has this reality not been declared aloud in Shi'ah books that Allah has created Paradise for the obedient persons even though they may be Ethiopian slaves and He has created Hell for the disobedient ones have also been quoted from the Holy Imams.

If the writer means intercession by the Holy Prophet or the Imams (peace be on them) for certain sinners, this is an entirely different topic which will be dealt with at its appropriate place. The question of "intercession" is, in brevity, one of the necessities of Islam and all sects of Muslims believe in it.[1]

Leaving this matter aside we repeat our previous words and say that even if it may be supposed that the

[1] In short it cannot be believed that a Muslim who respects the Holy Qur'an should decline to accept the very basis of intercession. However, intercession has some limits and particular meanings and conditions which too cannot be denied in toto.

Shi'ah have such a belief about the sinners among them and the Jews too have a similar belief about the followers of Judaism, does this similarity of belief justify anyone saying that Shi'ite Islam is deduced from Judaism or that the religion of the Jews has manifested itself in the religion of the Shi'ah? Can any wise person say that Abu Hanifah obtained his *Fiqah* (religious jurisprudence) from the Magi because in certain matters like marriage their views tally and especially because he is of Iranian descent? Will these baseless things leave any impression other than that of kindling the fire of hatred and enmity among different sects of Muslims?

Thereafter, Ahmad Amin adds: "Christian faith has also manifested itself in the Shi'ites because some Shi'ah believe that the relationship of Imam with Allah is the same as that of Jesus with Allah".

If Ahmad Amin, the author of **Fajrul Islam** wished to observe basic honesty, he should have made his object clear and should not have said irrelevant and illogical things. He should have stated clearly as to which Shi'ah professes such a belief about Imam and in which book this proposition is recorded. If he means those sects which are called the Ghulat like the Khitabiyah, Gharabiyah, Alya'iyah, Mukhammasa, Bazi'iyah and the like which have now fortunately become extinct. It may be said that, it is a great injustice to style them as Shi'ah because they are for all purposes akin with the sect of *Qaramata* and similar other sects who, in fact, are not bound with any religion. The **Imamiya** Shi'ah and their Imams (peace be on all of them) totally dissociate themselves from these sects.

Moreover, the said sects do not also have the same type of belief in the Imam as professed by Shi'ah Imamiya. On the other hand their belief and their perversion may be summarized in these words: "Imam is Allah or he has united himself with Him or has penetrated into Him". Many Sufis like Hallaj, Gilani, Rafa'i and Badawi are also said to have uttered similar remarks (and according to their own interpretations). Their words would rather give the apparent impression that they claim for themselves a position higher than Divinity itself (if such a position be possible). Similar nonsense and basless remarks have also been quoted from those who believe in *Wahdatul Wujud* (Pantheism) to *Wahdatul Mawjud*. (Unity of the Creator and Creation).

However, Shi'ah Imamiya i.e. people consisting of the majority of the population of Iran and millions of Muslims of Pakistan and India and hundreds of thousands of the inhabitants of Syria and Afghanistan and other places hate such beliefs and consider them to be the worst type of blasphemy and perversion. They do not believe in anything stated above except pure Oneness of Allah and His having no resemblance with anyone of the creation. They consider Allah to be free from the attributes of the creatures (like possibility, change and occurrence) as well as from whatever contradicts His pre-Existence and Eternity. And their books (especially on Philosophy and Scholastic Theology) are replete with such discussions, most common of these books being brief ones like Tajrid and detailed ones like Asfār and thousands of other books, a good many of which have fortunately been printed. In these books abundant cogent arguments in contradiction of Transmigration of Soul, Unity of the Creator and the Creation, Penetration and Incarnation can be observed and if a study thereof is made in a must and unbiased manner the worth of these unjustified and baseless imputations which the storms of modern changes have driven towards us will become absolutely clear and it will become known that we have never believed in Transmigration of Soul, Penetration, Unity of the Creator and the Creation or Incarnation and no one who seeks reality and is well-informed can impute such unreasonable things to us.

In short if Ahmad Amin meant by Shi'ah those sects which are now extinct and were absolute strangers to Islam and of whose followers there is no trace in the entire world, it is possible that we may agree that they did have such beliefs. But what have they to do with Shi'ah Imamiya and the followers of this faith? Is such an imposition not an open injustice and a grave error? If, in fact, by the word Shi'ah he meant this well-known and big community which consists millions of Muslims of the world he has been guilty of a great and unpardonable offence and we would like to demand a proof from him. We call upon him to produce testimony in support of his statement from any of the books written by Shi'ah scholars, either in the past or during the present times.

However, it is evident from this entire discussion that whatever has been said in **Fajrul Islam** about Shi'ah is baseless and all the claims of its author are without any documentary evidence or proof.

We do not wish to analyse the book **Fajrul Islam** in its entirety and explain all its weak and doubtful points and the erroneous and fallacious views of its author. We only wanted to present the attitude of contemporary writers and persons who are usually considered to be scholars on matters relating to the Shi'ah Faith.

When the writers and persons commonly styled as scholars adjudge about the Shi'ah in this manner what then could be expected of the common people?

THE SOURCE OF ADVERSITIES

We think that the source of all these adversities is the fact that for getting acquainted with Shi'ah faith such persons mostly rely on the words of Ibn Khaldun Barbari, the same Ibn Khaldun who, while sitting in the most far off point of Africa and Morocco wanted to pass a judgement on the Shi'ah of Iraq who were living in the most far off place of the East. Or else they consider the sayings of Ibn Abdu Rabbibi Undulusi to be their authority. And even if they make much more progress and wish to study and discuss matters relating to the Shi'ah in a wider perspective, they refer to the writings of the orientalists like Prof. Wilhosen and Prof. Dozie and look for decisive proofs therein. The thing which is not at all mentioned and none cares to think about is reference to the books of the Shi'ah themselves, in spite of the fact that the matter under discussion is Shi'ah and it is, therefore, necessary that in the first instance reference should be made to their books.

However, when a Shi'ah, whose belief rests on a firm

foundation, observes such discussions of modern writers about himself he is reminded of the strange story which has been related by Rāghib Isfahani in his famous book Muhāzirāt on the following lines: Someone approached Ja'far bin Sulaymān and said, "Such and such person is a heretic".

Ja'far bin Sulayman asked, "What is the proof?"

The man replied, "He is Khāriji, Mu'tazili, Nāsebi, Haruri, Jabri and Rāfezi. He abuses Ali bin Khattab, Umar bin Ali Quhāfa, Uthman bin Abi Talib and Abu Bakr bin Affan, and uses unbecoming words about Hajjaj who destroyed Kufa while fighting against Abu Sufyan and fought against Husayn bin Muawiyah on the day of Qatā'if (as if he meant by this the day of Taff or the day of Tā'if). After hearing all this rigmarole, Ja'far bin Sulayman said: "May you die! I do not know for what I should envy you — for your enormous knowledge of genealogies or for your information about beliefs and religions!"

ABDULLAH BIN SABA

Now as regards Abdullah bin Saba who is aligned to the Shi'ah or the Shi'ah are aligned to him and who is supposed to be the founder of the Shi'ah Faith. The best way of finding out the views of the Shi'ah about him is to refer to the books of Shi'ah. We find that in all such books, without any exception whatsoever, the Shi'ah have cursed him and dissociated themselves from him. The least that has been said about him in the books of biographies (Rijāl) under the letter "Ain" and the writers have contented themselves with it instead of going into details is this sentence: Abdullah bin Saba is too accursed to be made the subject of discussion (In this connection refer to the books on Rijāl by Bu Ali and other Shi'ah writers).

Besides what has been stated above, it is also not improbable that Abdullah bin Saba, Majnun Bani Āmir, Abu Hilāl and the like who are considered to be heroes of their respective stories, may also be a part of fables and fictions coined by the story writers in their fancy. Study of the history of Umayyads and Abbasids shows that people led a very luxurious life in their times. And it is quite natural that the more luxurious the life of the people is, the more brisk becomes the bazaar of fiction, visionary writing and tell-tale, so that people who are brought up in luxury and are drowned in pleasure should take more interest in these pursuits.[1]

[1]Very interesting and wonderful research has recently been carried out by our scholars about Abdullah bin Saba (the same person who, in the books written against the Shi'ah has been referred as the founder of the Shi'ite Islam). What has been stated in this context by Allama Kashiful Ghita as a possibility and, with his enormous wisdom, can be mentioned as not improbable, is in fact a reality. Especially in a book entitled **Abdullah bin Saba** written recently by Allama Murtaza Askari (which has fortunately been translated into Urdu, English, and Persian as well). Justice has been done to the subject in a very competent manner and the veil has been removed from the ambiguous face of this mythical person who has been the real hero of the concocted tales written against the Shi'ah during the span of the last thirteen centuries. In this book Allama Askari has, as a true researcher adopted a correct method for showing the real face of this mythical personality. He has commenced his study with the well-known documents like Kāmil Ibn Athir, Tarikh Ibn Khaldun, Tarikh Tabari, Ibn Kathir, Ibn Asākir and Zahabi and has endeavoured to find out the source of this fiction. After a complete research and study he has found that it is now more than 1000 years that the historians have quoted the story of Abdullah bin Saba and his activities from a person named Sayf bin Umar. Many of them like Tabari have quoted from him directly and other writers of recent past and present have quoted this story from Tabari and other historians mentioned above. Thereafter, he has directed his research to the identification of Sayf bin Umar because all talks about Abdullah bin Saba culminate in him. As a result of this research he has introduced Sayf bin Umar to us in the following terms in the light of clear documentary proof.

Sayf bin Umar was a person who died after 170 A.H. and handed down two books namely **al-Futuh wa al-Raddah** and **al-Jamal wa Masiru Ayesha wa Ali.**

Continued..

We think that the tales which Dr Taha Husayn and others like him have started narrating about the Holy Qur'an and Islam and the method which they have adopted in this age and the manner in which they wish to provide their sayings the dress of reality with speeches and melodies only are suited to the aforesaid visionary times and not to

The study of the particulars of Sayf in books on biographies and of what has been written about him by scholars from 3rd century until 10th century Hegira shows that he was an impostor, a pretender, originator of mythical stories and a narrator of fake tradition and who was sometimes referred to as Sayf bin Umar Zindiq (Atheist).

Study of his two books also confirms the fact that he possessed those qualities, because most of his narrations do not tally with any historical documents and have a perfect air of fiction.

All the documentary evidence collected in this behalf goes to show that Sayf bin Umar created a number of fictitious figures and it is also not improbable that he was commissioned by someone to do so. One of these fictious figures is this very Abdullah bin Saba.

In this manner we find with the deepest regret that this man (Abdullah bin Saba) who has, for more than 1000 years, served as a pretext for propaganda against the Shi'ah and who has been reported to be a Jew and the so-called founder of the Shi'ite Islam has had in fact no real existence but actually was the brainchild of that and a evil genius named Sayf bin Umar!

We invite the enlightened conscience of the Muslim sages for arbitration and ask: Is it proper that a religion whose root has been watered by the purest sources of inspiration viz. the Holy Progeny of the Holy Prophet should be subjected to such calumnies and unholy remarks may be passed against it on the authority of fictitious stories without any research or verification? Is this the justice to which the Holy Qur'an invites us to adhere to?

And is this the meaning of the commandment which we have been given regarding acceptance of news? *Believers, if one who publicly commits sins brings you any news, verify it, lest you harm people through ignorance and then regret thereafter.* (Surah al-Hujurat, 49:6) See: **Abdullah bin Saba**, Allama Murtaza Askari, the present age which is the age of research of facts, principles of honesty and sincerity of purpose.

We have drifted away from our real subject. It was not our intention to discuss these issues. On the other hand these words are only an introduction to the real theme. Keeping in view all these different factors of annoyance, calumnies, uncalled for sarcasm and sadness to which the Shi'ah are subjected, it was necessary for us to introduce a brief and condensed discussion about the beliefs and principles of Shi'ah and on the important matters of secondary nature which are unanimously accepted by Shi'ah scholars and which could be given the name of Shi'ah Faith. And this is our real object.

Evidently we cannot depend upon the beliefs of one or a few stray persons in this matter because such beliefs cannot be presented with the name of Shi'ah Faith, especially because the door of Ijtihad has been and is still open. Thus every scholar is entitled to express his view or give judgement by having recourse to reason if his view is respectable and is not opposed to the concensus of opinion of the ulema or clear commandments of the Holy Qur'an or authentic reports and traditions or exigencies of human intellect. Otherwise such a view or judgement will be treated as opposed to Shi'ah Faith in accordance with the rules and principles which need not be amplified here.

In short our ultimate objective is three-fold:
(i) To present the fundamentals of the Shi'ah Faith
(ii) To indicate its unanimity, and (iii) To show the absence of any dispute about it.

It is evident that I myself will explain all these matters. However, it is beyond the scope of this treatise to quote documents and proof for each of them. Hence, study of detailed books written on the subject may please be undertaken.

The purpose is to introduce to all the sects of Muslims including the scholars and the laymen, the Shi'ah and their beliefs, as they are, so that they (other sects of Muslims) may not do any more injustice to themselves and they may not impute baseless and false things to their brethren-in-faith and not personify them in their eyes like hounds of the jungle or wild beasts of the hot deserts of Africa or man-eaters. On the other hand they should know that by the Grace of Allah the Shi'ah are educated in the school of Islam and follow the sublime teachings of the Holy Qur'an and their share in faith and good morals is enormous. They do not depend upon anything except the Holy Qur'an, the tradition of the Holy Prophet and the decisive logical arguments. It is possible that in the light of these explanations, the ignorant people may become informed, the negligent may stand warned, the aspirants and frivolous may desist from their exaggerations and the fanatics may cast away fanaticism and come nearer to their brethren. It is, therefore, possible that in the wake of this warning and awakening and by creating mutual understanding, Allah may strengthen the bonds of unity among the Muslims so that they may assume the form of a strong column against their enemies and all should endeavour for the grandeur of Islam with one voice and one heart. The fulfilment of this desire of ours is not beyond the infinite Power of the Almighty![1]

[1]However, as it is quite evident, only the publication of books cannot fill these gaps and convert our dispersion into unity and brotherhood. On the other hand, besides the publication of books, it is necessary to set up a chain of channels for the exchange of knowledge, to conduct special meetings for mutual contacts of scholars of both sides and for their discussions in cordial atmosphere of reconciliation and sincerity, to organize conferences for finding the solution of the major problems of the Muslim world and most important of all to take full advantage of Hajj which is the greatest congregation of the Muslims of the world. This is so necessary that with Allah's Grace the inauspicious signs of dispersion, enmity and discord may gradually disappear from amongst the Muslims.

PART I

Towards Understanding Shi'ah Faith

SHI'AH IN THE DAYS OF THE HOLY PROPHET

When did Shi'ah Faith originate and how did it come into existence? Who was the first person to sow the seed of Shi'ah Faith? How did this sapling grow up and bear flowers and fruits so much so that even most of the statesmen of Islam believed in it and a number of Abbasid Caliph and some of their famous Ministers professed humility before it?

Who were the persons who watered this sapling with their blood? How did the people take refuge with the Holy Imams and the Progeny of the Holy Prophet as a consequence of the mis-representations and deviations of the Umayyad and the Abbasid Caliphs?

The first person who sowed the seed of Shi'ah Faith in the land of Islam was the Prophet of Allah, the Holy Prophet Muhammad, peace be on him. In other words the seed of Shi'ah Faith was sown simultaneously with that of Islam. The Holy Prophet watered it and looked after it consistently till the sapling grew up into a tree. Its branches were laden with flowers and it bore fruit after the passing away of the Holy Prophet. This statement is supported by the traditions *(Ahādith)* quoted from the Holy Prophet. Their narrators are not Shi'ah lest it should be said in the words of Ahmad Amin and others like him, that their statements are not credible as they believe in the concept of the **Return** or that it is only to achieve their own ends that they have narrated these traditions. No, not that but the narrators of these traditions are all distinguished Sunni ulema and have been quoted through reliable authorities so that no sensible person (keeping in view the circumstances thereof) can deny their authenticity or attribute to them any possibility of forgery or falsehood.

Here I would like to mention a few of these traditions in connection with the study of some other matters:

(i)   The famous Sunni scholar Suyuti while explaining the sublime Qur'anic verse (Surah Bayyina, 98:7) quotes from Ibn Asakir who quotes from Jabir bin Abdullah who quotes from the Holy Prophet: "We were with the Holy Prophet when Imam Ali was coming towards us. The Holy Prophet said: He and his Shi'ah will acquire salvation on the Day of Judgement. And it was at this time that the sublime verse: *The righteously striving believers are the best of all creatures* was revealed". (Tafsir al-Durr al-Manthur)

(ii)   He also quotes from Ibn Adi who quotes from Ibn Abbas to the effect that when the sacred verse of (Surah al-Bayyina, 98:7) was revealed, the Holy Prophet said to Imam Ali: "This is about you and your Shi'ah on the Day of Judgement. You will be pleased with Allah and He will be pleased with you".

(iii)   Similarly Ibn Marduyah quotes Imam Ali as saying: "The Holy Prophet said to me, 'Have you not heard that Almighty Allah says: *The righteously striving believers are the best of all creatures.* (Surah al-Bayyinah, 98:7) By this you and your Shi'ah are meant and whose rendezvous with me will be at the Fount of Kauthar. When different people will be called to account and present themselves in the court of the Almighty Allah, you will be called in such a condition that your foreheads, hands and feet will be shining". These three traditions have been quoted by Suyuti in al-Durr al-Manthur.

The next famous Sunni scholar Ibn Hajar has also quoted some of them in his book al-Sawā'iq al-Muhriqa from Dārqutni.

(iv)   Ibn Hajar also quotes from Mother of the Faithful Umme Salma to the effect that the Holy Prophet said,

"O Ali! You and your friends will be in Paradise".

(v) Ibn Athir also quotes in Nihāya to the effect that it is stated in the tradition related by Imam Ali that the Holy Prophet said to him: "You and your Shi'ah will soon meet Allah in such circumstances that you will be pleased with Him and He will be pleased with you and your enemies will meet you with dark faces in such a condition that their heads will be pulled up on account of tightened iron collars and chains round their necks".

It seems that this tradition, too, has been quoted by Ibn Hajar in Sawā'iq and also in other statements in a different manner. Hence, it can be concluded that this is one of the well-known traditions.

Zamakhshri in Rabi'ul Abrār quotes the Holy Prophet as saying, "O Ali! On the Day of Judgement I shall resort to Allah and you will resort to me and your children will resort to you and the Shi'ah will resort to them. Then you will see where they carry us (i.e. to Paradise)".

If books of traditions like Musnad of Ahmad bin Hambal, Khasā'is Nisā'i etc. are studied, it will be quite easy to collect many other similar traditions.

When the Holy Prophet of Islam repeatedly mentions the name of the Shi'ah of Ali bin Abi Talib in his discourses and says that they will be safe on the Day of Judgement and will acquire salvation and will be pleased with Allah and Allah will be pleased with them, there should be no doubt about the fact that all those who recognize the Holy Prophet to be the Messenger of Allah and have belief in his Prophethood and know that he does not say anything on the basis of his personal desire or wish will believe in what he has said in the above quoted traditions.

WHO WERE CALLED SHI'AH?

Incidentally, it can be concluded from the preceding traditions that this distinction (of being a Shi'ah) was for some particular companions of the Holy Prophet and not for all of them and these traditions are applicable to the former only. Hence, persons who have abandoned the real meaning of these traditions and have interpreted them to cover all the companions of the Holy Prophet have not reached the depth of their real import!

To explain the matter further, it may be said that it appears from books on Hadith and History that during the days of the Holy Prophet numerous companions (of the Holy Prophet) were close friends and attendants of Imam Ali who considered him to be their Imam and religious leader in the capacity of the missionary of the Holy Prophet and the expounder of his teachings and orders and who were, from that very time, identified as Shi'ah of Imam Ali. This fact can be verified by reference to the books of lexicographers like **Nihāya** of Ibn Athir, **Lisānul Arab** etc. They explain that the word "friends" or "supporters" by lapse of time became known as their proper name.

It goes without saying that if by the words "**Shi'ah of Ali**" the Holy Prophet had meant all the persons who were friendly towards him, or, at least, were not inimical towards him, in such a manner that the term should cover all or most of the Muslims (as comprehended by some ill-informed persons), the interpretation of the word *Shi'ah* in such a sense will not at all be appropriate, because being friendly towards someone or not being inimical towards him is not sufficient for the application of the title of Shi'ah to him but something more special is latent in its concept.

THE MEANING OF THE WORD SHI'AH

Shi'ah means a follower and an obedient person. As a matter of fact only following and obedience are also not sufficient. The meaning of the word implies that he should be loyal, staunch and constant.

Those who even have very little acquaintance with the usages and expressions of Arabic language will certainly understand the meaning of the word Shi'ah in such a manner that if it is used in any other sense it will certainly need further explanation.

In short it cannot be justified on the face of these and other similar traditions to deny the fact that what is meant by Shi'ah is a particular group of Muslims who had some special relations with Imam Ali and that this group was superior to other Muslims, although the hearts of those others were also not empty of love for him (not to talk of their being inimical towards him).

What we have said should not be misunderstood. We do not mean to say that those companions of the Holy Prophet who were not a part of this special group and who formed majority of the companions were, Allah forbid, against the Holy Prophet or did not display humility in the following of his teachings and orders. No, we do not at all mean this. Allah forbid that we shall have such an opinion about the friends and companions of the Holy Prophet when they were in their time the best people on the face of this earth.

Here the question is obvious. Possibly all of them did not hear these traditions and those who did hear them did not perhaps become acquainted with their real purport. In any case, the revered companions of the Holy Prophet enjoy a much higher position than that which lowly persons could aspire to reach.[1]

Let us not divert from the subject. The Holy Prophet of Islam took care of this sapling consistently and watered it with the sweet water of his words. He followed up this reality sometimes directly and sometimes indirectly. The traditions available in this context are very well-known to the distinguished Sunni traditionalists — not to speak of Shi'ah scholars — and most of them have been quoted in **Sahih Bukhari** and **Sahih Muslim** for example:

(i)   The famous tradition of *Manzilat* (similarity): In this

[1] Besides this, it is an admitted fact that all the companions did not enjoy the same rank in the matter of faith, knowledge and submission to what they heard from the Holy Prophet. To say that all the companions were purified and just is not compatible with any of the intellectual, logical, traditional and historical standards and has lost its value. Possibly there were persons among the companions who, on account of their age, or to safeguard their social and apparent status (or for other reasons), were not inclined to be called Shi'ah of Imam Ali, who was at that time in the prime of his life.

tradition the Holy Prophet says, "Ali is to me as Harun was to Musa.[1]

(ii) A famous tradition says: "None except the true believers are friendly towards you and none except the hypocrites are inimical towards you".

(iii) In the famous tradition called *Tayr* the Holy Prophet has been quoted as saying, "O Allah! Send your most favourite servant to me!" (And thereafter Imam Ali arrived in his presence!)"

(iv) One night, during the Battle of Khaybar the Holy Prophet was pleased to remark, "Tomorrow I shall give the Standard to the man who is loved by Allah and his Prophet and who also loves Allah and His Prophet".

(v) The tradition of *Thaqalayn*: In this tradition the Holy Prophet says: "I leave amongst you two very precious things — the Book of Allah and my Ahlul Bayt (Holy Progeny of the Holy Prophet)".[2]

---

[1]This is one of the most well-known traditions about Imam Ali which have been quoted in most of the books of Sunni like Sahih Muslim, Chapter on Attributes of Imam Ali (vol. II, p. 324) and similarly **al-Mustadrak al-Hākim** (vol. III, p. 109) and **Anwārul Muhammadiya min Mawāhibil Laduniyah** (p. 436) Sahih Bukhari (vol. III, p. 54), **Musnad Ahmad** (vol. I, p. 98), Isti'ab (vol. II, p. 473) and many other books.

[2]This is one of the most authentic and unambiguous traditions which clarifies the faith of the Holy Progeny of the Holy Prophet and their followers. In this tradition, the Holy Prophet has declared that to follow the members of his Progeny is just like following the Holy Qur'an and obeying them, protects one from perversion. According to this tradition, next to the Holy Qur'an, the members of the Holy Prophet's Progeny are the only competent authority, after the Holy Prophet to whom the Muslims should turn and they (the Muslims) cannot at all prevent themselves from following them. This tradition has been quoted by many distinguished Sunni sholars in their books such as: Musnad of Ahmad bin Hambal (vol. III, pp. 17, 26 and 59) Sahih Muslim (vol. II, p. 238), Sahih Tirmizi (vol. II, p. 308),

Continued...

(vi) A famous tradition says: "Ali is always with truth and truth is with Ali".

There are many examples of such traditions but we do not wish to mention them one by one in this small treatise. Fortunately we have been relieved of this responsibility by many detailed books which have been written on this subject. A reference thereto will make the position crystal clear. Out of these books one entitled **Abaqātul Anwār** has been written by the distinguished Indian scholar Sayyid Hāmid Husayn. This book consists of more than ten volumes — each volume being about as big as **Sahih Bukhari.** In this book he has quoted authorities for the aforesaid traditions from authentic Sunni sources and fully explained their applicability to the object. This scholar is one of hundreds and thousands of those who have, before or after him, discussed this matter and compiled books on it.

SHI'AH AFTER THE PROPHET

After the passing away of the Holy Prophet, some of his companions decided to hold back Caliphate (vicegerency) from Imam Ali, the excuse being that he was comparatively younger or that the Quraysh did not like that both Prophethood and Caliphate should be in the family of Bani Hashim (as if they thought that they wielded authority in the matter of Prophethood and Caliphate and could pass on to anyone they liked) or for some other reason with which we are not concerned for the present.

At this juncture Imam Ali refrained from swearing allegiance to the Caliph of the time and this is a fact which is admitted by the Ulema of both the sects (Shi'ah and Sunni). It has, however, been said in **Sahih Bukhari** in the chapter relating to the Battle of Khaybar that Imam Ali

Zakhā'irul Uqbā of Tabari p. 16, al-Mustadrak al-Hākim (vol. III, p. 109), Fakhr al-Rāzi in his Tafsir (vol. III, p. 18) and a large number of other traditionalists, exegetes and historians have also quoted this tradition in their books. Narration of their particulars will, however, make the account very lenghthy.

83

did not swear allegiance till after the passage of six months. Some other distinguished friends and companions of the Holy Prophet such as Ammar, Miqdād and Zubayr as well as some others followed Imam Ali and declined to take the oath of allegiance to Abu Bakr. However, when Imam Ali felt that his continued refusal to take the oath of allegiance might result in irreparable loss to Islam, he consented to take the oath of allegiance for two specific reasons: firstly, people knew that he had no greed for the seat of power and secondly, he never wanted Caliphate as an instrument to wield power and to establish his superiority. His conversation in this regard with Ibn Abbas at Ziqār[1] is well-known

---

[1]Ziqār is a town near Basra. While proceeding to Basra to suppress the revolt of the **People of the Camel**, Imam Ali alongwith his soldiers stayed at this place. Here he delivered a brief but forceful sermon in which he showed his determination to enforce the principles of truth and justice at all costs. This sermon has come down to us as his memorial and is recorded in **Nahjul Balaghah**. Before delivering the sermon, he was busy mending his shoes in his tent. Ibn Abbas insisted that he should come out of his tent as early as possible and deliver the sermon (It seems that Ibn Abbas considered the delivery of the sermon in question to be very important for strengthening the foundation of the rule of Imam Ali). Imam Ali, however, asked Ibn Abbas with absolute calmness, "What would be the approximate value of this shoe?" Ibn Abbas replied, "It has no value". Thereupon the Imam said, "By Allah! This shoe is more valuable in my eyes than your rule except that by assuming the reins of government one should uphold the truth and restrain falsehood". In fact nobody had understood the philosophy of government and statesmanship as Imam Ali had. He knew that this position (unless it is necessary to pursue a sacred object) is only an alluring landscape which is not desired by anyone except the world-loving persons who are not free from a mania of acquiring fame and position. Those are the people who are ready to apply themselves to everything to achieve their personal end.

Yes, his lofty spirit and intellect were much more elevated than could be enamoured of such a worthless object! For this very reason he did not fall a prey to any error and did not take a single step opposed to truth and justice for strengthening his position.

He wanted Caliphate only to strengthen Islam and to establish the principles of truth and justice.

On the other hand he observed that the first and second Caliphs were making efforts for the propagation of the Divine law and expansion of Islamic territories by conquests and did not display any despotism. For these reasons he reconciled himself with them after six months and renounced his indisputable right, lest the unanimity of the Muslims should be converted into dispersion and discord and people might revert to the Age of Ignorance.

During this period, the Shi'ah continued to exist under Imam Ali's protection and, benefiting from the light of his person, brightened their thoughts and soul. It is evident that in those days there was no opportunity for manifestation of Shi'ah Faith and the Muslims continued to advance on the same path which had been levelled for them by the Holy Prophet.

The Muslims continued their aforesaid journey till they reached the cross-roads of truth and falsehood. Falsehood now parted ways with truth, for Muawiya declined to take the oath of allegiance to Imam Ali and came out to fight against him at Siffin. At this juncture rest of the devoted companions of the Holy Prophet came round Imam Ali and met martyrdom under the shadow of his standard. On that day eighty distinguished companions of the Holy Prophet were with Imam Ali all of whom had the honour of being the heroes of Badr (i.e. those who participated in the Battle of Badr) or for having taken the oath of allegiance at Aqaba, like Ammar Yasir, Khuzayma Zush Shahādatayn, Abu Ayub Ansari and others.

After the martyrdom of Imam Ali and Muawiya's coming at the helm of affairs and after the termination of the period of orthodox Caliphs, Muawiya laid the foundations of his rule of despotism and personal will. He sowed the seeds of tyranny and injustice among the Muslims, invented heresies and did many other things which it is not possible to reckon or explain here. It is, however, an admitted fact and all the Muslims are unanimous about it that his ways were absolutely different from those of the preceding Caliphs and he ruled the Muslims against their will and desire.

CALIPHS' WORLDLINESS
AND PIETY OF AHLUL BAYT

The Commander of the Faithful Imam Ali used to observe piety and virtuousness in all aspects of his life. His dress and food were coarse and unwholesome. Deceit did not find any place either in his words or in his deeds, and Islam manifested itself in his person and throughout his life in its most sublime manner. On the contrary the ways of Muawiya in all these matters were quite the reverse of those of Imam Ali. The event of his assigning the vast land of Egypt to Amr bin Ās as a reward for his fraud, cunningness, dishonesty and deceitful schemes is well-known. And even more well-known is the unwillingness of the common Muslims to take the oath of allegiance to Yazid (after his nomination by Muawiya for the Caliphate) and acceptance by Muawiya of Zayd bin Abih as the son of his own father, Abu Sufyan.

Muawiya used to spread very colourful dinner carpets at the cost of hard earnings of common Muslims and of the Public Treasury and collected thereon all sorts of rich and tasty foods for himself and his companions.

In this connection Abu Sa'id Mansur bin Husayn Ābi (d. 422 A.H.) writes thus in his book entitled **Nathrud Durar:** Ahnaf bin Qays says, "One day I went to see Muawiya. He had laid a wonderful dinner carpet. He brought all sorts of hot, cold, sweet, and sour foods for me. I was wonderstruck. Later, as ordered by him, another dish of a different kind of food was brought in. I tried my best to find out what it was but did not succeed. I, therefore, enquired about it from Muawiya. He replied that it consisted of the intestines of a duck which had been filled with the marrow of the sheep and had then been fried in pistachio oil and finally sugar had been sprinkled on it. I began to weep. He asked me: "Why are you weeping?" I replied, "I have been reminded of the life of Imam Ali. I remember that one day I was with him. When the time for dinner and breaking the fast drew near he asked me to remain with him. A sealed leather case was brought to him. I asked him what it contained and he told me that there was barley flour in it". I asked him, "Why have you sealed it? Are you afraid that others may take some of it or do you not wish that anyone else should eat it?" He replied, "Who else? As a matter of fact I am afraid that my sons Hasan and Husayn may not taint it with butter or olive oil". I said, "O Commander of the Faithful! Is it prohibited?" He replied, "No. It is not prohibited. However, it is necessary for the true administrators and rulers to consider themselves to be the most deprived persons so that poverty and distress may not press and squeeze the indigent".

When I had said this, Muawiya interrupted and said: "You have mentioned a man whose excellence cannot be denied by anyone".[1]

Zamakhshari in **Rabi'ul Abrar** as well as others have narrated many wonderful anecdotes similar to the above which bear testimony to the authenticity of this claim.

The incidents and the conditions brought about by Muawiya belonged to a time when the people had not yet forgotten the things in the days of the Holy Prophet and the Caliphs and their indifference to the pomp and display of the worldly things.

[1]The Commander of the Faithful narrated this very philosophy in his letter addressed to Uthman bin Hunayf, the Governor of Basra. It is, no doubt, a very wonderful philosophy. The Imam says: "The ruler of a community should not remain content with titles and names only. On the other hand he should make his best efforts to solve the problems of persons, residing in the farthest areas, like a kind father. If the material resources at the disposal of the ruler do not suffice to meet the needs of the people, then the ruler should present to the people moral and spiritual values like contentment, patience and endurance to meet the challenge of their distress and poverty. The reason for this is that when their food, dress and lodging become similar to that of the rulers, they do not feel ashamed or distressed on account of their own condition. When they find their lives similar to the lives of the rulers, this spiritual strength removes more than half of their inner grief and discomfort". This is a valuable practice and an excellent human lesson which Imam Ali has taught to the statesmen of the world in general.

CALIPHS WERE INDIFFERENT TO ISLAM

This unpleasant situation continued till Muawiya flouted all the promises made by him to Imam Hasan at the time of concluding a Peace Pact and later got Imam Hasan poisoned as a consequence of which he met martyrdom. When he found the ground ready, he compelled the people to swear allegiance to his son Yazid, although even in those days people did not know anything better about him than we know today.

From here onwards the fire of anger and general discontentment against the organization of Bani Umayyah kindled up in the hearts of the Muslim community. All the Muslims realized that Muawiya was a worldly-minded person who did not have the least interest in the religion. As a matter of fact Muawiya has himself passed a very fair judgement on himself, for, as quoted by Zamakhshari in **Rabi'ul Abrār**, he says: "As regards Abu Bakr he left the world in peace and the world too remained in peace with him. As regards Umar he tried to manage and remedy it and the world also managed and remedied him. As regards Uthman he exploited it and the world too profited from him. But I have embraced the world completely and have united myself with it and, the world too has united itself with me".

From that day i.e. from the day of the commencement of the Caliphate of Muawiya and Yazid, the Divine rule became separated from the temporal rule, although during the days of the previous Caliphs they were united and the Caliph considered himself responsible for holding the reins of the spiritual affairs of the people with one hand and those of their temporal affairs with the other. From the time of Muawiya, however, the people realized that he had not the least interest in their religious and spiritual affairs and his entire attention was directed towards his politics in the material sphere.

In the circumstances they (the common people) realized that there was some other leader whom they had to refer to for guidance in religious and spiritual matters. And when they found none else more able and more authentic than Imam Ali and his sons in the matter of knowledge, piety, bravery and nobility of birth, they united with them. This situation coupled with the tradition which had been quoted about them (the Holy Progeny) from the Holy Prophet became the cause of the sapling of Shi'ah Faith becoming fruitful day by day and for its growth in the Islamic Ummah like a fresh spirit. In the wake of these conditions occurred the martyrdom of Imam Husayn and the pathetic and deplorably gruesome events of Karbala — the events which history will never forget and the tragic effects of which will continue to remain in our hearts for ever.

Imam Husayn was the son of the Holy Prophet, the rose of his garden and an apple of his eye. There were still alive some companions of the Holy Prophet, like Zayd bin Arqam, Jābir bin Abdullah Ansari, Sehl bin Sa'd Sā'idi and Anas bin Mālik who had observed the extreme love of the Holy Prophet for Imam Husayn and his brother (peace be on them). They had seen how the Holy Prophet lifted them on his shoulders and used to say, "What a fine ride you have and what fine riders you are!" Yes. These companions were still alive and they made known to the people whatever they had seen and heard from the Holy Prophet about the merits of Imam Husayn and other children of Imam Ali (peace be on them).

CRIMES OF BANI UMAYYAH AND BANI MARWAN
Bani Umayyah continued their indulgence in atrocities and crimes. Their hands and mouths were besmeared with the blood of the children of the Holy Prophet. Either they killed or poisoned them or made them their captives.

Naturally enough, these events in turn made Shi'ah Faith to take its root day by day and expanded its scope. It sowed the seed of the sapling of love for Imam Ali and his descendants in the hearts of the Muslims and established their extraordinary popularity.

Yes! Everyone knows that the unbearable condition of the oppressed ones plays the greatest role in making a mark on the hearts of the people at large!

On this account the more Bani Umayyah increased

their cruelties, despotism, obstinacy and murders of innocent persons for strengthening their tottering regime, the more the hearts of the people became inclined towards the Holy Progeny of the Holy Prophet. In other words by their own misdeed, they in fact provided considerable assistance to the Holy Progeny of the Holy Prophet and for the advancement of their object. The more they oppressed the Shi'ah and the friends of the Holy Progeny of the Holy Prophet and openly said unbecoming things about Imam Ali from the pulpits and tried to conceal their attributes, the more reverse was the effect on the people and greater was their failure in harming the Shi'ah. Greater, too, was the hostile reaction of other Muslims as has been described by Sha'bi to his son, "My son, whatever has been founded by faith and the faithful, cannot be destroyed by the world (materialistic forces) and whatever the world and the worldly people have founded, has been destroyed by faith. Think properly about Ali and his children. Bani Umayyah try to conceal their merits but in fact their action had a counter effect and led to their elevation. They endeavour to propagate the qualities of their own ancestors, but it is just like scattering the limbs of a corpse".

It is worth noticing that Sha'bi who is said to have spoken the above words is a person who has been accused of being inimical to Imam Ali. However, Zamakhshari, the well-known Sunni scholar, quotes him in his book **Rabi'ul Abrār** as saying, "Ali has created a difficulty for us. If we befriend him they will kill us and if we harbour grudge against him in our hearts we shall be destroyed".

The state of affairs continued like this till the Sufyani rule (i.e. of the sons and descendents of Abu Sufyan) came to an end and the Marwanis, headed by Abdul Malik bin Marwan, came at the helm of affairs.

Yes! Abdul Malik! The same man under whose orders his lieutenant Hajjaj erected catapults opposite the Holy Ka'bah and set the House of Allah on fire and destroyed it. He killed all those who had taken refuge in the Ka'bah and chopped off the head of Abdullah bin Zubayr in Masjid Harām between the Ka'bah and Maqām Ibrahim. Consequently, he desecrated the sanctity of Allah's Sanctuary of Peace which was held in high esteem even by the people of the Age of Ignorance who considered it a sin to shed therein even the blood of wild animals, not to say of human beings.

Another example of his cowardly and evil deed is that although he gave asylum to his cousin Amr bin Sa'id Ashdaq and promised not to interfere with him, he soon broke his promise and assassinated him in a dastardly manner, as satirized by Abdur Rahman bin Hakam in some of his poetic verses, one of which is as under:

"O sons of *Khayt Bātil*[1] (treacherous man), you were guilty of breach of trust with regard to Amr. Those like you always build their promises on the foundation of treachery.

Is a person who commits such shameful acts entitled to be called a Muslim? Not to speak of his being the Caliph of the Muslims and the Leader of the Faithful!"

Bani Marwan were always guilty of such wrongs and even more shameful acts. The only person among them whose object was different from others was Umar bin Abdul Aziz, a pious man.

When the time of the Abbasids came, according to the well-known sayings, they tuned up the tambourine to new melodies, so much so that a person who had witnessed the rule of both Bani Marwan and Bani Abbas says about them: "Would that the injustice of Bani Marwan had remained, and the justice of Bani Abbas had gone to Hell!"

This tyrannical rule brought matters to such a turn that the Alavis, wherever they were found, were put to death, their houses were destroyed and their traces were obliterated. And all this happened in spite of the fact that the Abbasids were the so-called cousins of the Alavis.

These atrocities were so wide spread that the poets of the time of Mutawakkil (with all the limitations and agitations that pervaded the atmosphere) opened their lips to

[1] In Arabic literature *Khayt Bātil* means a treacherous person. Possibly this is due to the fact that treacherous people are unreliable like a worn-out thread.

reproach Bani Abbas. One of them says: "I swear by Allah if Bani Umayyah cruelly murdered the son of the Holy Prophet, his cousins also repeated the same acts. This ruined grave of his, bears testimony to this fact. They (Bani Abbas) were sorry for not having participated in his murder. Consequently they meted out the same treatment to his sacred bones.

It would be better to place side by side with the savage behaviour of the Bani Marwan and the Abbasids and the behaviour of the descendants of Imam Ali and to compare them with each other and thereby to find out the secret of the expansion of Shi'ah Faith.

SHI'AH FAITH WAS AN ISLAMIC MOVEMENT

Fortunately in the light of living history it becomes clear that contrary to the futile views of some visionaries, the Shi'ah Faith was not an Iranian movement or something connected with Abdullah bin Saba. On the contrary, it was a purely Islamic Movement which had its origin in the special attachment and sentiments of the Muslims for the Prophet of Islam.

To understand this reality, we should study the life of the children of Imam Ali, the foremost among them being Imam Zaynul Abidin. After the martyrdom of his father, Imam Husayn, he withdrew from the scene of hustle and bustle − ridden environment of the world and the worldly people − and engaged himself in the worship of Allah, furtherance of morality and refinement of innerself and piety. It was he who opened this chapter for a number of *Tābi'in* like Hasan Basri, Tāwus Yamāni, Ibn Sirin, Umar bin Ubayd and others who had stepped into the world of piety and gnosticism. The Holy Imam undertook this task at a time when the conditions were such as might obliterate all sense of piety from the peoples' hearts and efface every trace and sign of Divinity from the world.

After Imam Zaynul Abidin his son Imam Muhammad Baqir and grandson Imam Ja'far Sadiq came at the helm of affairs and made efforts to strengthen the foundation of this faith. The period of interval was between the downfall of the regime of Bani Umayyah and the commencement of the reign of Bani Abbas. The first party was heading towards decline and definite fall whereas the second party was yet to gain sufficient strength.

This sensitive situation provided a good opportunity to Imam Ja'far Sadiq. The nightmare of injustice was removed and the veil of dissimulation was set aside. Imam Sadiq could now propagate everywhere the commandments of Allah and the traditions of the Holy Prophet which he had obtained from a pure and real source viz. his father, and his father from his grandfather, the Commander of the Faithful, who received it from the Prophet of Allah.

It was under Imam Ja'far Sadiq that the Shi'ah Faith spread with unprecedented rapidity. There was a group of narrators who learnt the traditions from him with utmost eagerness and enthusiasm. So great was their number and their enthusiasm that Abul Hasan Wash'ā, a resident of Kufa used to say: "In this very Masjid Kufa, I saw as many as 4000 distinguished and learned persons, everyone of whom said Ja'far bin Muhammad narrated this tradition for us". We do not wish to prolong this discussion by quoting different authorities and thus drift away from our real subject, especially so because the proposition is too clear to cast doubt in any mind.

What needs attention is that while the Umayyads and the Abbasids were exceptionally busy in strengthening the foundations of their reign and fighting against their enemies and had spread the carpet of merry-making and were openly engaged in pursuit of pleasure and amusements, the descendants of Imam Ali had invested their entire attention to the pursuit of knowledge, worship and piety. They were not at all concerned with the superficial allurements of life and did not take any part in politics — the same wretched politics which at that time was synonymous with falsehood, fraud and deceit.

It is evident that this difference had a great influence in spreading the Shi'ah Faith and attracting the attention of the Muslims towards the Holy Progeny of the Prophet. It turned public opinion against the Umayyads and the

Abbasids and inclined it towards the chosen descendants of the Holy Prophet.

It is also evident that although the people of those times, like those of all other times, had keen interest in material matters and their love for richness and wealth could not be denied, yet at the same time, sharpening of intellect, knowledge and spiritualism had not still been absolutely erased from their minds and souls. It was so, especially because they had not yet gone far from the time of the Holy Prophet and the traces of his teachings were still fresh in their minds. Furthermore, Islam, too, has a broad outlook and does not prohibit earning of wealth by lawful means.

On the one hand, Muslims could clearly see that Islam was the same religion which opened doors of blessings for them and made the stream of good luck and fortune flow for their society. Furthermore it had humiliated the kings of Iran and Byzantium before them and had given the keys of the treasures of East and West in their hands. In short it had granted them victories and honours even a small part of which had not been dreamt by them previously. Were they not, therefore, justified, in these circumstances, to wish to get acquainted with the principles, rules and regulations of this sublime religion? It is evident that they wished whole-heartedly to know what Islam said and what its programme was. At least they wanted to be aware of the duties pertaining to the society and to domestic affairs and matters related to the purity of human race etc.

On the other side, howsoever they endeavoured they did not find any signs of knowledge of these matters with the people who had occupied the office of Caliphate and assumed the titles of Caliph of the Muslims and Commander of the Faithful. However, after investigation they found this knowledge in its most complete and most sublime form with the chosen descendants of the Holy Prophet. Hence, it was not surprising that they had to believe in them and accept them as their Imams, the true successors (caliphs) of the Holy Prophet, the guardians of Islam and the real missionaries of the commands of Allah. This was another factor for the expansion of Shi'ah Faith.

This ardent faith and deep-rooted spiritual sentiment had kindled like a flame in the hearts of a number of Shi'ah and it was the same thing which encouraged them to embrace different kinds of dangers and offer sacrifices.

BRAVE MEN AND DEVOTED POETS

It would be appropriate if we look into the lives of Hujr bin Adi Kindi, Amr bin Humuq Khuzā'i, Rashid Hijri, Maytham Tammar, Abdullah bin Afif Azdi and others like them who ceaselessly waged a relentless war against perversion in religion and did not rest even for a moment till the perversion was completely eliminated.

Were these sincere sacrifices displayed by these brave men for securing any office or riches from the Holy Progeny of the Holy Prophet? Were they afraid of them especially when, in those ghastly times, the chosen descendants of the Holy Prophet's family were themselves homeless?

No, these sacrifices were not motivated by anything other than ardent faith and belief in a sacred object and it were these very things which brought such operations into existence.[1]

Now we shall look into the lives of the great poets of the 1st and the 2nd centuries A.H. They were no doubt very much dependent on the regime of the day from the

---

[1]If one studies the life-histories of Hujr, Maytham and Abdullah bin Afif, particularly the last days of their lives, one is stunned to see their hold as to how two of them, one an ordinary date-seller and the other a blind old man, could be so domineering that the entire edifice of the Umayyad regime shivered and shook before them. Of course they had been so mercilessly persecuted by the despotic Umayyad rulers that one becomes aghast to see their forebearance against those apalling tyrannies, and even against such odds they had been brave enough at the cost of their untiring efforts and selfless sacrifices to leave behind a group of devoted disciples for the preaching and propagation of the Shi'ah Faith and there was no reason as to why they should have not done so because as everyone of them was indeed one of the staunchest disciples of Imam Ali.

material view-point and looked to it for material help as well as security from distress. Yet, at the same time, neither fear nor covetousness (although the poets are usually worldly people!) nor the pressures of the regime and not even the drawn sword which was hanging over their heads, restrained them from supporting truth or from combating the enemies of Islam and disgracing them. Their numbers consisted of persons from Farazdaq up to Kumayt and from Sayyid Himyari to De'bal Khuza'i, to Dik al-Jinn, to Abi Tamām, to Bahtri and to Amir Abu Faras al-Hamadani, author of the famous panegyric wherein he says:

"You have torn the curtains of faith, trampled upon the Divine law and looted the properties of the Progeny of the Holy Prophet" (till the end of panegyric wherein he has brought interesting facts to light).

They stood up in support of truth in that turbulent atmosphere and defended the Progeny of the Holy Prophet with their powerful poetic verses. As a matter of fact, each one of them was a genius of his time in the field of poetry and literature and had to his credit a large number of exciting panegyrics and precious quatrains in the praise of the Holy Imams and in reproach of the Kings and Caliphs of the time and their atrocities and cruelties. In these poems they have expressed love for the family of the Holy Prophet and hatred for their opponents.

It is well-known that De'bal Khuzā'i used to say: "It is now forty years that I am carrying the gallows on my shoulder but I have not yet found anyone who should hang me on it". It was the same De'bal who satirized Harun Rashid, Mamun, Amin and Mu'tasim in his verses and eloquently praised Imam Sadiq, Imam Musa Kazim and Imam Ali Riza (peace be on them). His poetic verses in this regard are available in the books of history and literature.

It should also be remembered that all these persons belonged to the periods when Bani Umayyah and Bani Abbas wielded power and had complete control over the people. Observe carefully and ponder over the wonderful effect of the strength of faith and reality which enlightened hearts and souls of Muslims to make them fulfil the requirements of moral heroism, sacrifice and selflessness. History is generally replete with such deeds and particularly the history of Islam. However, we want to explain only the real origin of Shi'ah Faith and the source of the seed that was sown in the land of Islam as well as causes and factors for its rapid expansion. We have not followed up this discussion under the influence of religious sentiments. On the other hand whatever we have said is a logical analysis, free from all sorts of bias, depending on a chain of facts and authentic historical evidence and we think that with the grace of Allah we have done justice to the subject to some extent. Now it is up to you to take counsel from my words or feel aggrieved on their account.

Furthermore, there should be no misunderstanding that our intention is to ignore or deny some of the services of the Caliphs and the good deeds done by them for the sake of the world of Islam, because only obstinate people deny such things and, thank Allah, we are not obstinate and we hate vilification and slander.

We appreciate good things and, as far as possible, ignore bad things. We say, "They were the people who are now no more. If they did good deeds they will be rewarded for them. And if they have done bad deeds they will be held responsible for them. Their account is with Allah. If Allah forgives them it will be in consonance with His Kindness and Grace and if He punishes them He will have dealt with them in accordance with the canons of Justice".

We also wish to remind our readers that we are not inclined to mention the pangs of our heart and, as far as possible, do not permit our pen to repeat them. But what are we to do when some of our contemporary writers have imputed such cowardly and uncalled for calumnies to the Shi'ah except that we have been compelled to repeat some of these with pain.

In any case our real object was to introduce the real founder of Shi'ah Faith and the person who planted the first sapling of this faith. And as explained in the foregoing pages, this task was not performed by anyone other than the Holy Prophet of Islam himself. It has also been clarified

97

that the real factors of the spread and expansion of the Shi'ah faith were a chain of various causes linked with one another which have continued their effects in an inevitable manner.

So far as this part of the book is concerned, we content ourselves with what has been said. We now deal with the second part and commence discussions regarding the beliefs of the Shi'ah with reference to the basic principles of faith and articles of act.

* * * * * *

PART II

The Basic Principles of Shi'ah Faith

In this chapter we shall content ourselves with narrating the fundamentals of Shi'ah School in the matter of its articles of faith and articles of acts and, as far as possible, shall go into some details. However, we consider it necessary to repeat it that we shall depend only on those propositions which are accepted by Shi'ah scholars in general and which may be given the title of Shi'ah Faith and we shall ignore the beliefs held by a few stray persons.

ISLAM AND IMAN (SUBMISSION AND FAITH)

The entire Islamic system may be summarized into the following five divisions:
(i)   Recognition of Allah.
(ii) Recognition of the Prophets and their successors.
(iii) Recognition of Divine commands and to follow them.
(iv) Achieving moral virtue and renouncing indecent deeds.
(v)   Belief in the Day of Resurrection and Judgement.

Therefore, religion and faith is acquisition of religious knowledge and to act according to it. This faith and practice is Islam itself.

Islam and Iman are two synonymous words i.e. both of them point out the same reality which is founded on three bases: Monotheism, Prophethood and the Day of Judgement. If a person denies even one of these three fundamentals, he is neither a Muslim nor a Mo'min (Faithful). If, however, he believes in Monotheism, the Prophethood of the Holy Prophet of Islam and the Day of Judgement he is a real Muslim. Such a person will enjoy all the Islamic rights and his person, rank and status will be respected.

Sometimes the words Islam and Iman are used in a deeper and restricted sense. This happens when a fourth fundamental is added to the aforesaid three and that is Practice according to the five essentials of Islam namely *Salat* (Prayers) *Saum* (Fasting) *Zakat* (Religious tax) *Hajj* (Pilgrimage) and *Jihad* (Holy-war). It means the same thing when it is said that faith consists of believing from one's heart, professing by tongue and performing articles of acts according to the basic commands.[1]

As such, wherever the Holy Qur'an declares only faith in Allah and the Holy Prophet and the Day of Judgement, it conveys the first meaning but whenever good deeds are also added thereto, it conveys the second meaning.

In resorting to this division, we have acquired inspiration from the following verse: *The Bedouin Arabs say: "We are believers" Tell them: "You are not believers but you should say that you are Muslims. In fact belief has not yet entered your hearts".* (Surah al-Hujurat, 49:14)

Thereafter Almighty Allah adds by a subsequent verse: *The true belivers are only those who believe in Allah and His Prophet then never entertain the slightest doubt. They fight for the cause of Allah with their wealth and lives. They are the truthful ones'.* (Surah al-Hujurat, 49:15)

This means that Iman does not consist of professing Islam by tongue only. It must also be accompanied by belief and good deeds. These four fundamentals namely Monotheism, Prophethood, the Day of Judgement and practising the five essentials of the religion are acknowledged by Muslims in general, the basis of Islam and Iman (in its special sense).

THE SHI'AH AND OTHER MUSLIMS

However, the Shi'ah believe in Imamate as the fifth fundamental of Islam.

---

[1] This is not exactly a verse of the Holy Qur'an but its contents can be acquired from various verses.

The Shi'ah believe that Imamate like Prophethood is a sort of Divine office. Just as Allah selects anyone He likes for the office of a Prophet and empowers him to show miracles which are of the same worth as the message and the word of Allah, so does Allah select anyone He likes for the office of Imamate and orders the Prophet to introduce him to the people. The Imam has to perform the same functions as performed by the Prophet except that there is no revelation on him. On the other hand, he perceives Divine commands by the grace of Allah through the Prophet. Hence, whereas the Prophet is the missionary of Allah, the Imam is the missionary of the Prophet.

The Shi'ah believe that there are 12 Imams, each one of whom has clearly introduced his successor. The Shi'ah also believe that just like Prophet an Imam is infallible and impeccable because if it is not so, it will not be possible to rely on his words or deeds. It will not also be possible in that event to accept his words in the same manner as the words of Allah or Prophet or to treat his deeds as an example or specimen for others.

Allah addresses Prophet Ibrahim and says: *I have appointed you as the Imam of mankind. Ibrahim asked: Will this Imamate also continue through my descendants? Allah replied: The unjust do not have the right to excercise my authority.* (Surah al-Baqarah, 2:124)

The Shi'ah believe that an Imam should be superior to all the people of his age in the matter of knowledge, merits and wisdom because the purpose of appointment of an Imam is the refinement, reformation and perfection of humanity through knowledge and righteous deeds.

It is evident that a person who is himself imperfect cannot make others perfect. How can a man give what he does not possess himself!

Hence, from the view-point of status, an Imam is next to the Prophet and above all others.

Whoever owns this belief is considered by the Shi'ah a *"Mo'min"* in the special sense of the word. However, even if he believes only in the other four fundamentals he will be a Muslim or a Mo'min in the general sense and he will enjoy all the general laws and rights of Islam regarding his life and property. Therefore, lack of belief in Imamate, the fifth fundamental, does not occasion his expulsion from Islam nor the non-applicability of Islamic laws to him.

No doubt, the outcome of belief in Imamate will become apparent on the Day of Judgement in the shape of proximity to Almighty Allah. However, in this world all the Muslims, without exception, are equal and allied to one another from the view-point of Islamic laws. But there is no doubt about it that on the Day of Judgement there will be a vast difference between their positions and this difference will be related to their intentions and actions. Of course, only Almighty Allah is aware of the end of everyone and nobody can express a definite opinion about his own salvation.

In short we mean to say that the most important thing which distinguishes the Twelver Shi'ah (Shi'ah Imamiyah) from other sects of Muslim is their belief in the Imamate of the 12 Imams of the Holy progeny of the Holy Prophet. The reason for their being called Imamiyah is also the same, because all other sects which are called Shi'ah are not Imamiyah. For example, the title of Shi'ah is given to the Zaydiya, Ismailiya, Waqifiya, Fathiya sects etc. although they do not believe in the Imamate of the 12 Imams. This distinction could, of course, be possible if we had to discuss only those people who are considered to be Muslims. However, at times the term Shi'ah is given a wider scope and is made to cover sects which fall outside the limits of Islamic laws and beliefs, for example, the sect called Khitābiya or others like it. As a matter of fact if we wish to count the sects which assumed the title of Shi'ah their number will perhaps exceed 100 (most of these sects are, of course, now extinct and only their names are recorded in the history books.)

It is an admitted fact that the name Shi'ah is now particularly given to the Imamiyah sect which is the second biggest sect of Islam after Sunni. It may also be pointed out that belief in the 12 Caliphs is not something strange or of recent origion which may be inconsistant with the principles of Islam and the famous Islamic books, because we find that Bukhari and other distinguished Sunni scholars have quoted the traditions about 12 Caliphs in various ways.[1] For example:

(i) Bukhari quotes Jabir bin Samra from the Holy Prophet, as having said: "This affair (i.e. the affairs of the Muslims) will not be settled unless the 12 Caliphs rule over them". Thereafter he said some words in a low tone which I did not understand. I·asked my father who was also present in the meeting as to what the Holy Prophet had said. He told me that the Holy Prophet had said that all of them would be from among the Quraysh".

(ii) He narrates another tradition to the effect that the Holy Prophet sid: "The affairs of the Muslims will remain in order so long as twelve persons rule over them".

(iii) In another tradition quoted from the Holy Prophet it is said that: "Islam will be powerful so long as 12 Caliphs rule over the Muslims".

For the present we are not concerned as to who these twelve persons are.[2] What we mean is that belief in such a proposition is not something new or surprising so that it may become a pretext (for criticism) by some people. Of course, we come across a narration by Sunni scholars to the effect that the Holy Prophet said: "There will be thirty Caliphs after me and thereafter Caliphate will assume the shape of a perverted and shameful monarchy".

[1]The tradition about the 12 Caliphs has not been quoted by Bukhari only. It has also been quoted in other well-known books of tradition of Sunnis in different ways: Muslim has quoted it in his Sahih in a number of ways and it has also been quoted by Tirmizi and Abu Dawud in their Sihah, Ahmad bin Hambal in his Musnad and Hākim in al-Mustadrak 'Alas Sahihayn. All these books are the most authentic compilations by Sunni scholars.

[2]It, however, goes without saying that these traditions do not apply either to the first Caliphs or to the Caliphs of Bani Umayyah or Bani Abbas because besides there being other reason, the number 12 does not tally with them. In the circumstances can it carry any meaning
Continued...

For the present there is no occasion to offer arguments in favour of the Imamate of the twelve Imams and we do not wish to undertake such a discussion. Fortunately thousands of books are available on the subject which absolve us of this responsibility.

As has already been said, our object is only to explain the articles of Shi'ah Faith and its principal commandments on which there is general agreement, without offering arguments in their support, so that it may become clear as to what we say and what we believe. Of course, detailed books have been written by Shi'ah scholars in proof of each article of faith. We therefore, entrust the task of this discussion to them.

Let us not deviate from the main subject. As had already been pointed out Faith consists of a set of things worth knowing and practising i.e. acquisition of knowledge and practices. In other words it comprises of certain functions for intellect and soul and also some functions for the body. We shall, therefore, undertake this discussion in two parts.

* * * * * *

other than the 12 Imams of the Holy Prophet's Progeny? (There were 14 Caliphs among Bani Umayyah and 36 among Bani Abbas). The Sunni scholars have advanced very strange explanations for these traditions. Being unable to tally the number of 12 with the first Caliph or with others, they have selected, according to their own inclination some Caliphs out of Bani Umayyah and some out of Bani Abbas (whom they believe to be more acceptable) and put them together. Very strange conclusions have thus been drawn which are seriously at variance with one another. Those interested in further information on the subject should refer to the book entitled **al-Muntakhab al-Athar** (pp. 14—23) In any case the contents of these traditions are an evidence which does not conform to anything other than to the Shi'ah Faith.

The Basic Fundamentals

(i) MONOTHEISM

The Shi'ah believe that every wise person should recognize his Creator and should have faith in His Oneness. He should know that creation, sustenance, death and life are permanently in His Hands. As a matter of fact none except He Himself is permanently effective in the world. Hence, if anyone believes that creation, sustenance, death or life are in the hands of anyone other than Allah, he will be considered to be an infidel and a polytheist and outside the fold of Islam.

Similarly, according to the Shi'ah, it is only Allah who is to be worshipped. If a person worships anyone other than Allah or makes anyone a partner of Allah for purposes of worship (even though it may be with the excuse that worshipping anyone other than Allah is a means for access to Allah) even that person is an infidel and expelled from the ranks and files of Muslims.

Obedience, too, is specifically due to Allah and if it is necessary to obey the Prophets and the Imams it is for this reason that obedience to them is in fact obedience to Allah, because they are the missionaries of Divine commands Notwithstanding this, however, it is not permissible to worship them with the excuse that their worship is also the worship of Allah. This method of thinking is somewhat Satanic which pulls man down the precipice of polytheism. However, to seek blessing through them or to make their position and personalities a means for petition before

Allah and similarly to offer prayers to Allah near their sacred tombs are all permissible.[1]

We cannot imagine a person who cannot differentiate between offering prayers by the side of the tomb of a Prophet or Imam and praying to the Prophet or Imam himself. The Holy Qur'an says: *(This lamp is found) in houses which Allah has allowed to be exalted and that His name shall be remembered therein. Therein glorify Him in the morning and evening.* (Surah al-Nur, 24:36)

This is the gist of the belief of the Shi'ah in respect of monotheism regarding which there is general agreement among Shi'ah scholars and it is possible that severity in the matter may exceed even this. In any case the Shi'ah are exceptionally severe in this regard and anything which is in the least opposed to the propositions of the Oneness of Allah and Independence in Effect and Singularity of Deity is unacceptable from the Shi'ah view-point.

Of course, according to the Shi'ah, Monotheism has different degrees, for example Oneness of Being, Unity of Attributes, Unity of Action etc. However, this is not the place to explain these terms further.[2]

(ii) PROPHETHOOD

The Shi'ah believe that all the Prophets whom the Holy Qur'an refers to, were appointed by Allah. They were

[1] In fact as they are the object of Divine favours we pray to Allah near their tombs — not that we seek anything from them independently of Allah.

[2] Oneness of Being means that Allah has no partner and none is alike or similar to Him. His Sacred Being is Infinite and Absolute, and has no parts. Unity of Attributes means that all his ideal attributes which refer to His Being are inherent in His Being. Unity of the One to be worshipped which is also interpreted as Oneness of Allah means that there is none deserving to be worshipped except Allah, the Almighty and worship and prayers are only for His Being. Unity of Action means that One who is really effective in the entire world is Allah only and whatever effect or attribute any other being has, is derived from Him with His will and wish.

His Messengers who were nominated to guide the creatures. Muhammad, peace be on him, was the last and the greatest Prophet of Allah. He was bereft of any sin or error throughout his life and did not tread till the last moment of his life, but in the cause of Allah. The Shi'ah believe in *Me'rāj* (the Ascension) of the Holy Prophet to the heavens and believe that Allah made him travel during one night from Masjidul Harām (at Makkah) to Masjidul Aqsā (at Jerusalem) and then took him with his corporate body upto the Divine Screen and beyond the *Arsh* (the Throne), the *Kursi* (the Chair) and the *Hijāb* (the Divine Screen) the place of *Qāba Qausayn Aw Adna.*

The Shi'ah believe that the Holy Qur'an which is in the hands of the Muslims is the same Book which was revealed to the Holy Prophet by way of a miracle for teaching realities of Islam to the people, without the least addition, subtraction or alteration. There is a concensus of opinion of all the Shi'ah scholars on this point. If there are rare cases of some Shi'ah or Sunni holding the belief that the Holy Book has been altered, such persons are evidently mistaken. The Holy Qur'an contradicts them by saying: *Indeed We have revealed the Book and indeed We are its Guardian.* (Surah al-Hijr, 15:9)

Furthermore, even if there are some narrations of the Sunni as well as of the Shi'ah which mention that the Holy Qur'an has been tampered with, it should be understood that these narrations, besides being unauthentic, consist of solitary remarks, knowledge of which is not useful and which cannot be made a basis for adherence. Such statements should either be explained or totally ignored.

The Imamiyah believe that whoever claims after the Prophet of Islam that he is a Prophet or that anything is revealed to him or has faith in anyone who makes such a claim is not a Muslim and is liable to be dealt with according to rules pertaining to the infidels and non-Muslims.

(iii) IMAMATE

As has already been pointed out earlier, the main thing which distinguishes Twelver Shi'ah from other sects of Muslims is this very issue of Imamate. In fact the real and basic difference is the same. All other differences are secondary and accidental and resemble the differences found among the four sects of the Sunni (viz. Hanafi, Shāfi'i, Māliki and Hambali) themselves.

It has also been mentioned that from the Shi'ah point of view Imamate is a Divine office like Prophethood. Almighty Allah grants this office to whomsoever He likes and nominates him to this position through His Prophet. The Shi'ah believe that Almighty Allah ordered the Holy Prophet to introduce Imam Ali to the people as his successor. In a way the Holy Prophet also knew that the acceptance of this proposition might be difficult for a group of persons because all people were not equal in the matter of belief about Imam Ali's infallibility. It could be possible that some of them might consider this selection to be the outcome of the Holy Prophet's personal love for Imam Ali and their mutual relationship and his (Imam Ali) being son-in-law of the Holy Prophet. Nevertheless, Almighty Allah did not consider it necessary that the Holy Prophet should refrain from declaring this reality on this account. He, therefore, clearly ordered in the following verse that the succession of Imam Ali might be made known to the people: *O Prophet! Convey to the people that which Allah has revealed to you (regarding the succession of Ali). If you fail to do so, it would be as though you have not discharged the duty of Prophethood. Allah protects you from the people.* (Surah al-Maida, 5:67)

When the Divine order was conveyed with such emphasis, there was no alternative left for the Holy Prophet but to convey Allah's command to the people. Hence, at the time of his return from his last Hajj he delivered a sermon at Ghadir Khum, wherein he said inter alia with a loud voice so that all the people heard: "Do you not consider me superior to your ownselves? (i.e. Am I not your guardian and master?)". They replied, "Yes, you are". Then he said, 'Whoever considers me to be his master and patron; he should consider Ali also to be his master and patron". (See: Murtaza Mutahhery, Master and Mastership — ISP 1980).

108

Thereafter also the Holy Prophet emphasized this proposition on different occasions, sometimes openly and at other times by making allusion to it, and thus discharged the duty entrusted to him by Almighty Allah.

After the demise of the Holy Prophet, some elders among the Muslims interpreted this tradition according to their own way, "keeping in view the interests of Islam". They preferred some persons over others and said, "Every situation and every phenomenon has its own exigencies".[1]

[1] Some people may not accept so easily the statement that the Muslims, with all their attachment to the Holy Prophet should set aside his traditions. It may be asked whether they were not the same people who had made all sorts of sacrifices for the advancement of Islam. Then how could it be possible that they should ignore the Holy Prophet's words? As it happens, some Sunni scholars have raised this objection against us in their books. It should, however, be remembered that we will not be much surprised if we keep in view the true picture of those times and the circumstances and the way of thinking of the people of that age. We are all aware of the position of common people in such matters. They usually follow the elders of the community and have no opinion of their own. And even if they happen to have opposite views, they soon retreat in the face of the propaganda of the elders as well as of their strength and sway. As regards the elders of the nation it would appear from a study of the history of Islam that all the companions and friends of the Holy Prophet did not look upon him in the same manner as we do. We accept him to be the Messenger of Allah. We also believe that whatever he said is Divine revelation and that he did not say even a word which did not conform to it. We further believe that whatever he said is venerable and unalterable and is a guarantee for the welfare of the Muslims. However, among the companions of the Holy Prophet there were some who expressed their own views in the face of the orders and remarks of the Holy Prophet. Thus they practically assumed the role of Mujtahid and considered the Holy Prophet too, to be a Mujtahid. Consequently, they believed that there was no harm in changing some of the orders of Islam in the changed circumstances. For example the second Caliph who was the originator of

Continued...

109

Keeping in view these developments, Imam Ali and a group of other distinguished companions of the Holy Prophet declined to take the oath of allegiance to the Caliph who had been elected by the former group. But after some time, when they saw that refusal to take such an oath and not to make reconciliation might do great harm to the foundation of Islam and might root out the very sapling of Islam which had grown up only recently, they agreed to swear allegiance. And this was not very surprising because on the one hand Islam was so dear and honoured in the eyes of Imam Ali that he was prepared to sacrifice his own life as well as of his most near and dear ones for its sake. History of Islam will never forget Imam Ali's unparalleled sacrifice and bravery. It was he who on many occasions subjected his life to danger in order to safeguard Islam from harm. And on the other hand he saw that the person who had taken over Caliphate did not (apparently) refrain from making efforts to ensure the strength, grandeur and expansion of Islam and this was the desire and object which Imam Ali wanted to achieve. For these reasons, he did not oppose the Caliphate. However, during all these times, he did enjoy the status of Imamate

most of the events which took place after the Holy Prophet says thus in his well-known statement which has been reported by all scholars: "There were two Mut'a(s) which were permissible in the days of the Holy Prophet viz. Mut'a of Hajj and Mut'a of women (Fixed Time Marriage). I order them to be unpermissible and shall punish those who disobey these orders". Similar words have also been quoted from the said Caliph in other contexts. In the circumstances it should not be surprising that they ignored the orders of the Holy Prophet regarding succession also on the pretext of safeguarding the interests of Islam and Muslims.

Although presently there are no Muslim scholars or even ordinary persons who should give such a treatment to the words of the Holy Prophet but unfortunately the die has been cast and a tradition has been set and generation after generation has taken birth and been brought up in the pale of this tradition. As such it is not easy to bring about a change in the prevailing state of affairs.

110

because this was not such an office as could be relinquished or could become subject to decay, notwithstanding the fact that he remained silent for the sake of security of the interests of Muslims and renounced the status of public ruler.

Of course, when the time of Muawiya came, Imam Ali did not remain silent. The reason for this was that he knew perfectly well that reconciliation and co-operation with Muawiya and acceptance of his authority even over a small province, not to speak of his leadership of the Muslims, would entail huge losses and deplorable harm for the world of Islam. Consequently Imam Ali had no alternative left but to stand against him.[1]

In short the Imamiyah says: "We are Shi'ah and followers of Imam Ali. We make peace with those with whom he made peace and fight with those against whom he fought. We are friends of his friends, and enemies of his enemies. And in holding this belief we follow the Holy Prophet, who said, 'O Allah! Be his friend who befriends Ali and be his enemy who is inimical towards him'. Hence, our love for Imam Ali and his distinguished children is love for the Holy Prophet only as a token of obedience to his orders".

In order that we may not get diverted from our topic we revert back to our discussion about Imamate.

The Imamiyah believe that Allah never keeps the world without His *Hujjat* (Proof in the shape of Imam) whether he be visible or occult. Hence the Holy Prophet openly selected Imam Ali to be his successor. Imam Ali, too, introduced his son Imam Hasan as his successor. He also nominated his brother Imam Husayn to succeed him

---

[1]The spirit of the above statement can be found in Imam Ali's own words in Nahjul Balaghah, wherein he says: "O Allah! You know that whatever we have done in this context, has not been for the sake of snatching power or kingdom or to gain any material benefit. Rather we have done all this in order to restore truth and establish justice and to carry out reforms on the earth so that Your oppressed creatures may live in peace and Your suspended laws may be enforced again". (Muhammad Abdoh — Nahjul Balaghah, vol. II, p. 18).

and in the same manner nominations were made upto the Mahdi, the twelfth Imam.

This institution is not novel because all the Prophets of Allah from Adam up to Muhammad, the last Prophet of Islam (peace be on them) have acted on this schedule and nominated their successors.

A large number of religious scholars have written many books on this subject and have discussed at length the proof of the testament of the Holy Prophet about Imam Ali and of the Holy Imams about one another. We refer here to only those writers who wrote on this subject in the early days of Islam and before the 4th century A.H., under the caption **Kitabul Wasiyyah** by Hisham bin Hakām; Husayn bin Sa'id; Hakām bin Miskini; Ali bin Mughira; Ali bin Husayn bin Fazl; Muhammad bin Ali bin Fazl; Ibrahim bin Muhammad bin Sa'id bin Hilal; Ahmad bin Muhammad bin Khalid Barqi, the author of **Kitabul Mahāsin** and Abdul Aziz bin Yahya Judi, the distinguished historian.

Most of these scholars belonged to the 1st and 2nd centuries. In the 3rd century also a number of scholars wrote books on this subject under the caption, **Kitabul Wasiyyah** by Ali bin Ri'ab; Yahya bin Mustafād; Muhammad bin Ahmad Sabuni; Muhammad bin Hasan bin Farrukh; Ali bin Husayn Mas'udi, the distinguished historian and author of **Murujuz Zahab**; Shaykh Tā'ifa Muhammad bin Hasan Tusi; Muhammad bin Ali Shalmaghāni; Musa bin Hasan bin Āmir.

It is not, of course, possible to count the books written on this subject after the 4th century A.H.

Mas'udi, the well-known historian, writes in his book **Ithbātul Wasiyyah** that every Prophet had twelve successors. Then he gives their names with short accounts of their lives. Thereafter, he mentions the 12 Imams in detail.

These are specimens of the books which the Shi'ah scholars have written about the Imamate advancing logical arguments and documentary evidence in this behalf. However, as has already been pointed out, it is not our purpose to prove this proposition by such arguments. We only wish to set forth the basic Shi'ah beliefs without

112

advancing any proofs so that it may become known as to what we say and what is the worth of those unjustified calumnies imputed to us.

As has been observed, the fundamentals of Imamate in which the Shi‘ah believe are not something novel, incrediable or devoid of any argument or evidence so that one should find fault with us in this regard.

MAHDI AND HIS LONGEVITY

Of course, the belief about which other sects of Muslims and even non-Muslims have criticized us most is our belief in Imam Mahdi and his occultation. They have considered this belief to be false and baseless and have created a great fuss over it. However, if we study their remarks carefully and in an unbiased manner we find that only two kinds of criticism deserve discussion:

The first is the question of the longevity of the occult Imam. They ask as to how it could be believed that, opposed to principles of nature, a man could live for more than a thousand years. However, this objection is quite strange, especially when raised by a Muslim. It appears that they have ignored the longevity of Prophet Nuh about whom the Holy Qur'an clearly says that he remained busy guiding his people to the right path for as many as 950 years. As regards his total life, the minimum is stated to be 1600 years, and some have mentioned it to be 3000 years or even more than that.

Many Sunni traditionalists have mentioned some other persons also who lived longer than even Prophet Nuh. One of them is Nuvi, a distinguished Sunni traditionalist who, in his book **Tahzibul Asmā'** writes: "There is a difference of opinion regarding Khizr's longevity as well as the period of his Prophethood. Many scholars believe that he was a sage and not a Prophet, and is alive even now and lives, incognito, among the people. This proposition is also current among the gnostics. Many stories are told about people perceiving Khizr, contacting him and having dialogue with him and about knowledge gained from him and his appearance at the sacred places. These incidents are too well known to be related here". Shaykh Abu Amr bin Salāh says in his **Fatāwā**: "According to the belief of the majority of ulema and the gnostics, he (Khizr) is alive and most of the common people also hold this belief along with them. Only a few traditionalists deny his existence". (The statement of Nuvi ends here). I remember that he as well as Zamakhshari in Rabi'ul Abrār write thus: "Muslims are unanimous in their belief regarding four Prophets being alive viz. Idris and Isa who live in the heavens and Ilyās and Khizr who live on earth. As regards Khizr he was born during the time of Prophet Ibrahim".

Are there not persons besides those mentioned above who live much longer lives than usual, sometimes for centuries, and are called Longevals? Sayyid Murtaza in his book **Amāli**, and Shaykh Saduq have mentioned a large number of them.

We have also seen people in our own times who have lived unusually long for 120 years or even more.

Furthermore, such an objection is also not logical from the scientific and theoretical point of view,[1] because one who can keep a human being alive for one day, is also competent enough to keep him alive for thousands of years. All that can be said is that such things are opposed to general laws i.e. they are unusual. But is abnormality a novel thing in the matter of Prophets and Saints of Allah? How is it possible that we should consider the longevity of Mahdi, which is something abnormal, to be impossible, when we believe in the miracles of Prophets when these, too, are unusual and abnormal.[2]

[1]See: **The Awaited Saviour**, Ayatullah Baqir Sadr, ISP, 1979.

[2]Exception to the **Laws of Casuality** in the sense that something should be created in the Universe without any cause is not logical. However, there is nothing wrong with exceptions to the usual causes and changes in the course of causes and factors with which we are familiar and habituated because there is nothing to prevent other causes from replacing them and effects other than those so far found taking birth from them.

What has been said above is from the view-point of our religious and Islamic beliefs. Now as reagards views of other learned men, a number of renowned Western philosophers believe that from the scientific view-point there is no impediment to a total war being waged against death, so that it may be possible for man to lead eternal life. In support of this claim, they have advanced very forceful arguments, examples of which have been quoted in connection with articles written in previous issues of the magazine al-Muqtatif.

One of the renowned Western scholars says, "If Ali had not been martyred at the hands of Ibn Muljam it would have been possible for him to live eternally, because complete temperance in all aspects of life governed his self".

We, too, have a large number of arguments in this regard which need not be stated for the present.[1]

[1]Although in some of our writings, we have discussed the longevity of Mahdi in the light of present day science, it is necessary to introduce some of those discussions here. As a matter of principle the proposition of Normal Life for man is not more than a myth according to the recent researches of the biologists. It is this very proposition on which our opponents rely and say that the natural life of man is for a fixed period and ask as to how it could be possible that it should exceed that limit. In reply to the objections of such persons it should be said, "There is no scientist in these days who believes in the natural life of man, animal, or plant as being destined for a fixed period only. On the other hand all of them believe that with change in conditions, the length of the life of man or other animate beings or plants can undergo change and the limit of change is also not fixed. The following points bear testimony to this proposition:

(i) Today a large number of physicians and scientists are busy in studying ways and means for the longevity of man. They have also proposed a method for this. This proposition can be seen in many current magazines and scientific writings. If life of man had a fixed limit from a scientific view-point all these efforts and researches would have been meaningless.

(ii) Some time ago a Roman (or Greek) physician, named Prof.

Continued...

115

THE AWAITED SAVIOUR

Another point regarding the awaited Imam about which we are questioned is: "What is the use of the existence of an Imam who is hidden from the eyes of the people, and does his existence or otherwise make any difference at all?"

Anna Aslan, discovered a medicine consisting of Nokaien mixture for the treatment of old age which he proposed to hand over to the world after completion of research. The discoverer of this medicine believes that old age is nothing but fatigue of cells and this medicine has such an effect on the cells that it removes their fatigue. Interviews were obtained regarding the invention of such a medicine from some renowned physicians and they confirmed the possibility of such a result. (News pertaining to this subject were published in the papers in the month of Azar of the year 1338). This proposition also proves that the term Natural Age is meaningless.

(iii)   A number of experiments have been conducted regarding the lengthening of the span of life of plants and animals all of which confirm the fact that the proposition of Natural Age has no basis and the length of their ages can be changed by bringing about change in the relevant conditions.

Dr George Claber, a Professor of Hall University carried out experiments on grass named Saproline Magista and he could keep it alive for six years although its usual life span is not more than two weeks. If this proposition is applied to the human beings, our ages would become as long as 10,000 years (extract from the magazine al-Hilal, vol. IX of 23rd year, p. 77).

(iv)   Recently a fish was discovered in the snow-clad polar regions which belonged to a period of 5000 years earlier than the present times. This fish, which had been found frozen, was put in mild water. The people observed with great surprise that slowly and gradually the fish began to move and regained life. Hence, it became evident that it had not at all died during the period of 5000 years. This incident and several other similar observations and experiments have made the scientists think that they can benefit from this method while sending man to far-off spheres which would possibly require tens of thousands of years to reach.

Continued...

We do not know, however, whether or not the people who raise such objections believe that they have unveiled all the secrets of the Universe and mastered all the philosophies of Divine laws, and not a single doubtful point remains for them to be clarified, either with regard to the creation or in the matter of religion. If we sincerely believe that there are still many unknown things whose knowledge we have not been able to acquire, and we should certainly believe in this reality, what is the harm then if we accept the position that this proposition, too, is one of the secrets of the actions of Allah whose solution we have not been able to find so far! Besides the matters relating to the creation of the Universe about which we lack knowledge there have always existed some religious problems the secrets of which have not been revealed to us. Do we know the efficacy of kissing the Black Stone which forms a part of the ceremonies of Hajj and is one of the recommended articles of acts thereof, notwithstanding the fact that it is only a piece of stone which cannot do any good or harm to us? Similarly do we know why three *rakats* (units) have been fixed for Dusk prayers, four for Night prayers and two only for Dawn prayers?[1]

Our object in mentioning all these matters is to explain only the proposition viz. that from a scientific point of view there is no such thing as Natural Age which may provide a specific limit for the lives of men, plants or animals. And when the myth of Natural Age is explained all discussions regarding the longevity of Imam Mahdi will also come to an end, although the conditions of his longevity are admittedly different.

However, the thing which surprises us most is that pious persons who believe in Allah to be the controller of all natural and supernatural laws, and also believe in all the miracles relating to the Prophets of Allah, like Prophet Isa, Prophet Musa and the Prophet of Islam, deny the longevity of one person for one or a few thousand years, although that, too, is ordained by Allah. In any case, this is a simple matter from the view-point of natural sciences as well as philosophy and religious theories. See: **The Awaited Saviour**, ISP 1979.

[1]On the whole, religious matters may be divided into three catagories:

Continued...

The Holy Qur'an proclaims that there are some secrets in this world whose knowledge belongs to Allah only and even the great Prophets and Archangels are unaware of them, like the Day of Judgement and other similar matters. Allah says in the Holy Qur'an: *Only Allah knows the Hour of Doom. He sends down rain, and knows what is in the wombs. No one is aware of what he will earn tomorrow nor knows in which land he will die. Allah is all-knowing and all-aware.* (Surah Luqman, 31:34)

In any case the proposition of the Occultation of the Imam is not something novel, because, in Islam, there are many matters whose causes are not clearly known e.g. The Glorified Name, The Dignified Night, The Moment of Acceptance of Prayers etc.

In short, it is not surprising that Allah may do something or give some command the cause and philosophy of which may not be known to us; and no one can claim that

(i) Matters, the causes of which are known to us (e.g. the philosophy of the appointment of Prophets or philosophy of the necessity of prayers and zakat) or even if their causes were not known before they have now become known on account of expansion of knowledge (e.g. philosophy of forbidding the use of blood and flesh of swine and other similar matters).

(ii) The matters which have been explained for us by the religious leaders of which we were ignorant previously (e.g. the philosophy of fasting being essential during the sacred month of Ramazan and other similar matters).

(iii) Those matters which we are unable to understand by ourselves and which have also not been explained for us by the religious leaders (like the number of *rak'āts* of each prayer and other similar matters). As it happens, matters belonging to all these three categories exist in the world because the causes of some incidents of the material world are known to all and there are others which have been explained by the religious leader and there are still others which are veiled under secrecy. In any case the reason for the existence of such secrets in the material world as well as in religion is due to the knowledge of man being limited as compared to the unlimited hidden facts of the world.

such a thing is not possible. To end this discussion, the only point that remains is whether such a situation did or did not arise with regard to Imam Mahdi. In this regard also there remains no room for denial in the presence of authentic traditions quoted from the Prophet and his Successors about the Occult Imam and it is necessary that this fact which has been proved by positive arguments should be admitted. We are not at all bound to find out the philosophy and the causes underlying it, because there are many matters whose reality has been proved to us by reasonable proofs although we are not aware of their philosophy.

We have repeatedly pointed out that in these brief discussions all that we wish to do is to state clearly the text of the Shi'ah beliefs regarding the roots and branches of their faith without mentioning arguments in their support. Nevertheless, brief references are sometimes made to relevant arguments. Those interested in exhaustive arguments should refer to books written on the subject.

As regards the origin of the Occultation of Imam Mahdi, a number of traditions have been quoted from both Shi'ah and Sunni sources and are recorded in well-known books of both the sects. (See: **Awaited Saviour**, ISP 1979)

Although we have admitted our lack of absolute knowledge about the causes of Imam Mahdi's existence and the conditions of his Occultation, but in reply to a question put to us by some Shi'ah in this regard, we have mentioned reasons therefore which may explain the secret of this proposition to a considerable extent. It may, however, be pointed out that we cannot depend on them by way of a decisive chain of arguments with regard to this mysterious matter. Especially so, because at times it happens that one perceives a matter but cannot do justice while narrating it.[1]

The last observation which is proposed to be made in this regard is this that after adducing final arguments

---

[1] The distinguished author has discussed the philosophy of Occultation of the Imam of the Age in his book **Jannatul Ma'wā**.

regarding the necessity of the existence of an Imam in every age we come to believe that the world should not be devoid of Allah's Proof and Sign and also that in the person of the Imam there is *Lutf* (Grace of Allah) and his rule will be another Grace of Allah. Hence it is not in the fitness of things to reveal the secrets and the philosophy of this proposition any further.[1]

(iv) JUSTICE

According to Twelver Shi'ah the fourth fundamental of faith is belief in the Justice of Allah. It signifies that Allah is not unjust to anyone and does not perform any act which is considered indecent and obscene by healthy intellect. The Shi'ah consider it to be one of the fundamentals of their religious beliefs and discuss it as an independent proposition.

Although in view of the fact that Justice is one of the attributes of Allah it should be discussed along with the Oneness and Attributes of Allah and treated as a part of discussion with regard thereto, yet one point has been the cause for the Shi'ah to particularly treat it as a separate fundamental. That point is this that *Ashā'ira* (disciples of Abul Hasan Ash'ari who form a large part of the Sunni) believe that our reason is not at all capable of perceiving good or bad (decency or indecency) and it is incumbent on us to derive guidance for this purpose from Divine laws alone. Whatever religion declares anything to be good should be taken as good and whatever it condemns as bad should be treated as bad. In other words, the fact is that goodness and badness have no existence as defined by religion so

[1] In the terminology of theology, *Lutf* means all the resources which are made available by Allah for the guidance of human beings and for bringing them nearer to good fortune as well as making them obedient to the commands of Allah. *Lutf* may pertain to mean religion (e.g. sending a Prophet or appointing an Imam) or it may pertain to mean creation of strength (e.g. strength of different kinds provided to us by Allah) which assists in traversing the right path and obedience to His orders.

much so that if Almighty Allah permanently keeps the good and faithful people in Hell and the evil-doers and unbelieving ones in Paradise, He has not done anything wrong, because all things and all persons belong to Him and He may deal with His belongings in any manner He likes. As Allah proclaims in the Holy Qur'an: *Nobody has a right to dispute His authority.* (Surah al-Ambiya, 21:23)

This would mean that man has no intellectual function to perform and nothing is obligatory on human beings from the standpoint of reason. All functions and responsibilities should be specified by religion so much so that even the necessity of recognizing Allah and of studying the claim of a person to Prophethood and his miracles should also be proved through religion, because reason is not in a position to prove any proposition.

In case, however, we wish to solve these problems also through religious orders, we are caught in a strange whirlwind of contradictions, because before we recognize Allah or the Prophet would it not be necessary for us to conduct investigation regarding recognition of Allah and the Prophet? Now the question arises as to why it should be necessary to conduct an investigation. Would such an investigation be according to the dictates of religion — the same religion whose bases of Oneness of Allah and Prophethood have not been established? As such it is necessary that before we recognize Allah and the Prophet we should know religion (i.e. Allah and the Prophet). In view of this it is beyond doubt that such matters should be governed by reason and consequently the position of reason is not that of a deposed ruler.

As opposed to the belief of the *Ashā'ira*, the *Adliya* i.e. Shi'ah, and a group of Sunni who are the disciples of Wāsil bin Ata and are popularly known as *Mo'atazila* believe that the absolute ruler in such matters is reason and religion does not and cannot have any role to play except that of guidance and recommendation for the decrees of reason.

In the same manner reason perceives independently the good and evil about many things. Reason says that it is impossible that Allah should do anything indecent or obscene because He is Wise and the consequences of indecent and undesirable deeds are opposed to wisdom. Reason says that it is unjust to punish good people and injustice is something indecent. On this account Allah does not do any such thing that is unjust.

In the manner as detailed above the Shi'ah scholars have proved the Attribute of Justice for Allah and have made it the object of discussion as separate topic and have not mixed it up with the issue of Attributes of Allah to make a clear distinction between Asha'ira and themselves.

However, the Asha'ira do not in fact deny the Justice of Allah, so much so that according to their belief whatever Allah does is Just.[1]

As such, if He punishes good people, it will be quite in keeping with Justice. They only deny the independence and rule of reason regarding the assessment of goodness or indecency of actions relating to Allah whereas the Shi'ah and Mo'tazila believe in it. They think that reason has no right to interfere in the matter and to say that so far as Almighty Allah is concerned such and such action is admissible and such and such action is not admissible.[2]

Those who believe in Justice (i.e. the Shi'ah and the Mo'tazila) have solved a number of problems on the basis of this priciple e.g. the Priciple of Grace; necessity of thanking the Beneficient; necessity of examination and

[1]We believe that according to this view Justice has absolutely no meaning vis-a-vis Allah, because when injustice has no meaning and whatever He does is Just, Justice too, will be devoid of any meaning. The reason for this is that these two can exist only side by side.

[2]As we have already said the confusion and fallacy which has taken place over here is that (the Asha'ira) pretend as if by accepting the proposition of good or bad according to reason we wish to impose a duty on Allah and make Him subservient to reason, although the reality is otherwise. Basically reason has no authority. What it possesses is the perception of a chain of realities. Is it imposing a duty on Allah to perceive the reality that injustice is not compatible with the laws of creation and the order of life enforced by Allah?

study of the claim of a claimant of Prophethood.

Out of the many problems which originate from the proposition of Justice, one is Fatalism and Free Will which is one of the most important and complicated problems to be discussed. Ashā'ira believe in Fatalism or in something which eventually ends in Fatalism. On the other hand Mo'tazila believe in Free Will and consider man to be independent in his actions, so much so that according to them this freedom of will has been given to man by Allah in the same manner in which He has given him the real existence. On this account just as Allah has created words, the Attributes of Authority totally belong to Allah and partially to us (i.e. in the matter of benefit from the attribute of free will and actions in consequence thereof).

Almighty Allah does not compel anyone to do something or to refrain from it — it is for His creatures to choose one of the two courses. It is for this reason that if men perform good acts they merit reward in the eyes of wise men and if they commit bad deeds, they are subjected to blame and rebuke. If men had not been free in their actions, reward and punishment would have borne no meaning and the appointment of Prophets and revelation of Divine Books would also have been of no use.[1]

We do not wish to discuss here the issue of Fatalism and Free Will any more, because it does not form a part of the subject under consideration. We have discussed this topic in detail in the end of the first volume of our book **al Din wal Islam** and propounded the proposition in such a manner that it should be intelligible to persons possessing average knowledge. Here we wish to explain only this point that one of the fundamental beliefs of Shi'ah Imamiya is the Justice of Allah and the Free Will of human beings.

[1]As a matter of principle all invitations to religion and all canons of morality are based on the principle of Free Will and have no meaning in its absence. If we consider man to be a machine whose person rotates without his own control and his activities are forced ones, especially because they are the effects of a chain of some internal and external factors than what will be the purpose of sending Prophets and revealing sacred Books and of the teachings of morality?

(v) THE DAY OF RESURRECTION

The Shi'ah, like all other Muslims, believe in the Day of Resurrection. It is an article of their faith that Almighty Allah will call persons to life after their death for reward or punishment for their deeds. Resurrection will take place with this very soul and body, so that if a man is seen by another man they will recognize each other.

Much has been said about Resurrection. Will the return of the dead be of the category of re-establishment of the extinct? Will man become completely non-existence and then acquire a new existence or of the appearance of the existent (i.e. man is not destroyed completely and on the Day of Resurrection the same being appears again in the original shape?) These are propositions, ignorance of whose details does not affect faith on the Day of Resurrection. Hence, it is not necessary to acquire knowledge about them after having belief in the basic thing (i.e. Resurrection).[1]

The Shi'ah believe in all matters related to Resurrection and life in the Hereafter which have been mentioned in the Holy Qur'an and authentic traditions like *Jannat* (Paradise) and *Nār* (Hell) and their respective blessings and tortures, *Mizān, Sirāt* (which the righteous only will be able to cross on the passage to Paradise), *A'rāf* (place between Hell and Paradise) and the Book of Deeds in which all the doings of the human beings will be recorded in detail. They also believe that everyone will be repaid for his deeds — he will get good reward for his good deeds and punishment for his bad deeds.

They also believe in other similar matters which have been proved by way of revelation of the Holy Qur'an or authentic traditions.

* * * * * *

---

[1]However, if anyone wishes to acquire belief about a part of these matters or all their details it is necessary that he should depend on logical conclusion and rational proof.

124

Bida and Taqayyah

Here we consider it necessary to bring under discussion two propositions for which the Shi'ah are criticized most and to explain the true Shi'ah belief in this regard.

(i) **Belief in Bidā**: Some persons think that the Shi'ah belief with regard to *Bidā* means that some matters are concealed from Almighty Allah and later become known through passage of time (and He repents some of His actions which He had performed previously due to lack of knowledge about them). However, can any sane and sensible Muslim entertain such an opinion about Allah? Is not this thing a clear and shocking ignorance about Allah to consider Him to be subject to changes and accidents viz. that He does not know something on one day and becomes aware of it on the other.

God forbid that such an erroneous belief should be entertained by Twelver Shi'ah or by any other sect of Islam, a belief which is total ignorance and perversion. Of course some such rotten and bogus beliefs were held by the sect called Mujassama. However, their beliefs cannot be taken into account of religion or faith because they are more akin to superstitions and fables than to religion, so much so that some very ridiculous propositions have been quoted from them which make every sane person feel ashamed. For example one of them says about the body of Allah: "Excuse us from discussing His beard and male organ and ask about anything else you like". (He possesses everything besides these also, but these two should not even be discussed).

However, Bidā in which the Shi'ah believe is the one which is considered to be one of the mysteries of the descendants of the Holy Prophet and has been treated to be so important that it is thus referred in the traditions of the members of the Holy Progeny: "None have worshipped Allah in the same manner in which He has been worshipped by those, who believe in *Bidā*. He who does not believe in *Bidā* has not recognized Allah properly".

Bidā consists of the fact that the occurrence of an incident has been anticipated in *Mahvo Ithbāt* (Tablet of Obliteration and Affirmation) and the Prophet is informed about the occurrence of this incident through one of the angels who are aware of the contents of the said table. The Prophet in his turn informs his disciples that such an event is going to happen.[1]

If this incident does not occur in the future, it is due to the fact that the incidents anticipated in the **Tablet of Obliteration and Affirmation** are (as is evident from its very name) alterable and it is possible that Almighty Allah may obliterate one incident and substitute it by another. And none except Himself is aware of this fact as all these

---

[1] A number of scholars believe that the **Tablet of Obliteration and Affirmation** means the very Law of Causality (Imperfect Cause). On this account knowledge of this tablet means knowledge of the circumstances and causes of different incidents although full knowledge of their conditions and impediments may not be in hand. It is possible that the incidents which have been so anticipated should take place in this manner that the causes of the incident may be concurrent with the conditions as well as lack of impediments. It is also possible that these incidents may not take place due to absence of pre-conditions and presence of impediments. It is for this reason that the name of obliteration and affirmation has been given to them. However, the Protected Tablet means the perfect causes for various incidents and occurrences. Knowledge of these causes which are a collection of courses, conditions and absence of impediments rests with Almighty Allah only. As is evident, no change can take place in this destiny.

126

positions consist of the occult and special knowledge of Allah and no Prophet or Angel has access to them. All these incidents are recorded in *Lawhul Mahfuz* (the Protected Tablet) which has been construed in the Holy Qur'an as *Ummul Kitab* (the Mother of Books).

As regards the Prophets and the Angels they are aware of the realities of the Tablet of Obliteration and Affirmation and their knowledge does not go beyond that. This has been expressed in the Holy Qur'an thus: *Allah effaces or establishes whatever He wants and with Him is the original Book.* (Surah al-Ra'd, 13:39)

It is possible that some ignorant persons may raise the objection here that this concealment of reality and making known something else which takes place through the Tablet of Obliteration and Affirmation amounts to a statement contrary to facts and a source of furtherance of ignorance, is in fact not proper. It should, however, be kept in view that such matters are definitely governed by exigencies and philosophies which are beyond our comprehension. For making the position clear it would be appropriate to make a comparison between *Naskh* (Supersession) and *Bidā*. We are aware that supersession of orders is permissible in Islam. In other words it is possible that an order may be enforced and the people may think from its appearance that it is an eternal order. However, after lapse of some time this order may be declared as superseded by the Holy Prophet himself and a new order may be substituted for it. Thus though the first order is decidedly eternal its later supersession carries wisdom and expediency. That is the case with Bidā also. At the most *Bidā* belongs to the world of genesis and is subject to the occurrences of creation whereas *Naskh* is related to the religious law. For this reason just as *Naskh* carries wisdom and philosophy, in the same manner *Bidā* and the secrecy of a reality of creation and its subsequent disclosure with the lapse of time has also its expediency which is not deprived of reality on account of our lack of knowledge about it.

Besides this there is another kind of *Bidā* which takes place in the metaphysical world by the union of the sacred souls of the Prophets. It is possible that on account of this relationship they may become aware of the root of occurrence of an accident but may not acquire knowledge of its conditions and impediments.

There is a story reported from Jesus Christ we find that he warned in regard to a bride that she would die the very night of the consummation of her marriage. In other words the sacred soul of Christ had realized the reality of this proposition on account of his connection with the spiritual world. However, he did not take into consideration that the occurrence of this incident was conditional on the part of the people of the bride failing to give alms to an indigent person. By chance it so happened that the bride's mother had helped a poor man. Consequently as opposed to the foretelling of Christ the bride remained hail and hearty. When asked about this development, he said: Perhaps you have given alms in this behalf. Alms ward off confirmed calamities!

At times the utility of episode of this type lies in testing the preparedness of people in the path of obedience to Allah. This is observed in the matter of Prophet Ibrahim being commissioned to sacrifice his son Ismā'il.

As a matter of principle if the proposition of Bidā had not been there, prayers, intercession and giving of alms to ward off calamities would have been meaningless. Similarly the weepings and implorings of the Prophets and friends of Allah in extreme fear of Allah on their part would not have carried much sense, because they had not set their foot contrary to Allah's commands even for the twinkling of an eye. However, they were afraid of the realities which are in the occult knolwedge of Allah and no one else is aware of them. They were afraid lest some development should take place which may change their condition. This is the very knolwedge from which *Bidā* gains capital.

We have conducted detailed discussion about *Bidā* and other similar matters like predestination and the Tablet of Obliteration and Affirmation in *al Din wal Islam*. Those interested may acquire detailed information on these matters from that book.

128

(ii) **Belief in Taqayyah**: Another topic which has occasioned criticism on the Shi'ah and is considered to be one of the faults of the followers of this faith is the proposition of *Taqayyah* (Dissimulation). However, the root cause of all criticism in this regard is that the critics have not understood the object of *Taqayyah* and the reality about it. Unfortunately they have also not made any research in this behalf, although if they had done so and displayed patience they would have easily realized the fact that the Shi'ah are not alone in holding this belief. On the other hand *Taqayyah* in itself is a categorical order which accords perfectly with human nature and instincts.

We are also aware that in the matter of all its basic laws and orders Islam moves along with reason and knowledge and does not separate itself even a little bit from these two. Is it not a part of human nature that one should protect and defend one's life which is the dearest thing in the eyes of man? It is true that at times man is ready to stake even his life for sublime objects like safeguarding of honour, establishing of truth and eradication of falsehood. However, can a sane person say that it is permissible that man should endanger his life for other purposes not carrying such sacred and just cause? It is evident that neither reason nor religious law gives such permission, and all that *Taqayyah* means is that in such circumstances man should not submit his life to annihilation.

Islam has clearly permitted that if the life, property or honour of a man is in danger and the statement of truth is harmful for him, he should forsake it temporarily and perform his functions secretly, as the Holy Qur'an says: *Except that you wish to observe Taqayyah from your enemies*. (Surah Ale Imran, 3:28). And again says: *Except those who are forced to reject faith in Him openly, but whose hearts are satisfied and comforted with His faith*. (Surah al-Nahl, 16:106)

History of Islam has not yet forgotten the tale of Ammar Yasir and his parents who were caught in the clutches of the idol-worshippers who put them to torture so that they might dissociate themselves from Islam.

129

(See: Ammar Yasir, ISP 1984). Ammar's parents declined to do so and were killed at the hands of idol-worshippers. Ammar, however, said what they desired and later, weeping owing to fear of Almighty Allah, ran into the presence of the Holy Prophet. The Holy Prophet told him: "If you are caught by them again say what they want you to say". Thus the Holy Prophet pacified his agitation of mind, fear and weeping.

The point which needs perfect attention is that the same orders do not apply to *Taqayyah* in all circumstances. On the other hand it is sometimes obligatory, at other times unlawful and still at other times permissible.

Taqayyah becomes obligatory when human life falls in danger without any corresponding gain in view. It is permissible in such circumstances that its abandonment may amount to a sort of defence and strength for truth. In that event it is upto man to make a sacrifice to achieve the object or to ignore it and save his life.

However, *Taqayyah* is unlawful and forbidden in case it becomes a source of promotion of falsehood, perversion of the people and strengthening of cruelty and injustice. In such circumstances one should display selflessness and combat all dangers.

From what has been stated above the real meaning of *Taqayyah* and the logical belief of the Shi'ah in this regard become as clear as daylight. Incidentally it should also be kept in mind that if *Taqayyah* deserves blame and admonition, should be directed towards those who have deprived the Shi'ah of freedom of faith and compelled them to resort to *Taqayyah*. It is those people, and not the Shi'ah, who deserve reproach.

We read in history books that Muawiya assumed the reins of Islamic government without the approval of Muslims and became so obstinate that he meddled with the laws and orders of Islam in any manner he liked and had no regard for anyone. He pursued the Shi'ah of Imam Ali in particular and killed them when and where they were found, so much so that he did not spare even those who were suspected or accused of being Shi'ah. Other Caliphs of Bani Umayyah and Bani Marwan also followed this evil policy and dirty politics. Then came the turn of the Abbasids. They too not only repeated the evils of Bani Umayyah but tuned to a new pitch in this field which had no precedent.

What could the Shi'ah do in those circumstances except to conceal their belief at one time and divulge it at another, according to the demands of defence of truth and reality and campaign against ignorance and perversion? In such circumstances the Shi'ah did not refuse to express their beliefs in order that argument may be completed and the path of truth and reality may not remain totally hidden from the people. Consequently we see that a large number of the Shi'ah and their leaders abandoned *Taqayyah* and submitted their own bodies to the gallows and the altars of tyranny and injustice in the capacity of victims of cruelty in the path of righteousness.

History can never forget the heart-rending tragedy of the martyrs of Marjul 'Azra (a village in Syria). They were followers and leaders of the Shi'ah community numbering fourteen. Their leader was the same distinguished companion whose strong skeleton and knotty muscles had been exhausted by worship and abstemiousness. He was none else than Hujr bin Adi Kindi.

To introduce him more fully it may be said that he was one of the Commanders of the army of Islam which conquered Syria. However, Muawiya killed all these fourteen persons by subjecting them to horrible tortures. Later he used to say, "Whomsoever I killed there was some reason for it, except Hujr bin Adi, about whom I do not know what his crime was".

However, I would like to tell Muawiya what crime Hujr had committed. His only crime was that he had abandoned *Taqayyah* in order to prove the perversion of Bani Umayyah and their not having any connection with Islam. Yes! He had not committed any sin except the expression of truth for the sake of this sacred object.

Is it possible to forget the event of the revered companion Amr bin Humuq Khuza'i and Abdur Rahman bin Hassān Anza whom Zayd got buried alive in Qassul Nātif? Can the saddening remembrance of the murder of Maytham Tammar, Rashid Hijri and Abdullah bin Yaqtar be forgotten who were hanged in Kufa at a place where refuse was dumped? These and hundreds of others like them were persons who gladly sacrificed their lives in the path of righteousness and struck their bright foreheads on the rocks of falsehood of the enemies so severely that their foreheads did not break unless they had broken those rocks. Of course, they did not at all know in which farm *Taqayyah* grows. They considered *Taqayyah* unlawful for themselves and they were justified in doing so, because if they too had kept silent and adopted *Taqayyah* truth and reality would have been obliterated completely and the religion of Islam would have adopted the shape of the religion of fraud, dishonesty and hypocrisy and a source of all sorts of mean qualities. How could such a religion be compared with the religion of Islam which inspires all kinds of virtues?

Of course these were the people who sacrificed their lives for the sake of Islam. They were the martyrs in the path of truth and virtue!

The tragedy of the martyrs of Taf, Imam Husayn and his respected companions, is known to everyone. They were the leaders of the path of truth and heads of the hierarchy of men who never submitted to injustice. Of course, they considered *Taqayyah* unlawful for themselves, whereas some others, who were faced with conditions totally different from the conditions mentioned above, considered *Taqayyah* obligatory and similarly another group of persons whose circumstances differed from either of the two mentioned above considered it to be lawful. All these different views were the outcome of different conditions, circumstances and environments.

I remember to have seen in some narrations that the imposter, Musaylima Kazzāb captured two Muslims and asked them to testify: "I am the prophet of Allah and Muhammad too is the Prophet of Allah".

One of those two persons said: "I testify that

Muhammad is the Prophet of Allah and you are a liar".
He was executed under Musaylima's order. As regards the
other he said what Musaylima wished and was set free.
When this news reached the Holy Prophet he said: "The
first person made hurry and carried himself to Paradise.
The second person also acted according to permission and
each one of them will get his own reward".

O dear Muslims! Please fear Allah and do not do any
thing which compels your brethren to observe *Taqayyah*
and then turn round and blame and admonish them as to
why they have resorted to *Taqayyah* (Dissimulation).

We pray to Almighty Allah that He may make our
and your affairs well and grant all of us unity of expression
in the path of truth and reality.

Allah's peace, grace and blessings be upon you!

This was the gist of the Shi'ah Faith. Now we shall
study the Articles of Acts.

* * * * * *

PART III

Articles of Acts

Ijtihād: Before discussing the beliefs of Twelver Shi'ah regarding practical matters and practical fulfilments, it would appear necessary to set forth an introductory statement.

The Shi'ah believe that in Islam an order or command is laid down for every matter in life so much so that if a person inflicts a scratch on the body of another, the amount of conciliation money has been prescribed for it. In short an order has been laid down in Islam for every matter which has been the subject of human requirement or will be so till the Day of Judgement and there is no single matter which is not covered by a relevant command.

The collection of these commands was communicated by Almighty Allah to the Holy Prophet through revelation or inspiration. The Holy Prophet also communicated these commands gradually to the Muslims according to different occurrences, events and needs with which they were confronted. He communicated them generally to those who remained with him during day and night so that they might communicate them to others and thus perform the duty of the propagation of religion.

However, a considerable number of these commands still remained to be communicated. The reason for this was either that factors for their propagation did not arise in the days of the Holy Prophet or that they were not in fact related to the problems and needs of the people of that time or some other reasons necessitated that their propagation should not be resorted to during that period. In short it was expedient that these commands should be spread gradually keeping in view the exigencies of requirements and the conditions of environments. Hence, a considerable number of these orders were propagated whereas the remaining ones remained unpropagated.

Nevertheless, the Holy Prophet of Islam entrusted all these instructions to his successors (the Holy Imams) so that they might gradually communicate them to the people at appropriate times, keeping in view their interests and requirements.

There were many general instructions which possessed particularlity and their particular features were not made public during the days of the Holy Prophet as it was not considered expedient to do so. These were, however, made known to the people by the successors of the Holy Prophet. There were many other briefly-worded instructions also which were explained by them as and when necessity arose. This was one side of the picture. As regards the other side, the companions and friends of the Holy Prophet differed in their capacity to understand his words because their intellect and capability differed widely and it is evident that everyone benefited from that boundless ocean of knowledge and wisdom according to his intellect and capability. Allah says: *He sent down water from the sky, that flows in the valleys according to their capacities.* (Surah al-Ra'd, 13:17)

Or, as says a poet: "However, everyone benefits from my thoughts according to his capacity".

Often it so happened that one of the companions heard an order from the Holy Prophet and another heard from him a contrary order regarding an affair resembling the former. Apparently these two orders appeared to contradict each other, but in reality there was some distinction between the two matters which was the cause of difference between the two orders. However, the person who narrated the tradition did not pay heed to this distinction and even if he took note of it he did not mention it while narrating the tradition. That is why in the present times two traditions appear to us contradicting each other although the factual position is otherwise and each of them is related to a different matter.

Owing to this as well as other reasons, all the Muslims and even the companions and friends of the Holy Prophet, who had been associated with him, were obliged, in order to comprehend the tenets of Islam, to study the traditions very carefully and compare them with one another and to scrutinize the context, particulars and conditions of issuance of particular tradition. As it happens so often that the wording of a tradition appears to give one meaning but on concentrating on the context it is realized that its import is different. This close study for comprehending the orders is the very thing to which we give the name of *Ijtihad*.

It is evident that all the companions of the Holy Prophet were not competent to infer and deduce orders from the traditions. And in case those amongst them who possessed such competence quoted the exact words of the tradition which they had heard, they were treated to be only narrators. However, if they explained to others the orders deduced by them from that tradition keeping in view other traditions and various contexts which were associated with it they were treated to be *Mujtahids* and those who acted according to their opinions were called their *Muqallids* (Followers) such developments took place during the days of the Holy Prophet and even in his lifetime. At times the Holy Prophet himself instructed such persons who did not possess perfect capability to understand the orders to refer to some of his companions who knew better so that they could perfectly follow and understand an accomplished fact.

By giving a careful thought to what has been stated above we come to the conclusion that, not to talk of other periods, the door of *Ijtihad* was open even in the days of the Holy Prophet. It should not, however, be forgotten that there is a great difference between the *Ijtihad* during the days of the Holy Prophet and that of our times. In those days *Ijtihad* was simple and easy because the companions were living in the days of the Holy Prophet and the means for understanding the meaning of the tradition were abundant. Furthermore, if there was any confusion or complication in any matter, they could refer directly to the Holy Prophet himself and obtain clarification. However, as we are becoming distant from the period of the Holy Prophet the manner of *Ijtihad* is also becoming more and more different and complicated and greater need is being felt for concerted research and care for collecting the traditions, differentiation of the authentic from the forged and their preference inter se. This is due to a large number of opinions, association of Arabs with others, gradual changes in the Arabic language as well as on account of the abundance of traditions − especially due to the fact that for various reasons interested and incompetent persons meddled with the traditions and forged a number of them. Consequently as the distance from the period of the Prophet increased, and as Islam expanded and the number of scholars and narrators grew, the task of *Mujtahid* became more difficult and complicated. However, the door of *Ijtihad* which was admittedly open in the days of the Prophet is similarly open today and this is a fact which cannot be denied.

Hence, the people always consist of two groups namely the learned and the ignorant. It is also evident that according to the dictates of nature and logic the ignorant persons refer to the learned people in matters about which they themselves are not aware with the result that some people will always be *Mujtahid* and others will always be *Muqallid*.[1]

---

[1] In fact *Ijtihad* and *Taqlid* (the Following) have a much wider meaning which covers the entire life of the human beings and does not particularly concern religious matters. As it is not naturally possible that an individual should specialize himself in all arts and sciences and the specialization of one person is limited to one or at the most a few branches of knowledge, the field of specialization of each person is the field of his *Ijtihad* and he is obliged to follow other specialists in their respective fields. For this reason many saints and sages of the world have followed others (specialists in other fields) in

Continued...

137

It is also an admitted fact among the Muslims that Islamic orders should be obtained from one of the following four sources: (i) *Kitab,* the Holy Qur'an. (ii) *Sunnah,* traditions of the Holy Prophet. (iii) *Aql,* dictates of reason. (iv) *Ijmā',* consensus of opinion of all Muslims.

There is no difference in this regard between the Shi'ah Imamiyah and others. However, in some matters the Shi'ah differ from others:

(i)   The Shi'ah do not at all follow *Qiyās* (Analogy)[1] and

many important matters related to human life. As such it is not something novel that persons not coversant with religious matters should refer to the learned in this field. On the other hand it is a general principle related to entire human life.

[1] In religious terminology, analogy means application of an order relating to one matter to another matter resembling the former. For example, if we say that as alcoholic beverages are impure, therefore all intoxicating things are impure.

From the Shi'ah point of view analogy is something entirely false and not reliable for decision in any matter. A number of tradition have been quoted from the Imams of the Prophet's Progeny prohibiting action on analogy. (Refer to **Wasā'ilush Shi'ah**, vol. III, chapter of *Qaza*). As a matter of fact one of the factors which have made the Sunni ulema act on analogy is, according to them, the deficiency of evidence with regard to certain orders. As is well-known the numer of authentic traditions relating to all branches of Jurisprudence which Abu Hanifa had in view, does not exceed thirty. Those conversant with the differnent extensive branches of Jurisprudence are aware that if these traditions relate to one branch only, they will not suffice for problems relating to other branches. How can it, therefore, be possible to base the entire Jurisprudence on this limited number of traditions only? Consequently their jurists have been compelled to extend their hand to analogy, *Istehsān* (Approval) and *Ijtihad* (in a special sense which will be explained later) to solve the juridical problems. However, as the Shi'ah possess large collection of traditions from the Holy Prophet narrated and explained by his Progeny they do not feel any need to resort to analogy (leaving aside the defects and difficulties which are encountered by acting on it).

Continued...

138

number of traditions have been quoted on this subject from the Holy Imams of the Prophet's Progeny to the effect that if analogy is resorted to in religious laws the foundation of religion will be demolished. The concept of invalidity of analogy, however, needs detailed discussion which is beyond the scope of this book.

(ii) The Imamiyah believe that traditions of the Holy Prophet should be accepted through the channel of narrations by the people of the Holy Prophet's Progeny. For example, those traditions should be accepted which are quoted by Imam Ja'far Sadiq from his father Imam Baqir and by him from his father Imam Sajjad and by him from his father Imam Husayn and by him from his father Imam Ali and by him from the Holy Prophet. In this manner the Shi'ah receive the tradition of the Holy Prophet through proper channel which ends with the chosen descendants of the Holy Prophet and not through persons like Abu Hurayra, Samrah bin Jundab, Marwan bin Hakām, Imran bin Hattan Khāriji, Amr bin Ās and others of that type, because they (Shi'ah) do not attach any importance to the

One of the clear arguments about the invalidity of action on the basis of Analogy is that the secrets of many religious orders are not fully known to us. Often it so happens that so far as we can perceive some matters resemble one another but according to Islamic laws different orders have been specified for them. For example we cannot comprehend the difference between alcoholic beverage and other narcotic and intoxicating things although the former are impure and the latter are are pure (although the use of all of them may be prohibited). Instances of such distinction are abundant in matters relating to Jurisprudence. On the other hand in many cases we feel that there is too much difference between two matters but according to religious law they are governed by one and the same law. For example, a barren woman has to observe the same *Idda* (during which a divorced or widowed woman may not be married to another man) as is observed by another woman although usually *Idda* is observed to find out whether the woman is pregnant. These matters clearly show that we are not entitled to deduce inferences by Analogy regarding religious laws.

narrations of people of this type and their real posture is too well-known to need any explanation. This is so clear that even some learned men among the Sunni have disclosed in their books the weak points of these people in religious as well as moral affairs.[1]

(iii) The Imamiyah consider the door of *Ijtihad* to be always open and as already pointed out their reasoning in this behalf is quite clear. Others have, however, closed this door on the scholars and wise men of the Ummah. However, I am not aware as to when, why and how this door has been closed. It is a matter of great regret that I have not yet met any Sunni scholar who should give satisfactory replies to these questions although it is their duty to provide us sufficient explanation in this regard and tell us why the door of *Ijtihad* has been closed on them.[2]

---

[1] It goes without saying that the distinguished author does not mean to say that there were no reliable persons among the friends and companions of the Holy Prophet whose traditions would be incredible. Certainly there were such reliable companions and the traditions quoted by them would be acceptable. However, the concept of purity of the companions and the view that traditions narrated by anyone who is called a companion should be accepted without dispute (as believed by most of the Sunni scholars) cannot be agreed upon and is not compatible with any logic. The history of Islam and even the history books written by distinguished Sunni historians are replete with accounts of offences committed by some of the persons who are counted among the companions of the Holy Prophet. Is it possible to deny the contents of all these history books and ignore all these offences and silently accept every tradition, the narration of which ends with anyone of the companions? Can any enlightened conscience accept such a proposition?

[2] One of the matters which is very well-known among the Sunnis and for which no proof exists is the concept of restricting faith to the four famous schools and in other words restricting the right of *Ijtihad* to only four persons and depriving others. None of their scholars has furnished a satisfactory argument for this unjustified privilege and discrimination. I remember that when I had the honour to go to Makkah to perform the pilgrimage of the House of Allah,

Continued...

There is no difference between the Shi'ah and other
Muslims regarding the principles of jurisprudence except in

I, along with some other learned friends, went to see a Sunni scholar,
who was one of the teachers of sacred precinct of Ka'bah and an
author of many books. No doubt he was an enlightened and learned
scholar with good disposition. On our way we were thinking of
propounding a theoretical issue for discussion and benefiting from
his knowledge. I thought of the question of restricting faith to four
schools. After going through the usual formalities of introduction
etc. I asked him, "O our Shaykh! What is the proof of restricting
faith to four religious schools?" I was ready for a detailed discussion
on the subject between him and myself so that it should lead to the
questions of opening the door of *Ijtihad*. However, I suddenly found
that the said scholar remarked in reply to my question without any
hesitation or pause and with perfect clarity and sincerity, "There is
no proof on this proposition".

However, it appears that in the eyes of the Sunnis the real
object of this restriction is to prevent diversity and dispersion in the
Muslim society, although this thinking is absolutely erroneous,
because diversity and dispersion has not only not been prevented but
has stabilized itself in a pungent form in the four schools and has
brought about stagnancy and disorder, particularly in their Jurisprudence. On the other hand Shi'ah Jurisprudence has acquired unusual
expansion and special stimulation on account of the door of *Ijtihad*
has been kept open and especially due to the following the decrees
of the dead scholars (the scholars and Jurists who are no longer
alive) being declared unlawful, except when *Taqlid* (of decrees given
by such Jurists during their lifetime) is adhered to (after their death).
As it happens, therefore, the distance between the followers of two
Shi'ah Mujtahids is much lesser than the distance between the
followers of the four schools (of Sunnis).

And if the principle of "Following the most learned scholar"
which is well-known among the Shi'ah is practised properly and after
the passing away of one great authority the ulema of the highest
order sit together and select the most learned person this will accord
with all the juridical standards and as a result thereof the consensus
of all people of one period in secondary matters will also be ensured.

the above mentioned three points[1] and even if there are some differences they are about legal matters of secondary nature. For example, it is possible that the Shi'ah may consider something essential which others may not consider to be essential and vice versa. However, examples of such differences may be found among Sunni scholars or Shi'ah scholars also although their source is the same and such differences occur in the *Ijtihad* of individuals inter se.

Another point which should be mentioned here is that from the Shi'ah view-point, a *Mujtahid* is a person who acquires acumen for *Ijtihad* after deep and extensive study of the arguments relating to religious laws. In other words he acquires scientific and intellectual strength by means of which he deduces religious laws from relevant sources and arguments. Such a person can give his opinion on religious matters by dint of his *Ijtihad*. However, only this much is not sufficient for others to follow him. On the other hand to acquire the status of an authority to guide,

[1] Besides these, *Ijtihad* has a fundamental and basic difference between us and the Sunnis, because from our point of view *Ijtihad* is deducing of religious laws from different sources viz. the Holy Qur'an, traditions, logical arguments and consensus of opinion of Muslim community, but according to the Sunni Jurists it is a sort of legislation. To explain the point further it may be said that when a matter is not discussed in the text and no law with regard to it exists in the Holy Qur'an and traditions of the Holy Prophet, they (the Sunni Ulema) sit down and considering the good and evil of the matter, coin an order or formulate a law (because they believe that in fact no order exists on the subject and the matter has been left over to us).

They call formulation of law on these lines as *Ijtihad*. However, it goes without saying that this type of *Ijtihad* means that the religious laws are incomplete and depend on the Muslim community for formulation of orders. The Shi'ah do not, however, agree with this and believe that in Islam a law exists for every affair and has been promulgated in advance either in the shape of a general rule or in a special manner. Further explanation of the subject is beyond the capacity of this treatise.

it is necessary to fulfil some other conditions also besides those essential for *Ijtihad* – the most important being the attribute of justice.

Attribute of justice is a spiritual state of piety which keeps man away from sins and guides him to the performance of duties and fulfilment of essentials. This state has different stages, of which the most sublime and deeply rooted is the stage of purity which is one of the pre-requisites of the offices of the Prophet and Imam.

Of course, the concept of *Ijtihad* and *Taqlid* does not arise in evident and admitted religious matters which are quite well-known to everybody (e.g. Prayers being obligatory and Usury being prohibited etc.) Similarly *Taqlid* is not permissible in matters related to fundamental beliefs (e.g. Monotheism, Prophethood and the Day of Judgement). On the other hand it is necessary that everyone should acquire knowledge about them with decisive proofs as it suits him because such matters are fundamentals of faith which should be perceived by everyone with proof as articles of faith (although this proof may be quite simple). In these matters neither conjectures and opinions are sufficient nor following others is permissible.

In articles of acts, however, it is correct to follow one's own *Ijtihad* as well as to observe *Taqlid* viz. *Ijtihad* by those who are competent to draw inferences and *Taqlid* for those who do not possess sufficient religious knowledge.

The point which appears necessary to be explained at the end of this discussion is that the adults have to perform religious duties with the clear knowledge of the precepts and commands either by way of *Ijtihad* or *Taqlid* under the following two conditions:
the following two conditions:

(i) **Worship:** Worship consists of functions, the object of which is to strengthen the relationship of mankind with Allah. Hence its validity is based upon intention of proximity.

Worship is of two kinds viz. (i) Physical like Prayers and Fasting and (ii) Financial like *Zakat* and *Khums.*

(ii) **Transactions:** Transactions mean all matters which define dealings with one another or with regard to themselves. These too are of three kinds, viz. matters which are bilateral, for example, purchase and sale, marriage etc. and matters which are unilateral like divorce and setting the slaves free and matters which relate to man himself like the manner of eating food or wearing dress etc.

Fiqh is the branch of knowledge which explains the laws relating to the subjects falling under four headings: **worship, transactions, unilateral obligations** and **regulations.**

Basic worship consists of six things of which two are purely physical (Prayers and Fasting), two purely financial (Zakat and Khums) and two physical as well as financial (Hajj and Jihad).

As regards *Kaffarah* (expiations or atonements) they are special punishments which apply to specific crimes. (The above matters will be explained further in the following discussions).

* * * * *

Prayers: From the view-point of the Shi'ah as well as all other Muslims, *Salāt* (Prayer) is the pillar of the faith which means communication between man and Allah and the spiritual ascension of the Faithful. If a person gives up offering Prayers, relationship between him and Allah comes to an end. As such it has been said in the traditions of the members of Holy Prophet's Progeny: "The distance between a Musim and infidelity is only the abandonment of one or two obligatory Prayers".

The superiority of Prayers among Islamic articles of worship is such that none of them is equal to it in position. All Shi'ah scholars and ulema are agreed on this point that whoever abandons Prayers is a sinner and a libertine and is not entitled to any respect. Speaking ill of him in his absence is permissible and he loses all credit. In short the Shi'ah are extraordinarily strict on the subject of Prayers.[1]

From the Shi'ah point of view there are five kinds of obligatory Prayers (according to basic faith) viz. Five daily

---

[1]It is possible that some people may be surprised to note as to why the late Allama Kashiful Ghita had persisted in emphasizing that the Shi'ah attach much importance to Prayers. The point is that unfortunately some self-interested and separatist persons accuse the Shi'ah that they do not offer Prayers at all. Why are we people so much detached from one another that we have no information about the clearest matters relating to us? Who is guilty? We believe that all of us are guilty.

Prayers, Friday Prayers, Eidul Fitr and Eidul Azha Prayers, *Āyāt* (Sign) Prayers and *Tawāf* (Circumambulation) Prayers. However, it is possible that at times one who has reached the age of puberty may make Prayers obligatory for himself by means of a vow, a pledge, or an oath for his own sake or for the sake of another person. This type of Prayer is not obligatory from the point of view of religion. On the other hand the person concerned has made it obligatory for himself.

Prayers other than those mentioned above, are *Mustahab* (Recommended). The most important recommended Prayers are the daily Nafilah Prayers which are twice as many as the five obligatory Prayers (i.e. thirty four rak'ats). On this account, according to Shi'ah the total number of rakats of obligatory and recommended Prayers comes to fifty one.

Here I happen to recollect an interesting story which it will not be out of place to mention. This story has been related by Raghib Isfahani in his valuable and useful book entitled **Muhazirāt**: In the days of Ahmad bin Abdul Aziz, there lived in Isfahan a man named Kanāni, who was a supporter of Ahlul Bayt (Progeny of the Holy Prophet). Ahmad bin Abdul Aziz used to take lessons from him on the subject of Imamate. One day Ahmad's mother chanced to peep in and saw the scene in the study room. She suddenly shouted and addressing Kanāni said, "You are a bad man. You have made my son Rāfizi". Kanani thereupon replied, "O' foolish woman! The Rafizi offer Prayers daily consisting of 51 rak'ats whereas your son does not offer Prayers consisting of even one rakat. Then how has he become a Rāfizi?"

After the daily *Nafilah* Prayers the most important recommended Prayers are the *Nafilah* of the sacred month of Ramazan which consist of 1000 rak'ats (of course over and above the daily *Nafilah* Prayers). In this matter there is no difference between us and our Sunni brethren except that we offer these Prayers individually and do not consider it permissible that they should be offered congregationally whereas they offer these Prayers congregationally and call them *Tarāwih*.

146

Orders regarding Friday Prayers, Eidul Fitr and Eidul Azha Prayers, Sign Prayers and other recommended Prayers should be studied in detailed books written on this subject by Shi'ah ulema and scholars. The number of such books exceeds tens of thousands.

Each of these Prayers has special formalities, recitations and supplications which are recorded in books written specially on the subject. The number of such books is also unusually large.

Now as regards the essence of Prayers. From our view-point the essence of Prayers consists of three parts:

Pre-conditions: The pre-conditions of Prayers consist of descriptions and circumstances abstracted from a chain of matters not forming part of Prayers. Bases of these conditions are the following six things without which the Prayers would be void:
(i) *Taharat* (Ceremonial purification). (ii) Time. (iii) *Qibla* (Direction to which one has to turn while praying). (iv) Dress of the person offering Prayers. (v) Intentioning (to offer Prayers). (vi) Place utilized by the person concerned for offering Prayers.

Of course place is not in essence a part of these conditions but it is a necessity for existence of every human being, because the person who offers Prayers cannot (like every other person) do without a place. It is, however, essential that the place where Prayers are offered should not have been usurped and the place of prostration (the place which the forehead touches) should also be clean and pure.

Ingredients of Prayers: Ingredients of Prayers consist of items of which Prayers are composed. They too, in their turn, are of two kinds. In the first category fall the ingredients which are the essentials of Prayers and without which the Prayers become void (whether these essentials are abandoned purposely or by mistake). They consist of four things namely *Takbiratul Ihram* (saying *Allaho Akbar* viz. Allah is the Greatest at the commencement of prayers) *Qiyam* (Standing up), *Ruku'* (Bowing) and *Sujud* (Prostrations).

147

To the second category belong the ingredients which are not the essentials of Prayers. If they are, however, abandoned purposely the Prayers will become void for example, *Qir'at* (recitation of Surah Hamd and another sura, *Zikr, Tashahhud* and *Salām*). During the performance of prayers *Tuma'ninat* (well-composed manner) is essential. However, Azan and *Iqamah* may fall in the category of *Mustahab Mu'akkad* (emphatically recommended). Rather, it is not unlikely that there is ample time *Iqamah* may be obligatory.[1]

Impediments of Prayers: As the very phrase indicates, are things that make Prayers void and they too fall into two categories. In the first category fall the basic impediments which make Prayers void in all circumstances, (whether relevant actions are done intentionally or unintentionally) and they are three: (i) Turning ones back to *Qibla*, (ii) Things which make *Wuzu* (ablution) void; and (iii) Excessive action which obliterates the very shape of Prayers.[2]

In the second category the actions which if done intentionally, make the Prayers void and they consist of speaking, laughing or weeping with sound, turning the face towards right or left, eating and drinking.[3]

Taharāt (ceremonial purification) which has been referred to as one of the pre-conditions of Prayers consists of ablution and *Ghusl* (ceremonial bath) and there are causes as a consequence whereof each one of them becomes obligatory. In case water is not available for ablution or

---

[1] It is not clear whether *Iqamah* is obligatory. The fact is that it is *Mustahab Muakkad.*

[2] Instead of saying excessive action, it would be appropriate to say, action obliterating the shape of prayers (whether excessive or not) e.g. jumping or clapping hands in the middle of prayers obliterates and makes void the shape of prayers notwithstanding the fact that it is not an excessive action.

[3] These are not the only impediments of Prayers. There are many other things which make Prayers void. For this reference should be made to relevant books.

bath or though water may be available, it may not be possible for the person concerned to utilize it on account of illness of severe winter or shortage of time he should perform *Tayammum* (ceremonial purification of body with sand or dust) instead, just as the Holy Qur'an says: *O you who believe! approach not Prayers with a mind befogged until you can understand all that you say nor in a state of ceremonial impurity (except when travelling) until after the ceremonial bath. If you are ill, or on a journey, or if you have moved your bowels, or you have been in contact with your wives, and you find no water, then strike your hands on clean sand and rub your face and hands with it. Allah pardons such things and He is Forgiving.* (Surah al-Nisa, 4:43)

As regards the meaning of the word *saeed* used in the sacred verse reproduced above, there is a difference of opinion among the jurists and lexicographers. Some of them believe that the word *saeed* means soil only, whereas others give it a wider meaning and are of the view that whatever covers the face of the earth generally, whether it be soil, gravel, sand, stone or other similar things is covered by the word *saeed* so much so that mineral stones are also a part of *saeed* before they are baked and assume the shape of chalk, lime etc. The latter view appears to be more correct.

This was a short account of the view of Shi'ah regarding Prayers. However, as has already been pointed out each ingredient of this subject needs detailed discussions. This is a task which can be accomplished only by writing a number of voluminous books.

* * * * * *

From the view-point of Shi'ah Fasting is one of the pillars of Islamic articles of worship. From the religious standpoint it is divided into three categories:

(i) **Obligatory Fasting:** This too is of two kinds viz. Fast which is obligatory by itself (fasting during the sacred month of Ramazan) and the Fast which becomes obligatory for various reasons like Expiatory Fast and Fast as substitute for a sacrifice and Fasting on behalf of another and Fast as a consequence of a vow etc.

(ii) **Recommended Fasting:** Like Fasts of the months of Rajab and Sha'ban and other recommended Fasts which are large in number.

(iii) **Forbidden Fasting:** Fasting on the festival days of Eidul Fitr and Eidul Azha.

Some Shi'ah scholars have also mentioned a fourth kind of Fast namely abominable Fast e.g. Fasting on the day of Ashura (10th of Muharram) and *Arafa* (9th of Zilhajj). It should, however, be remembered that such fasts are not abominable in the sense that it is preferable to forsake rather than to observe them. On the other hand their abomination is relative viz. as compared to other Fasts their reward and desirability is lesser.

Fasting has many pre-conditions, which are mentioned in books on the subject written by Shi'ah scholars. The

150

number of such books exceeds thousands.

In all circumstances the Shi'ah are so much bound over to the Fasts of the month of Ramazan that they are not prepared to break the Fast notwithstanding the fact that due to intense thirst and uneasiness their condition may become serious.

This was the brief explanation of two articles of Islamic worship which possess physical aspect only.

* * * * * *

Zakat

From Shi'ah point of view *Zakat* is the most important article of worship next to Prayers, so much so that in some of the narrations of Imams belonging to the Holy Prophet's Progeny it has been said, "The Prayers of a person who does not pay *Zakat* are not acceptable".

The Shi'ah, like other Muslims, consider the payment of *Zakat* obligatory with regard to nine things, namely, three kinds of quadrupeds (sheep, cow and camel) four kinds of cereals (wheat, barley, dates and raisins) and gold and silver coins. In some cases payment of *Zakat* has been recommended viz. for merchandise, horses and the total proceeds of farming.

As regards the payment of *Zakat* for the above-mentioned nine things being obligatory, it carries certain preconditions and fixed limits of taxation which are laid down in relevant books.

It is also necessary to point out that all the conditions and limitations of payment of *Zakat* in which the Shi'ah believe, tally with at least one of the four schools of Sunni. From the Shi'ah point of view the items of expenditure of *Zakat* are eight as mentioned by the Holy Qur'an. *Zakat is for the poor, the indigent, non-believers whose hearts are inclined towards Islam, debtors, pious and Divine causes and for those who have become needy on a journey.* (Surah al-Tawbah, 9:60)

152

Zakatul Fitr: It is a type of *Zakat* payable at the time of Eidul Fitr (Islamic festival). Its payment is compulsory for every sane and adult on his own behalf as well as on behalf of all persons dependent upon him whether young or old. The quantity of *Zakatul Fitr* per head is one *Sā'* (3 kilos approx) of articles of usual diet of the people viz. wheat, barley, dates and the like.

There is no difference between the Shi'ah and Sunni in the basic priciples of *Zakatul Fitr*.

* * * * * *

Khums

The Shi'ah consider payment of *Khums* obligatory in respect of following seven things:
(i) Booty of war. (ii) Things obtained from the sea by diving. (iii) Treasure-trove. (iv) Minerals. (v) Lawful wealth mixed up with unlawful wealth. (vi) Land transferred by a Muslim to a *Zimmi* infidel (who pays tribute and is under the protection of Muslims). (vii) Income from trades.

The sacred verse of the Holy Qur'an proclaims: *Know that whatever property you gain one fifth belongs to Allah, the Prophet, (Prophet's) near relatives, orphans, the needy, and the wayfarer — if you do believe in Allah and in the revelation We sent down to our Servant on the Day of Testing (Badr) — when the armies confronted each other the two forces. For Allah has power over all things.* (Surah al-Anfal, 8:41) forms the basis for this discussion. According to this verse *Khums* is obligatory on all sorts of *Ghanimat* (profits).[1]

---

[1] The literal meaning of the word *Ghanimat* is quite wide. It covers every income earned by a person and is not confined to booty of war only. In the narrations of the Holy Prophet's Progeny also it has been interpreted in the same sense. In this way *Khums* is related to all earnings. In fact it is a kind of Islamic tax on income which is payable on the balance left at the end of the year after meeting the necessary expenses of life. It is true that the sacred verse has occurred in the Holy Qur'an among the verses related to *Jihad*. However, if a

Continued...

154

We believe that the Almighty Allah arranged *Khums* for the members of the Holy Prophet's Progeny instead of *Zakat* (which is unlawful for them) and it should be divided into six parts. Three shares belong to Almighty Allah, the Holy Prophet and his Ahlul Bayt (as mentioned in the Holy Qur'an). During the period of the presence of an Imam these three shares should be entrusted to him so that he may spend them according to his discretion. During the period of Occultation of the Imam these shares should be handed over to a righteous *Mujtahid* (who is considered to be the deputy of the Imam) so that they may be spent under his supervision for the security of Islamic laws and Islamic countries and for the propagation of religion and in connection with other important religious and social matters such as assistance to the poor and needy members of the society.

SHOULD THE SHARE OF THE IMAM BE PLACED AT SARDAB?

It is not as Mahmud Ālusi says by way of mocking in his exegesis: "It is appropriate that the Shi'ah should leave these shares in these days (i.e. during the period of Occultation of the Imam) at *Sardab* (Cellar)". His object by saying this is the same false accusation which has been attributed to the Shi'ah time and again and it has been said that they (Shi'ah) believe that the Imam of the Age is hidden in the Cave.

We have repeatedly said that these are unjustified accusations ascribed to us by the Sunni from olden times. They have also written in their books that the Shi'ah believe that the Imam is hidden in Sardāb. The fact,

verse falls within the range of verses related to one topic, it is not an argument for the unity of the subject; because we know that the verses of the Holy Qur'an were not revealed one after the other and without any interruption between them. Often it so happened that one day a verse was revealed relating to one matter and a week later another verse was revealed relating to another matter. In these circumstances unity of context of verses cannot be treated as a proof of the unity of their subject.

155

however, is that the Sardab in question has the least connection with the Occultation of the Imam and it is not known on the basis of which evidence and which writing of the Shi'ah they have made these uncalled for statements against us. Possibly the source of this error is that they (Sunni) see that we visit the said cave. In fact the real position is that we visit the said place on account of its being the place of worship of the Imam of the Age and his forefathers namely Imam Hasan Askari and Imam Hadi. At this place they stood in the presence of Allah, prostrated before Him and had invocations with Him.

As regards the remaining three shares of *Khums*, they have been allocated to destitutes and needy Sayyids (instead of *Zakat* which is unlawful for them to take).[1]

From the Shi'ah point of view these have been the laws relating to *Khums* from the time of the Holy Prophet to the present day. However, after the passing away of the Holy Prophet, the Sunni cut off the right of *Khums* of Bani Hashim and made it a part of the Treasury. Consequently the needy persons among Bani Hashim were deprived of *Khums* as *Zakat* was prohibited to them.

It seems that in his well-known book entitled **Um,** Imam Shāfi'i refers to this very point and says: "As regards

---

[1] In fact *Khums* is a ceremonial previlege for the preservation of the dignity of the Progeny of the Holy Prophet, otherwise, in reality it does not establish any difference between the needy Sayyids and non-Sayyids. The needy Sayyids are entitled to benefit from *Khums* to the extent of their needs and if the amount of three shares of *Khums*, which is the right of Sayyids, exceeds their requirements, the balance reverts to the Islamic treasury in the same way in which their requirements are to be met from the treasury in case the amount of *Khums* falls short of them. That is to say the amount of benefit drawn by Sayyids from three shares of *Khums* is just equal to that drawn by non-Sayyids from *Zakat*. Notwithstanding the fact, therefore, the Sayyids are deprived of *Zakat* there remains no financial disparity between them and others and *Khums* carries only the aspect of respect and preservation of the dignity of the Progeny of the Holy Prophet.

the family of the Holy Prophet for whom *Khums* has been prescribed instead of *Zakat*, they cannot, on any account, benefit from *Zakat* and obligatory alms and in case any person gives them something (i.e. by way of *Zakat* or alms) it does not suffice and he is not absolved of his responsibility (to pay them *Khums*)".

Consequently the Sunni jurists have practically eliminated the Chapter of *Khums* from their writings and do not undertake any discussion in their books under this heading. However, so far as Shi'ah jurists are concerned they conduct discussion on *Khums* just as on *Zakat*, in their books on Jurisprudence.

Only the famous scholar named Abu Ubaydul Qasim bin Salām (d. 224 A.H.) has conducted a detailed discussion about usages and other orders relevant to *Khums*, in his book entitled **Kitabul Amwāl**, which is one of the most excellent Islamic books. Most of its contents conform to the well-known beliefs of the Shi'ah. Those interested may refer to pp. 303 — 349.

This was a brief discussion of Shi'ah belief regarding two items of Islamic worship which have a financial aspect only viz. *Khums* and *Zakat*. Now as regards the articles of worship which have two aspects (viz. physical and financial) they are *Hajj* and *Jihad*.

* * * * * *

157

Hajj

According to the Shi'ah one of the main elements of Islam is *Hajj* and in accordance with the traditions quoted in our books whoever forsakes it, dies either as a Jew or as a Christian. Such a person is on the threshold of infidelity as the sacred verse points out: *Whoever disbelieves (Hajj), then verily, Allah is self-sufficiently independent of the worships.* (Surah Ale Imran, 3:97)

As a matter of fact *Hajj* is a sort of physical and financial *Jihad*. *Hajj* is a spiritual *Jihad* while *Jihad*, in its true sense, is a real *Hajj*[1] and when one thinks deeply into the mysteries and formalities of these two main Islamic elements, he very easily feels a sort of unity and harmony between them.

When a person satisfies the prerequisite conditions (viz. being adult and sane) as well as the special conditions (viz. possessing necessary means i.e. provisions for journey, ride, health and security of passage) it is obligatory for him to perform *Hajj* once in his lifetime. Of course, it is an immediate obligation and cannot be postponed.

Hajj is of three kinds: *Ifrād*, *Qirān* and *Tamatto*:

(i) *Hajjul Ifrād* to which the following verse refers: *.... Pilgrimage to the House is a duty to Allah incumbent on all..........* (Surah Ale Imran, 3:97).

(ii) *Hajjul Qirān*, which has been referred to in this verse: *Complete the pilgrimage (Hajj) and Umra for the sake of Allah.* (Surah al-Baqarah, 2:197)

---

[1] Here *Hajj* means to prepare oneself to meet Allah.

158

(iii) *Hajjut Tamatto,* which is provided for in this verse:
. . . .*Whoever profits by combining the visit (umra)
with the pilgrimage (Hajj)* . . . . . (Surah al-Baqarah, 2:196)
For each of these kinds of pilgrimage there are sufficient orders and discussions which have been explained in
books written on the subject. I have studied many books
written by Sunni scholars about pilgrimage and have found
that, except for a few points about which there are differences, they tally with the writings of Shi'ah scholars.

The history of Shi'ah Faith and study of the affairs of
the Shi'ah in the past and present abundantly reveal that
they have always given special importance to pilgrimage
and thousands of persons have had the honour of performing this great Islamic obligation every year, although they
were confronted with various dangers and discomforts
from thousands of those who considered it permissible to
plunder their belongings and even shed their blood. However, none of these arduous difficulties prevented them
from performing this great duty. They have made sacrifices
in this behalf and have not refrained in any way from
laying down their lives and property for this purpose. How
surprising it is that in spite of all these sacrifices on the
part of Shi'ah it is said that they want to destroy the very
foundation of Islam!

* * * * *

Jihad - The Holy War

Major Jihad and Minor Jihad: *Jihad* is one of the most important foundations of Islam and the real pillars of its edifice. It is *Jihad* which has erected the palace of Islam and made it lofty. If *Jihad* had not been there Islam would have not been the source of salvation and the means of grace and blessings in the manner in which it is.

Jihad is nothing except firmness in the face of aggression by the enemy. Resistance against injustice and mischief and sacrificing one's life and property and considering no sacrifice dearer in this path is called *Jihad*.

According to the belief of the Shi'ah, *Jihad* is of two kinds: **Major Jihad** and **Minor Jihad.**

Major Jihad is the very resistance against inner enemy viz. unruly passions and campaign against mean desires and moral degradations like ignorance, fear, injustice, pride, selfishness, envy, stinginess etc. Thus it has been rightly said: "Your arch-enemy is your refractory passion".

Minor Jihad is campaign against external enemies, enemies of truth, enemies of justice, enemies of reforms and enemies of virtue and faith.

In view of the fact that campaign against moral deviations and indecent and abominable deeds and actions which have taken roots in human soul is a very difficult task, the Holy Prophet of Islam has, in some of his traditions, called this type of campaign as Major *Jihad*. (See: **Jihad Akbar** by Imam Khumayni).

The respected comrades and companions of the Holy

160

Prophet were also always engaged in these two kinds of campaigns throughout their lives and made Islam attain the zenith of its honour and distinction under its wing.

However, there still remains one point which should be mentioned and it is this that if we wish to permit our pen to delineate the picture of the manner of *Jihad* of Muslims of the past and their sacrifices and bravery for the grandeur and exaltation of Islam, compared to what we see today, it would be most appropriate that tears of regret should flow down from our eyes and our hearts should break with extreme grief and sadness!

However, are you aware as to why I refrain from writing on this point although flames of sadness and grief are rising in my bosom and choking my heart so much so that the power of explaining this matter has been taken away from me?[1]

We have the explanation of this separation and this pang of the loss of our life-blood for the present and postpone it for some other time.

Old problems of race have been revived and Arab Nationalism has been made the object of worship instead

---

[1] It is a matter of great regret that during the present times *Jihad* has taken the shape of internal hot and cold wars, political and religious campaigns and conflicts among the Muslims themselves. We are waving our swords on the heads of each other, the swords which should have fallen on the heads of those enemies who are threatening our very existence. And instead of mobilizing all our physical and spiritual strength for the renewal of the past glory and utilizing the abundant resources which Almighty Allah has been kind enough to place at our disposal, we have, by our differences, prepared the ground for foreign influence and infiltration.

'There are some others who are assisting this dispersion by adopting local and individualistic attitude in social, political and religious matters. There are still others who have aligned themselves with different blocs. They have thus lost their identity and complete idependence and have assumed the shape of a limb attached to others. The result of this is the very condition which we are observing these days and with which we are grappling.

of Islam so much so that efforts are being made to give racial colour even to Islam and to Arab Islamic Culture, which has been selected as their motto. In this manner those concerned have separated themselves from the overall majority of Muslims and restricted their frontierless Islam within limited tracts of lands. Those persons have neither correct knowledge of Islam nor of the conditions and circustances of this age. It is an admitted fact that the Arab thinkers have not endorsed this erroneous way of thinking and will never do so.

* * * * * *

Two Important Commandments

According to the belief of the Shi'ah *Amr bil Ma'ruf* (enjoining good) and *Nahi 'anil Munkar* (campaigning against corruption) are a part of the most important and sublime commands of Islam about whose necessity reason as well as religion are unanimous.

These two great functions are considered to be the most fundamental bases of Islam. They range from the best prayers and worship to one of the different kinds of *Jihad.* If any nation ignores these two fundamentals, Almighty Allah certainly subjects them to degradation and misfortunes. Such communities readily fall a prey to the human looking rapacious animals and tyrants and unjust men. It is for this reason that the Prophet of Islam and our infallible Imams have been quoted to have spoken in moving words regarding the necessity of discharging these two great duties and the mischief and harm caused to human society by their abandonmnet, the very thought of which makes one shiver.

Unfortunately, today we see openly with our own eyes the mischief and harm which originate from laziness in the performance of these two functions. However, we wish that this process should have ended here and we might have remained content with the abandonment of these two functions and things should not have come to such a pass that permissible should have become unpermissible and vice versa so much so that those who invite others to truth and excellence should themselves recalci-

163

trate against truth and those who prohibit others from doing bad deeds should themselves be involved in various kinds of unlawful matters. This is an onerous and unbearable calamity. As a result of bad deeds of the people, mischief has become patent everywhere. And all this is in spite of the fact that we have been told: "Accursed are those who invite others to goodness and forsake it themselves and also those who prohibit others from committing sins but commit sins themselves!"

Truly, Islam deserves to be praised for its laws as well as for the extent and comprehensiveness of its commands, because it foresaw all that which is necessary for the spiritual and material life of man as well as the source of his advancement and prosperity.

On the one hand, it has formulated comprehensive and potent laws for mankind and this in fact amounts to authority for legislation. As is evident, authority for legislation cannot bring the desired results without necessary power to enforce it. Hence in the first instance all Muslims have been made responsible to guarantee its enforcement and it has been declared that it is the duty of every individual to enjoin others to do good things and to forbid them from doing bad things so that everyone of them may become the enforcing authority for the relevant rules and regulations. All should supervise the actions of one another and all should be answerable to one another. However, as it is possible that in certain circumstances this guarantee for enforcement may not suffice and some persons may hold back from putting the laws in action, extensive powers have been given in the second stage to the Islamic State and its ruler and the person absolutely reponsible for the affairs of Muslim society, viz. the Imam or person nominated by him for the purpose.

Islamic regime is responsible to enforce the penal laws of Islam, punish the offenders, campaign against corruption, injustice and mischief and make efforts to safeguard the independence of Muslims and strengthen the frontiers of the country.

In short the benefits and vital effects of these two

great Islamic Commands (to enjoin others to do good and to refrain from evil) are too numerous to be narrated. Is it possible to find such sublime social policies in any other religion of the world? Is there any school of thought or philosophy more profound than this wherein all individuals supervise the conduct of others in three things viz. (i) to learn and act upon it; (ii) to educate others; and (iii) to persuade others to learn and act, should be compulsory for everyone? It is here that man wonders at the grandeur of this religion and its sublime training centre. However, more surprising than this is the deplorable condition of the Muslims of the present age who, in spite of such a manifesto, have fallen into the ditch of degradation!

These are the fundamentals of Islamic worship from the Shi'ah view-point. We have contented ourselves with making brief reference to them and leave their explanation to detailed books written by the Shi'ah scholars and ulema since the early days of Islam upto the present times. As has already been pointed out the number of such books is so large that even those which have survived till today consist of hundreds of thousands of volumes, leaving aside those which have perished and have been destroyed due to various reasons and have not come down to us.

* * * * * *

Contracts and Transactions

As has already been pointed out, transactions are of various kinds:

Mutual Transactions: Such transactions are commitments which necessitate two parties. One is called the seller and the other is called the buyer. For example if a person says: "I have sold" he will be the seller and another person who says: "I have bought" will be the buyer.

If the transaction rotates on the pivot of property it is called compensation. Compensation is of two kinds:

(i) *Uqudul Lāzim* (Binding or enforceable contract) e.g. purchase and sale, lease, exchange, mortgage, gift, gift by exchange etc. Such transactions are sometimes termed *Uqudul Mughābina* (Contracts to avoid cheating) also because each of the parties endeavours that it may not be cheated and may profit more from the transaction.

(ii) *Uqudul Jā'iz* (Voidable Contracts) i.e. transactions which may be revoked by one or both the parties e.g. debt, gift without consideration, *Ju'āla*[1] and the like.

Orders and conditions relating to enforceable as well as voidable contracts have been explained in our detailed as well as concise books on Jurisprudence. The point

---

[1] *Ju'āla* may be to the effect that one may say: "I shall give so much money or a sum of money to the person who does such and such thing for me". (In *Ju'āla* no particular acceptance by a specified person is necessary). Other conditions of such a transaction should be seen in the books on Jurisprudence.

which must be mentioned here is that the Shi'ah ulema do not allow the slightest deviation from the Holy Qur'an and the Sunnah of the Holy Prophet and the rules deduced from them, whether it be in the matter of transactions or in the matters of worship. We do not at all permit any person to embark on acquisition of wealth and property except through lawful means like trade, farming, industry and the like. In our opinion every property which is acquired by way of usurpation, interest, misappropriation, fraud and cheating is unlawful. We do not allow anyone to practise fraud and swindling even in the case of infidels by usurping their property. We consider the payment of deposits to be one of the most important obligations and not to talk of the Muslim property, we do not regard any misappropriation to be permissible even in the case of unbelievers.

So much about the financial transactions. However, there are some mutual transactions and contracts which do not have a financial aspect although it is possible that they may also guarantee some financial rights. An example of such contracts is marriage, the real object of which is the preservation of the race, welfare of the family and the survival of mankind.

From Shi'ah point of view marriage is of two types viz. Permanent Marriage and Fixed Time Marriage. As regards the first type of marriage there is a consensus of opinion of all Muslims about it. As regards the second type of marriage (viz. Fixed Time Marriage which is also called *Mut'ah*,) it is one of the special features of the Shi'ah Faith only and the Holy Qur'an bears clear testimony about its being lawful: *If you marry for the appointed time you must pay their dowries.* (Surah al-Nisa, 4:24)

We say that this type of marriage is still lawful in the same manner in which it was made lawful in the early days of Islam and shall remain so for ever. However, there has always been serious conflict between us and others on this issue and the history of this dispute dates back to the days of the companions of the Holy Prophet. In view of the fact that for various reasons this issue carries importance, hence, to explain its truths for enlightening the minds of all Muslim brethren becomes essential.

167

Fixed-time Marriage

One of the. undeniable propositions about which no one with the least knowledge of Islamic laws and orders can have any doubt is that Fixed Time Marriage i.e. marriage which is for a limited and specified time, was declared lawful by the Holy Prophet himself and many of his companions availed themselves of the permission under this law during his lifetime as well as after his death.

The exegetes of Islam are unanimous on this point that a number of distinguished companions of the Holy Prophet e.g. Abdullah bin Abbas, Jabir bin Abdullah Ansari, Imran bin Hasin, Abdullah bin Mas'ud, Abi bin Ka'b and the like gave verdicts in favour of permissibility of Fixed Time Marriage and used to read the aforesaid verse in this manner: "Give those women their dowries as fixed reward whom you marry for a fixed period".[1]

Certainly, it was not their idea that an alteration had taken place in the Holy Qur'an and something had been omitted from it. No. Never! On the contrary their object was to narrate the commentary which they had heard from the Holy Prophet i.e. the very person on whom this Sublime Divine Book had been revealed, although from the narrations recorded by Ibn Jarir Tabari in his commentary, it apparently seems that the verse "Give those women their dowries as a fixed reward whom you

---

[1]See: **Tafsir Kabir** by Fakhruddin Rāzi, vol. III, p. 201 and **Tafsir Tabari**, p. 9.

marry for a specified period" originally formed a part of the Holy Qur'an, for he says: "Abu Nasira narrates thus: 'I read this verse before Ibn Abbas'. He said, 'Read for a specified period'. I said: I do not read it like this. He said, 'I swear by Allah that it has been revealed like this (He repeated these words thrice)' ".

However, the status of Ibn Abbas who had been given the title of the Saint of Islam *(Hibrul Ummah)* is certainly much above attributing alteration in the Holy Qur'an. If this report be authentic, he certainly meant that the explanation of the verse had come down like this.

MYTH OF ABROGATION OF THE VERSE

In any case there is consensus of opinion of the ulema of Islam on this point, rather it is a necessity of faith, that in the beginning Fixed Time Marraige was permissible and Muslims practised it in the early days of Islam except that the opponents of this assert that later the relevant verse was abrogated and Fixed Time Marraage became unlawful. However, there is a difference of opinion regarding the abrogation of the verse and the traditions which are adduced by the said persons in support of their claim are conflicting.

It is evident that so far as such traditions are concerned they are not only incredible but they should not also lead to any conjecture or suspicion because according to juridical rules a final order cannot be taken to be abrogated without the existence of a definite proof.

To explain further, it may be said that as regards the abrogation of the verse, they sometimes claim that the Holy Prophet himself permitted the Fixed Time Marriage in the first instance and later declared it to be unlawful and on this account the verse was abrogated by the tradition of the Holy Prophet.

At another time they say that the said verse was abrogated by other verses of the Holy Qur'an. There is also a difference of opinion among them as to which verse abrogated it. Some say that it was abrogated by the verse relating to divorce: *If you divorce women, divorce them* during the proper period of Iddah (when their period of menses is over and you have not had sexual intercourse with them). (Surah al-Talaq, 65:1)

Others say that the verse in question has been abrogated by the verse relating to the inheritance of husband and wife: *In what your wives leave, your share is half, if they leave no child.* (Surah al-Nisa, 4:12)

We think that these claims are so feeble and baseless that they do not necessitate any reply because these verses (verses relating to inheritance and divorce) do not have the least relevance with the verse relating to Fixed Time Marriage so that it could be said that one concels the other. We shall explain later that Fixed Time Marriage is a sort of real marriage and the woman who gets married in this manner is really the wife and spouse of the man and all the orders relating to marriage apply to her.[1] Some of the opponents claim that the verse in question has been abrogated through the verse: *Except with their wives or those whom their right hands possess for then verily they are not blameable.* (Surah al-Mo'minun, 23:6) because this verse introduces the legality of intercourse of man and woman in two cases viz. actual marriage or in the case of the master of a slave girl, and the Fixed Time Marriage satisfies neither of the two conditions.

The well-known Sunni scholar Ālusi says thus in his commentary: The Shi'ah cannot claim that the woman who contracts a Fixed Time Marriage is a sort of a slave girl because this proposition would be patently fasle. They cannot also claim that she is equivalent to a wife because the effects and orders of wifehood like inheritance, *Iddah*, subsistence and divorce do not apply to her''.

This reasoning of Ālusi is very queer. The Shi'ah say that the woman who contracts Fixed Time Marriage is a real wife and Ālusi's remark that she does not fulfil the necessary conditions of this office is absolutely baseless and incorrect for the following reasons:

[1]With the exception of a few orders which are necessary concomitants of a permanent marriage and not of all types of marriages as shall be explained later.

Firstly, if he means that the essentials and the effects to which he has referred (inheritance, subsistence etc.) exist in all types of marriages, this claim is absolutely untenable because such effects exist definitely in the case of only one marriage. If, however, it is meant that in most kinds of marriages these necessities are proved we too accept this fact. However, their non-existence in some cases (Fixed Time Marriage) does not cause any harm.

From the various types of evidence which is available, it would appear that these necessities do not exist in all cases because we find that in most instances the wife does not inherit but still she is a wife. For example, the wife, who is an infidel, does not inherit and similarly the wife who attempts murder of her husband is not entitled to inherit from him. Furthermore, if a man, suffering from some ailment, marries a woman but dies before any sexual intercourse takes place, his wife will not inherit from him (although the marriage in all these cases have been Permanent Marriages).

On the contrary we find instances wherein marriages are totally dissolved on account of divorce but the right of inheritance remains in tact. For example if a man divorces his wife during his illness which culminates in his death and her *Iddah* also expires and subsequently the man dies before the completion of one year, the woman will inherit from him.

Secondly, even if we suppose that all these effects including inheritance are necessary concomitants of wifehood the said arguments would still remain indecisive because it is not an established fact that a woman who is married temporarily is not entitled to inheritance. On the other hand some Shi'ah scholars believe that such a woman also inherits like one with whom permanent marriage is accomplished. Some other scholars are, however, of the view that normally she does not inherit but a stipulation can be made for inheritance i.e. condition can be laid down in the text of the marriage contract that the parties will inherit from each other. In such a case they will inherit like permanent spouses. Still other jurists believe

171

that she (the woman with whom Fixed Time Marriage is accomplished) inherits in all circumstances except when it is stipulated to the contrary i.e. it is made clear at the time of marriage that they will not inherit from each other. Only in that event the woman who contracts a Fixed Time Marriage will not inherit.

In the above circumstances how can it be said that deprivation of a temporarily married woman from inheritance is an established fact?[1]

According to the principles of jurisprudence which are available with us and exigency of conjunction between the verses (verse relating to Fixed Time Marriage and verse relating to marriage (in Surah al-Mo'minun), the true position is that a woman with whom Fixed Time Marriage is accomplished is a wife and all orders relating to marriage apply to her − except when decisive proof excludes her from the application of certain orders.

However, as regards *Iddah*, all Shi'ah ulema and jurists agree that *Iddah* is proved in the case of Fixed Time Marriage and there is not a single person who does not consider it to be compulsory. (Under the circumstances, it is not known as to how Ālusi should have imputed such an irregularity to Shi'ah).

[1]Another point which deserves attention is that according to the principles of jurisprudence, it has been established that if a special order is given on a subject and a general order opposed to it is also given (of course, after the special order has been acted upon) then, just as it is probable that the general order may abrogate the special order, it is also possible that because of the special order, the general order may be appropriated (i.e. devoted to a special purpose). And as the number of orders abrogated is very small and as opposed to it appropriation has taken place to a large extent, it is appropriate that the second possibility may be given preference and appropriation should be relied upon. Hence, with a view to prove that inheritance is not admissible in the case of temporary marriage, the verse relating to inheritance should be treated as appropriated instead of treating the order regarding Fixed Time Marriage as abrogated. (However, this would be possible in case the verse relating to inheritance was revealed after the one relating to Fixed Time Marriage).

Nevertheless, subsistence is not one of the necessities of marriage because a woman who is not prepared for sexual intercourse with her husband and does not condescend to it, is not entitled to subsistence, although she is admittedly a spouse.

As regards divorce it should be remembered that in the case of Fixed Time Marriage there is a thing which is equivalent to divorce and that is the remission of the period of marriage because the husband can remit the remaining period of marriage and get separated from the woman. In that case the need for divorce does not arise.

Secondly, the abrogation of the verse relating to Fixed Time Marriage by the verse regarding marriage (Azwāj) (Surah al-Mo'minun, 23:6) is basically impossible because the verse relating to Fixed Time Marriage is in Surah al-Nisa and this Surah is one of those revealed in Madina, whereas the verse relating to marriage is in Surah al-Mo'minun and Surah al-Ma'arij both of which were revealed in Makkah. Hence, from historical point of view the first verse was revealed later and it is not possible that a verse revealed earlier should abrogate it.

Thirdly, a number of distinguished Sunni ulema have quoted narrations according to which the verse relating to Fixed Time Marriage has not been abrogated. Out of them Zamakhshari quotes, in his exegesis entitled Kash'shāf, from Ibn Abbas that the verse relating to Fixed Time Marriage is one of the Muhkamāt (i.e. verses admitting of no allegorical interpretation). Some others quote from Hakam bin Ayina that in reply to the question as to whether the verse relating to Fixed Time Marriage had been abrogated, he clearly said, 'No'.

In short, our opponents, after admitting the Fixed Time Marriage to have been permissible, claim that the order relating thereto was later abrogated and sometimes consider that a verse of the Holy Qur'an has abrogated it. However, the value of such a claim has become evident. At other times they claim that the said verse has been abrogated by tradition (of the Holy Prohphet) and treat this tradition quoted by Bukhari and Muslim to be the testimony for their claim: "The Holy Prophet forbade Fixed Time Marriage and the meat of domestic donkeys and this development took place during the time of the conquest of Makkah or Khaybar or at the time of the Battle of Awtās.[1] As will be observed this tradition is peculiarly conflicting and incoherent. Consequently those who claim that the order relating to Fixed Time Marriage has been abrogated through any tradition, have said a number of things, so much so that those like Qazi Ayaz have quoted that according to the belief of some persons the proposition of Fixed Time Marriage has twice been added to the list of permissible things and twice declared unlawful!

However, if we extend the area of study of this subject and carefully examine the relevant books we will find that there is much self-contradiction and diversity of opinions in this matter.

In some of their books it is stated that the abrogation of this order took place at the time of the last Hajj 10 A.H.) and in others it is said that it occurred at the time of the Battle of Tabuk (9 A.H.)

According to one report it took place during the Battle of Awtās or Hunayn (month of Shawwal in the year 8 A.H.) and according to another report it happened on the conquest of Makkah (during the month of Ramazan).

Some say the Holy Prophet permitted it at the time of the conquest of Makkah and after a few days declared it unlawful at the same place.

However, what is well-known among them is that this order was abrogated at the time of the Battle of Khaybar (7 A.H.) or during *Umratul Qaza* (during Zil Hajj in the same year).

If we accept all these remarks by way of narrations we should agree that this proposition was permitted five or six times and later declared unlawful — and not only twice

[1]After the Battle of Hunayn some infidel soldiers escaped to Awtās, a place located at three days journey from Makkah. The Prophet sent Muslim soldiers after them to defeat and disperse them. They very soon captivated and scattered them.

or thrice as stated by the Sunni scholar Nouvi and some others in commentary on Sahih Muslim.

O ulema of Islam! What a game you have played with religious matters? Can an iota of any reason approve it? It is evident that in the circumstances explained above not the least reliance can be placed on the statements made regarding the abrogation of the verse in question and the fable of its abrogation is unacceptable for the following reasons:

(i) The abrogation of a verse by a single report (i.e. a tradition narrated by one person only) is not admissible.

(ii) The traditions, claiming to prove the cancellation of the verse in question, are opposed to other traditions which clearly negate the abrogation of that verse. Such traditions are many and have been quoted by Sunni sources.

(iii) From a number of traditions quoted in the well-known books of the Sunni, it can be learnt very clearly that this order was operative in the days of the Holy Prophet and even during the time of the first Caliph; and only the second Caliph opposed it. Among others, Bukhari remarks thus in his **Sahih**: Abu Rijā quotes from Imrān bin Hasin that the verse relating to *Mut'ah* was revealed in the Holy Qur'an and we along with the Holy Prophet acted on this verse and no verse disallowing *Mut'ah* was revealed and the Holy Prophet, too, did not prohibit it in his lifetime. Thereafter someone said something about it according to his own thinking. It is said that this man was Umar (Bukhari's tradition ends).

Muslim, too, quotes on his own authority from Ata to this effect that Jābir bin Abdullah Ansari came to Makkah for Umra. We went to see him at his residence. Those present asked him questions and later enquired about *Mut'ah*. He replied, "Yes, we practised *Mut'ah* in the days of the Holy Prophet and acted on this order even in the days of Abu Bakr and Umar".

It has again been quoted thus in another tradition in **Sahih Muslim** from Jābir, "In the days of the Holy Prophet we practised *Mut'ah* for a few days against a small dowry and did so in the time of Abu Bakr till Umar prohibited it in the case of Amr bin Hārith".

In the same book Abu Nazar is quoted as saying: "I was with Jābir bin Abdullah and told him that Abdullah bin Abbas and Abdullah bin Zubayr differed with each other in the matter of *Mut'ah* and *Hajjut Tamatto* (which is a kind of *Hajj*)". Jābir replied, "We performed both of them with the Holy Prophet. Later Umar prohibited both and we too did not dispute over the matter".

However, it goes without saying that Jābir's forbearance on the subject was due to the fear of the Caliph because the latter applied the penalty of adultery in the case of Fixed Time Marriage and subjected the persons concerned to a shower of stones.

Indeed if we study **Sahih Muslim** carefully and analyse the tradition quoted therein for and against the legality of *Mut'ah* we come across very interesting results.

Jahni says: "During the year of the conquest of Makkah, on our arrival in that city, the Holy Prophet declared *Mut'ah* lawful but before we departed from there he withdrew the order".

Sometimes they say that the Holy Prophet abrogated this order. At other times they assert that this order was operative in the days of the Holy Prophet and Abu Bakr and it was abrogated by Umar. At times they say that Imam Ali repeatedly objected to the view of Ibn Abbas and dissuaded him from *Mut'ah* and this repeated objection by Imam Ali was the cause for Ibn Abbas reviewing his belief and forsaking his view regarding *Mut'ah*. This is notwithstanding the fact that he quotes about Abdullah bin Zubayr that one day he rose in Makkah and said: "There are people whose hearts have been blinded by Allah like their eyes. (He meant Abdullah bin Abbas who had become blind by that time). They pass verdict regarding *Mut'ah* as being lawful! Ibn Abbas heard these words and shouted, "You are an ignorant, brainless and disrespectful person. I swear by my life that *Mut'ah* was practised in the days of Imam Ali, the Commander of the Faithful".

It is clear from this narration that Ibn Abbas persistently held his views in favour of *Mut'ah* till the end of his life and even during the rule of Abdullah bin Zubayr. However, the thing which is most surprising is associating the decision regarding inadmissibility of Fixed Time Marriage with the Commander of the Faithful Imam Ali because the decision regarding the legality of this institution is considered to be one of the maxims adopted by the people of the Holy Prophet's Progeny especially so because a number of narrations have been quoted from the Commander of the Faithful contradicting the abrogation of Fixed Time Marriage. One of the well-known remarks of Imam Ali which has acquired the position of a proverb is: "If Umar had not forbidden Fixed Time Marriage none except the vicious persons would have been guilty of adultery". In his great Tafsir, Tabari has quoted him as saying: "If Umar had not forbidden people from *Mut'ah* none except the vicious people or a very small number of persons would have been involved in adultery".

Imam Ja'far Sadiq has also been quoted in reliable narrations as saying: "There are three things about which we need not dissimulate from anyone viz. *Hajjut Tamatto*, *Mut'ah* and wiping of feet" (i.e. about performance of *Hajjut Tamatto*, admissibility of Fixed Time Marriage and wiping of feet from the fingers up to the ankle by hands while performing ablution).

Apart from all this there is no room for denying that according to the admitted principles of Jurisprudence when certain traditions and narrations on a subject are opposed to each other and are on equal footing, they are not reliable and fall under the category of being ambiguous. In such circumstances they should be abandoned and efforts made to find out those which need no interpretation but having apparent meaning and clear evidence.[1]

Taking into account the contradiction of the tradi-

[1]Of course this is to be done when the narrations are definite from the point of view of authority but are at variance with one another from the point of view of applicability. However, if the authorities are doubtful, the rule is that after equilibration and adjustment in different ways *Takhyir* should be resorted to i.e. anyone of them may be acted upon.

tions it may be said about the proposition under discussion that the thing about which the Muslims are generally unanimous is that the Fixed Time Marriage was lawful and permissible in the beginning. Now the rule of *Istishāb* and the rule of the Basis of non-abrogation which are the two established rules of Jurisprudence ordain that this matter continued to retain its original position. As such there is no course open till today but to accept and decide that it (Fixed Time Marriage) is permissible!

QUESTION OF MUT'AH AND ITS SOLUTION

If we wish to do justice to this problem in the light of facts and realities and to find out the secret of all the intricacies and contradictory discussions, we will find out after necessary studies and research that the source of all these disputes is only one point, viz. that Umar, the second Caliph, according to his own thinking and in view of special considerations occasioned by the conditions prevailing at the time, declared Fixed Time Marriage to be illegal. This illegality was, however, statutory and secular and not religious or canonical. Hence this sentence has been repeatedly quoted from him: "During the time of the Holy Prophet two *Mut'ah* were permissible but I have prohibited them and will punish those who act to the contrary — they are *Mut'ah* of *Hajj (Hajjut Tamatto)* and *Mut'ah* (Fixed Time Marriage). As will be observed the second Caliph has not associated the order of illegality with the Holy Prophet. On the other hand he says: "I have prohibited them and shall punish the offenders". He does not say that Allah will punish them. Why so? The reason is that it appears very improbable that a person like the second Caliph who displayed insistence and severity in the application of Islamic punishments and penalties should declare unlawful what Allah has made lawful or introduce anything which is not a part of the commands of Islam. This is so because he knew that: **Whatever has been declared lawful by the Holy Prophet shall remain lawful till the Day of Judgement and whatever has been declared by him to be unlawful shall remain unlawful till the Day of Judgement.** He knew that

Almighty Allah says about the Holy Prophet: *Had the Prophet attributed some false statements to Us, definitely We would have seized him by the right hand, and then would surely have cut his life-vein, and none of you could have defended him.* (Surah al-Ḥāqqah, 69:44 — 47)

Under the circumstances, how can it be imagined that the Caliph intended declaring unlawful what Allah has made lawful? He definitely intended ordering a sort of statutory and secular prohibition for that period only.[1]

Unfortunately, however, some traditionalists who were his (Umar's) contemporaries and some other simple-minded traditionalists ignored this subtle point and considering it improbable that a person like Umar, whose duty was to safeguard the orders of Islam, should declare unlawful what Allah had made lawful and should transgress the limits fixed by Almighty Allah, thought of creating a justification for Umar's action. And to achieve this end they did not find any way out except to claim that the Holy Prophet had first allowed and later prohibited it (i.e. Fixed Time Marriage). However, as this claim was not in keeping with the reality, they were, while explaining the

[1]The explanation of the distinguished author regarding the action the second Caliph is a sort of magnanimous explanation coupled with a very favourable opinion and indulgence with regard to certain aspects of the matter. However, there is also another probability which may possibly appear to accord more with the incident quoted about the second Caliph. And that probability is that the way of thinking of the Caliph about the Islamic orders and penalities was not in consonance with ours. It appears that he did not consider all the commands of Islam to be eternal and at least some of the orders were subject to the conditions and exigencies of environments and could be changed. Hence he says: "In the days of the Holy Prophet the law was like this". Evidently this way of thinking is not in conformity with the rules and regulations of Islam and places revelation at par with ordinary human intellect and practically binds the Holy Prophet and his laws and commands within the limits of time and place and particular conditions. Can any Muslim scholar of the present times agree with this type of thinking?

179

case, caught in the snare of contradictions and disputes, although, in case they had explained the action of the Caliph in the way we have done they would not have been compelled to make contradictory statements or to take so many pains in the matter. The narration in **Sahih Muslim** which we have previously quoted from Jabir bin Abdullah Ansari bears testimony to this. He says: "In the days of the Holy Prophet as well as during the time of the first Caliph, we used to accomplish Fixed Time Marriage against small dowry till Umar prohibited it as a consequence of the incident of Amr bin Hurayth".

In the commentary on **Sahih Muslim** entitled **Ikmāl al-Mu'allim** written by the Sunni scholar Wishtāni Ābi he says: "Some say this prohibition was ordered at the end of Umar's Caliphate while others say that it took place during his Caliphate. He (Umar) used to say: "I will stone to death every married man brought before me on the charge of contracting Fixed Time Marriage and shall subject to lashes every unmarried man for the same offence".

Amr bin Hurayth contracted Fixed Time Marriage during the time of the Holy Prophet. This marriage continued till Umar's Caliphate. Umar heard about the matter. He called the woman concerned in his presence and enquired from her about the incident. She confirmed the position. Umar asked her: "Who is your witness?" She introduced her parents as witnesses. Umar said: "Why have you not produced any other person as witness?" Thereafter he prohibited Fixed Time Marriage.

Although the details of this incident (of Amr bin Hurayth) are not known to us we are quite aware of the mentality of the second Caliph. He was very severe and harsh in all matters. Often it so happened that in particular circumstances some incident which he did not like took place. This prompted him to ban such a thing totally lest a similar incident should be repeated. Hence as already explained, the source of all disputes which have taken place with regard to this subject was the very prohibitive order of the second Caliph. Otherwise the admissibility of Fixed Time Marriage after clarification by the Holy Qur'an and action of Holy Prophet and his companions during his time and thereafter during the Caliphate of Abu Bakr and a part of the Caliphate of Umar is too clear to need dependence on these lengthy disputes and discussions. Incidentally from the history of Islam, it transpires that Fixed Time Marriage was prevalent even among the noble men and companions of the Holy Prophet and dignitaries of Quraysh in the days of the Holy Prophet and many of their distinguished descendants were the offsprings of Fixed Time Marriage. An example of such incident is the one quoted by Rāghib Isfahani who was one of the celebrated ulema of the Sunni and a pious and reliable person. He says: "Abdullah bin Zubayr used to admonish Ibn Abbas for believing in Fixed Time Marriage as lawful. The latter told him to go to his (Abdullah's) mother and ask her as to how fragrant smells emitted betwixt his father and mother (here ceremonies of marriage are hinted upon). Abdullah enquired about the matter from his mother whereupon she swore by Allah and said that he did not come into the world except through Fixed Time Marriage".

This incident has been quoted by the famous Sunni scholar, Rāghib Isfahani. However, are you aware as to who Abdullah bin Zubayr's mother was? She was Asmā, daughter of Abu Bakr and sister of the mother of the Faithful Ayesha and her husband Zubayr was one of the disciples of the Holy Prophet. Notwithstanding all this he contracted Fixed Time Marriage with her. Now with such a clear evidence why should we be obstinate about this issue?

After mentioning this event Raghib quotes another incident and says: "Yahya bin Aktham (the famous Chief Justice) asked one of the distinguished men of Basra, 'Whom do you follow in the matters of the legality of Fixed Time Marriage?" He replied, "Umar bin Khattab". Yahya inquired, 'What do you mean? Umar was one of the greatest opponents of Fixed Time Marriage". He replied, "Yes. It has, however, been reported in reliable tradition that he mounted the pulpit and said, 'O people! There were two *Mut'ab* which were permitted by Allah and His

Prophet and I hereby declare them to be unlawful and shall punish those who contract them'. We do not accept his decision regarding the illegality of the *Mut'ah*".

A similar incident has been reported by Abdullah bin Umar. However, it should be kept in mind that the language which one of the dignitaries of Basra has attributed to Umar regarding the following statement is very harsh and repulsive: (Allah and Prophet made them admissible for you but I disallow them).

Of course, all the Muslims may not like this interpretation. The language used by the second Caliph as reported in the well-known tradition is much milder (There were two *Mut'ah* during the time of the Holy Prophet which I prohibit). There is certainly a clear difference between the two interpretations and if the object of the Caliph was the same as hinted upon by us earlier (viz. statutory and secular inadmissibility and not religious inadmissibility and the former too for a specified period) the matters would become much easier.

When I reached here while discussing this subject I came across the statement of Muhaqqiq Muhammad bin Idris Hilli (one of the Shi'ah scholars of the sixth century A.H.) which, from many angles, conformed to what I have said. I, therefore, became inclined to quote it for confirmation of the conclusions already arrived at. He says thus in his book entitled **Sarā'ir** which is one of the best books on Jurisprudence and tradition: "Fixed Time Marriage is permissible in Islamic law. All Muslims believe that it was allowed in the Holy Qur'an as well as through repeated traditions. Only some of them claim that this order has been abrogated. However, it is necessary that they should produce some proof in support of this claim. But wherefrom can they produce such a proof?"

Besides this, according to authentic evidences which we have in hand, everything which carries some gain and does not involve any harm in this world or in the next life is permissible according to the dictates of reason. In the case of Fixed Time Marriage this condition is fulfilled viz. it carries gain and does not also involve any harm in the next life. On this account also we can declare it to be lawful. If any person objects as to how we can claim that this act does not involve any harm in the next life when there is a dispute among the Muslims regarding its legality? We would say in reply: Firstly, one who claims that it is illegal, should produce proof in support of his claim and in the absence of such proof, reason would ordain its admissibility; secondly, as has already been pointed out, there is no dispute about the fact that this type of marriage was permissible during the days of the Holy Prophet. At the most it is claimed by some that this order has been abrogated although no authentic evidence is available regarding its abrogation. When its being permissible basically is an admitted fact and its abrogation is not proved, therefore, it is evident that a law cannot be ignored unless its abrogation is proved.

If it be said that tradition have been quoted from the Holy Prophet regarding its abrogation and illegality, the reply thereto is quite clear viz. even if these traditions are sound from the point of view of authority, they are in the category single report (i.e. they have been reported only once by a person) and such reports are neither a means of knowledge nor reliable for purposes of practice. It is not, therefore, appropriate to abandon final and admitted facts on this account.

Besides this, the Holy Qur'an, after mentioning the women with whom marriage is illegal, says:

Married women are forbidden to you except the slave-girls whom you own. Such is the decree of Allah. Beside these, it is lawful for you to marry other women if you pay their dowries, maintain chastity and do not commit indecency. If you marry for a Fixed Time you must pay their dowries as a fixed reward; and it shall not be a sin on you in whatever you mutually agree (to vary) after the fixed reward. Verily Allah is All-knowing, All-Wise. (Surah al-Nisa, 4:24).

The phrase *Istamta'tum* used in this verse bears one of the two meanings. Either it carries the literal meaning of gain, relish and benefit or it means Fixed Time Marriage as per religious terminology.

183

Admittedly the first meaning is not intended here for two reasons:

(i)   It is an admitted fact among the scholars of the principles of jurisprudence that if a word occurs in the Holy Qur'an which can bear two meanings, viz. literal meaning as well as meaning according to religious terminology, it should be taken to have the latter meaning. It is for this reason that literal meaning of the words *Salāt*, *Saum*, *Zakat* and *Hajj* occurring in the Holy Qur'an have not been adopted. On the other hand their meanings as per religious terminology have been relied upon.

(ii)   A large number of the companions of the Holy Prophet and Tābi'in (people who lived after the companions of the Holy Prophet) have admitted the legality of *Mut'ah*.

The Commander of the Faithful Imam Ali and Ibn Abbas and all others have quoted it, so much so that even poets have mentioned it in their poetry. One of them says: "When the discussion and session of Shaykh (about this topic) becomes lengthy we ask him whether he has any objection to the verdict of Ibn Abbas as well (who was one of the distinguished companions).

Similarly Abdullah bin Mas'ud, Mujahid, Ata, Jabir bin Abdullah Ansari, Salma bin Akwa', Abu Sa'id Khudari, Mughaira bin Sho'ba, Sa'id bin Jubayr and Ibn Jurayh have all passed verdicts in favour of Fixed Time Marriage and this thing by itself confirms the second meaning. Hence the claim of the opponents that the inadmissibility of Fixed Time Marriage is an admitted fact is a baseless assertion". (End of the statement of Ibn Idris).

The sound manner of discussion and the forceful and logical reasoning of this scholar is evident to the wise and learned men.

MORAL AND SOCIAL ASPECT

The discussion so far conducted in this matter was from the religious and historical aspects as well as from legal evidence and principles of jurisprudence. However, its moral and social aspects also deserve consideration.

There is no doubt about the fact that Islam is a

Heavenly message and a Divine melody which has blown in the world of humanity along with the zephyr of the blessings of Allah. It is the source of prosperity and has come for the welfare of mankind and not for creating misfortune. Islam is the greatest blessing of Allah and not a calamity. Islam advances in all walks of life along with the time and takes steps forward with the caravan of progress. Islam inspires blessings and meets all the needs of human beings in the material and spiritual fields. Islam brings blessings and welfare to human society and fights against evil. Islam has not at all come to make the burden of human beings heavier, or to imprison them in the narrow gorge of difficulties or to confront them with misfortunes and adversity. No, not at all!

Islam is the source of blessings and prosperity for the people of the world. It levels the paths of comfort, tranquillity and good fortune for man and places the sources of affluence under his control.

It is for these reasons that Islam is the most accomplished of all the religions, the best of the faiths and the last Divine law. It has ignored nothing which could be efficacious for the prosperity of mankind. It has not a single weak point with regard to any aspect of life so that another religion should rectify it.

Now as regards another aspect of the matter. Has not the question of travelling and remoteness from one's home land been one of the necessities of man's life ever since he has recognized himself viz. the same travelling which is undertaken at times for purposes of trade, at other times for acquisition of knowledge and still at other times for purposes of defence, administration, touring, recreation etc.? Can the need for such journeys be denied?[1] And on the other hand, has not Almighty Allah endowed human beings with the instinct of lust and interest in the opposite

[1]The respected author has relied to a larger extent on the question of travelling in the matter of the philosophy of Fixed Time Marriage although the necessity of this issue has no particular relationship with travelling in the modern times.

sex to ensure the preservation of mankind? And if this instinct had weakened or ceased to exist could any trace of mankind be found today on the face of the earth? Replies to these questions are quite clear.

It also goes without saying that usually those who travel to different places cannot afford to make the members of their families (viz. wives and children) accompany them or to contract permanent marriages at those places because permanent marriage carries pre-requisites which do not conform to the situation and means of a traveller. Nevertheless it is necessary that this instinct should be satisfied, especially during long journeys which are undertaken for education or trade or for administrative or defence purposes. In such circumstances, permanent marriage is not possible for most of the people and there is also no practical way out of this difficulty. With this state of affairs is any solution of this problem available than Fixed Time Marriage, especially when the majority of the people who perform journeys for various purposes (especially long journeys) is of those who are in the prime of their youth and subject to the urges of refractory sexual instinct? It is young people who perform such journeys and it is also the same people who are engulfed in the struggle of this instinct. If Fixed Time Marriage is disallowed what is the proper course for such people to pursue? Evidently they have only two ways open to them.

The first path is that they should remain contented and make efforts to control the sexual instinct and fall a prey to a number of ailments which are the necessary consequences of this instinct in human beings. It may be asked whether the spirit of Islam which is a practical and simple religion, comforms to such unusual rigour, notwithstanding the fact that the Holy Qur'an says: *Allah does not impose any hardship on you. He desires comfort for you.* (Surah al-Baqarah, 2:185) and further declares: *Allah has chosen you, and has imposed no hardship on you in religion.* (Surah al-Hajj, 22:78)

The second path which such people can follow in the event of abandonment of contentment and self-control is falling into the quagmire of unchastity, the same shameful act, the evils and adversities of which have filled the world today.

I swear by Allah and by the sublimity of truth that if the Muslims of the world had acted according to the excellent laws and regulations of the eternal religion of Islam, the Divine blessings would have descended upon them and they would have regained their past glory, self-respect and honour.

One of those excellent laws is the law relating to Fixed Time Marriage. If the Muslims had enforced this law in an appropriate manner (with proper regard for enforcement of marriage, observance of *Iddah*, protection of the pedigree of the children and their maintenance), the gates of corrupt clubs and centres of prostitution would have been closed or at least, immorality, corruption and sin would have been reduced considerably. Many women who have fallen into the lap of infamy and mischief would have acquired salvation. The human race would have been healthy and there would have been legitimate children. People would have been relieved of the innocent children who are abandoned every now and then on roads. The condition of public morals would have improved. In short the proper enforcement of this law would have brought in its wake a large number of benefits to human society.

The scholar of Bani Hashim and the saint of Muslim Community, Abdullah bin Abbas, has said something very sublime in a brief and eternal sentence which has been quoted by Ibn Athir in his book **Nihaya** and by Zamakhshari in **Fā'iq** and by others in their own books. He says: "Mut'ah is nothing but a blessing of Allah on the followers of Muhammad. If the second Caliph had not prohibited it, none except a few would have indulged in adultery". In fact, Ibn Abbas obtained this remark from his teacher and instructor, the Commander of the Faithful Imam Ali and truly speaking this Islamic law is a great grace and blessing for the Muslims. Unfortunately Muslims have destroyed this blessing with their own hands and have consequently been deprived of its precious fruits and fallen into the abyss of corruption, unchastity and disgrace in this world. Allah says: *Will you exchange the better for the worse?* (Surah al-Baqarah, 2:61)

KHĀDIMUL ULEMA AND MUT'AH

However is not the discourse reproduced by the writer of the Magazine A'tidāl printed in the 161st issue of its First Volume surprising which bears the heading: "There is no alternative but to hold a syringe in the hand instead of a pen and inject facts in the brains?"

To explain the matter it may be stated that, in the first instance, he has reproduced the objection which the narrator had raised against Fixed Time Marriage. Then he has inserted, in the begining of this issue, the letter received under the signatures of Ibn Mā'is Samā[1] in defence of the issue of Fixed Time Marriage and in reply to the said object. Then he makes the following addition:

A letter was received from Baghdad under the signature of Khādimul Ulema. He repeated the objections raised by some people against Fixed Time Marriage (fault in the pedigree of the offspring and marriage with every passerby and stranger). Thereafter, this unknown writer has added that Ibn Ma'is Samā had not touched the ambiguous point under consideration till he says:

"What do you say about the periodical Fixed Time Marriage? Supposing that three, four or ten men pronounce the formula (i.e. complete the ceremonies) of marriage with a woman and every hour one of them shares her bed and consequently a child is born how will his pedigree be decided? Whose child will it be and which of those men will be recognized to be its father?"

Yes! The Shi'ah consider all types of Fixed Time Marriage (even periodical *Mut'ah*) to be permissible and lawful. Notwithstanding this, the issue of *Mut'ah* is so repulsive that even the virtuous Shi'ah themselves abstain

---

[1]Ibn Ma'is Samā (son of the water of the sky) and Khadimul Ulema are assumed names which have been used for the real ones. The real names of these writers are not known.

from it. We have never heard anyone saying: I attended the Fixed Time Marriage party of such and such gentleman and such and such lady in the manner in which people say, I attended the marriage party of Mr. so and so and Miss so and so. As such Fixed Time Marriage is prevalent only among the mean and low people. Does it not mean that Fixed Time Marriage is only a means of indulgence in one's desires, although it is likely that a child may also be born?

Has the time not arrived that Allamah Kashiful Ghita who has stood up to edify the principles of Shi'ite Islam should refine the morals of the followers of this religion and bid them to purity? We pray to Allah for his success in this mission!" — Khādimul Ulema.

The Editor of the Magazine has thus written in reply to the said letter: The said letter has been received by the office of the Magazine A'tidal from an unknown writer and the gist of the subject of his letter is that in the third issue of the Magazine he has read a letter written by Ibn Ma'il Sama which does not conform to the real objection. Thereafter the said writer has repeated the very objection raised by the narrator against Fixed Time Marriage to the effect that such a marriage would become the cause of the disturbance of the family order and doubtful pedigree and ruination of children who are the offspring of such a marriage.

The objections have been raised notwithstanding the fact that Ibn Mā'is Samā has replied to them in a very clear and excellent manner and pointed out that the method of fore-stalling confusion in the matter of pedigree and disturbance of family order is *Iddah*. *Iddah* is compulsory and obligatory in the case of Fixed Time Marriage in the same manner as it is necessary in the case of Permanent Marriage (in the event of divorce). No one has a right to contract Fixed Time Marriage with a woman with whom Fixed Time Marriage had been contracted previously by another man unless and until the period of her *Iddah* has expired and if a man acts otherwise he will be treated as guilty of adultery. In that event neither the seeds get mixed up nor any disturbance occurs in the order of the family or in the pedigree.

189

Thereafter, this unknown writer (Khadimul Ulema) writes: "Why has Ibn Ma'is Samā not touched the ambiguous point which deserves attention and that is: 'If a traveller or an unknown person contracts Fixed Time Marriage with a woman and after sometimes a child is born where should the father of this child be located?'"

It seems that this Khadim has not studied the entire discourse of Ibn Ma'is Samā and even if he has studied it, he has not understood its import. Or else it is possible to give a clearer reply than that give by him. He says: "It is necessary for man that he should fully recognize the woman with whom he is contracting Fixed Time Marriage so that, if a child is born, it shoud be associated with him and the pedigree should remain safe. Similarly woman should observe *Iddah* after the expiry of the period of Fixed Time Marriage, so that her condition regarding her being pregnant or otherwise should become clear. Furthermore, she should fully recognize her husband so that, if she gives birth to his child, she may return it to him after the expiry of the period of lactation".

Under the circumstances is any ambiguous point left which has not been clarified in his discourse? In case the unknown writer does not realize this clear reality, there is no alternative but to hold a syringe in the hand instead of a pen and inject facts in the brains!

Now as regards the periodic Fixed Time Marriage mentioned by you and about which you believe that three, four or ten Shi'ah contract Fixed Time Marriage with a woman alternately and every hour one of them sleeps with her and you have been disturbed about the children whom the woman concerned may give birth and want to know as to which man should be treated to be its father, it may be stated that: Firstly, it is necessary for you to mention at least one book written by ignorant and unknowledgeable Shi'ah, not to talk of ulema and scholars, wherein such a shameful and disgraceful affair should have been declared permissible. However, if you do not inform us of any such book, it would be appropriate that you should be punished for falsehood and calumny according to the religious law!

190

Are you not aware that all the Shi'ah Imamiya, without exception, consider observance of *Iddah* in Fixed Time Marriage to be absolutely necessary and its minimum limit is 45 days? Is not in these circumstances the myth of Fixed Time Marriage by alternate men in consecutive hours ridiculous?

If you mean to say that possibly some common, ignorant and unruly persons who do not care much about sins indulge in such activities, it may be said in reply that, besides the fact that such affairs are not particular to the Shi'ah and are perhaps more prevalent among others, they cannot also be given permission for such deeds. Admissibility and permission are connected with the verdicts of the ulema of religion and not with the deeds of impious and sinful persons. If in fact such a practice does exist and is not only a fable, it is not at all different from adultery from the view-point of Shi'ah ulema and the persons guilty of it should be punished accordingly. The child born of such an intercourse is also illegitimate and is not associated with anyone of them. It is as the Holy Prophet has said: "The child belongs to the bed (husband and wife) and the one guilty of adultery gets nothing except stones".

As regards abstention of noble, pious and virtuous persons among the Shi'ah from contracting Fixed Time Marriage it is to be noted that it is not on account of obscenity or indecency of the issue. On the contrary this attitude is a sort of high mindedness, heedlessness, self-restraint and contentment with permanent wives on their part and especially so because Islam permits polygamy. If occasionally they wished to contract Fixed Time Marriage and there are reasons for doing so, they do contract such a marriage and there can be no objection to it. Chiefs of clans and wealthy Shaykhs of tribes are occasionally seen who have contracted Fixed Time Marrriage (and even if this action of theirs is objected to for other reasons it is not criticized on account of their marriages being Fixed Time Marriage or Permanent).

In any case abstention of noble persons from Fixed Time Marriage cannot be a proof of its being abominable what to say of its being unlawful or inadmissible.[1]

We learn from the history of Islam that a number of companions of the Holy Prophet and after them the Muslims had slave-girls who gave birth to their children and those children grew up to be very distinguished personalities. However, in the present times, self-possessed and dignified people desist from such action and consider it improper for themselves. Similarly in the present times pious and noble persons refrain from divorcing their wives, so much so that we have not heard about anyone of them having divorced his wife. Is this fact a proof of divorce being unlawful from the view-point of Islam?[2]

Thereafter, the said Magazine adds, "Now as regards the unknown writer saying that Allama Kashiful Ghita who has stood up to edify the principles of Shi'ite Islam should refine the morals of the followers of this religion and bid them to purity". Of course, this is something true and there can be no dispute about a true thing. This magnanimous person continuously makes efforts for refinement and guidance, not only of the Shi'ah but also of all the Muslims of the world because all enjoy equal status in his eyes. However, this is not the duty of only the said gentleman but of all the ulema of Islam, and probably also the duty of the ulema and scholars of those countries and cities where corruption is greater and obscenity is

[1]We think that abstention of virtuous and respectable men from contracting Fixed Time Marriage is due to another important reason as well. That reason is that on account of its misuse by some of our ignorant people and adverse propaganda by the opponents, Fixed Time Marriage has acquired a meaning opposed to its reality and if we can effectively forestall these two things, the conditions will become totally different. As matters stand at present Fixed Time Marriage is considered to be a sort of prostitution although in fact it is a kind of pure marriage and an effective means for a campaign against corruption and fornication. A matter of great regret indeed!

[2]This last portion which relates to reasons for abstention of respectable and pious persons from Fixed Time Marriage has not been published in the magazne A'tidal.

resorted to publicly to a larger extent. As the situation becomes serious the responsibility of the ulema and scholars also increases.

We do not wish to deviate from the usual policy of this magazine. Otherwise we would have quoted some moral corruptions of others so that it could become clear that not to speak of the noble classes of the Shi'ah, even their common people are more chaste, pious and innocent than others. However, following the instructions of the distinguished teacher Allama Kashiful Ghita we refrain from everything which leads to dispute between the parties and kindles the fire of religious differences. Under his directions we direct our efforts towards the unity of purpose and filling the gaps which exist between different Muslim communities. This great reformer always teaches us that Islam is the religion of alliance and unity and not of difference and dispersion. He says, "Interests of the Muslims of the world demand that all mutual differences should be uprooted". He always advises: "O Muslims! Purify your hearts from all sorts of misgivings and bad intentions. Keep your tongues free from vilification and slander and your pens from writing ironically of one another so that you may become happy and prosperous. Make efforts like your ancestors to tell the truth and to act sincerely".

Khadimul Ulema! These are the ingredients of purity not the calumnies that you are ascribing to the Shi'ah when we were thinking that contentions and disputes on this subject had come to an end and their traces had disappeared totally after the convincing reply by Ibn Mā'is Samā. What is surprising is this as to how a person who calls himself the servant of the ulema wishes to renew these controversies and to scatter the dust of dispute in all directions and to draw a veil on the face of reality — the same reality which tears the veils and casts aside curtains and manifests itself.

CONCLUSION

From the discussions which have so far been conducted we come to the following conclusions:

Marriage consists of a sort of interest and special relationship between man and woman which envisages different rights. Marriage needs a special contract which takes place by acceptance under specified conditions.

If marriage has no limitations of time, it is called Permanent Marriage which continues for ever unless it is terminated by things like divorce etc. However, if the period of marriage is limited (for a day, a month, a year or more) it is a Fixed Time Marriage. There is no difference between them from the point of view of concept of marriage The only difference between them is the difference in the length of their duration.

Most of the orders relating to these two types of marriage as well as their effects are identical and they differ on very few points. The difference is not, however, in principle or essence. On the other hand, it is a difference like that between two classes of one species (e.g. difference between black and white races) coupled with the preservation of the unity of essence. The difference in quality is not, however, particular to marriage and partnership of two human beings in life. On the other hand examples of such a difference can be observed in different types of transaction and ownership which take place from purchases and sales. For example it sometimes happens that a person concludes an absolute transaction without any condition. The result of such a transaction is eternal ownership which cannot be determined except by a few voluntary means like a new purchase and sale, gift, etc. or involuntary means like wear and tear, death etc.

However, at times the ownership is for a limited period from the very outset in the sense that the condition of annulment is laid down in the contract itself. It is evident that the duration of such ownership would be brief and limited to the period agreed upon by the parties (till the time of automatic annulment). In any case these are matters on which reason and religion are unanimous.

Hence, O' scholars and ulema of Islam and O' writers! what for is all this hullabaloo about Fixed Time Marriage which is a kind of ordinary marriage? Does this matter justify rebuke so that you should be attacking and rebuking the Shi'ah continuously on this account? Is this concise and brief discussion not sufficient to keep you from kindling the fire of enmity between the Muslims and to oblige you to submit before truth? I swear by the greatness of truth and sublimity of reality that whatever I have said has been for the sake of truth and not on account of any bias. And even if I have offered criticism it was solely against falsehood. We depend on Allah and all of us have to return to Him.

We content ourselves with what has already been said about marriage from the Shi'ah point of view. However, there still remains a large number of discussions about orders regarding the ceremonies of marriage as well as orders regarding children, subsistence, kinds of *Iddah* etc. which are beyond the capacity of this small book and should be perused in the valuable books on Jurisprudence written by Shi'ah scholars. Fortunately various books have been written and notwithstanding their brevity they deal with all branches of Jurisprudence from *Taha'rat* (purification) up to *Hudud* (penalties) and *Diyāt* (compensations) so that they explain all these matters in about a hundred pages of usual size. On the other hand there are some detailed books also as many as twenty volumes (each volume being approximately of the size of **Sahih Bukhari** and **Sahih Muslim**) for example *Jawāhir* and *Hadā'iq*.[1]

[1] Jurisprudence is the very branch of Islamic learning which the Shi'ah, has completed its evolutionary course. Truly speaking the vastness, authenticity and precision of the Shi'ah Jurisprudence is unparalleled and unless a person makes deep study of it he will not believe this fact. Various difficult and complicated matters and even secondary judicial matters of rare type have been studied and discussed threadbare in detailed Shi'ah books on Jurisprudence, so much so that many books have been written on problems which have cropped up in our own time like insurance, goodwill, different kinds of partnerships, copyright etc. For this achievement the Shi'ah are highly indebted to the Imams of the Holy Prophet's progeny who have opened the door of *Ijtihad* upon them and guided them in different ways. (See: Murtaza Mutahhery, Woman and her Rights ISP, 1982).

Divorce

It has become clear that the spirit of marriage is a type of mutual contract and a special liaison and relationship which is established between man and woman and this very fact becomes the cause of the application of the title of a "couple" to them. This interpretation is for the sake of relationship and connection between them which brings them together like two eyes, two ears and two hands, although before their marriage they were treated to be two separate beings absolutely apart from each other. This mutual contract creates such a strong and deep relationship between them that a tie more sublime than this cannot be imagined. Certainly a wording more expressive and more appropriate than that of this verse cannot be found for explaining this profound relationship: *Women are your garments and you are their garments.* (Surah al-Baqarah, 2:187)[1]

It has also become clear that if at the time of entering into the contract no stipulation is made regarding its duration the result and tenor thereof will be permanent marriage whose effects will remain till death and even thereafter, except when causes for its annulment become

[1]Perhaps the reason for giving a simile of garments of each other to men and women is this that the garment conceals one's private parts, is a means of decoration and protection against vagaries of nature and, being attached to the body, is fully aware of its secrets. The relationship between the two spouses should, therefore, be like this.

196

apparent. On the other hand it often happens that needs, conditions and special circumstances necessitate that in some cases relationship of marriage may be terminated. It is also possible that termination of such a relationship may be in mutual interests or at least it may be in the interest of one party and which may not make any difference to the other. Hence ways and means for achieving this purpose have been provided in Islamic law so that the relationship may thereby be terminated. Now if the permanent marriage is repulsive to the man only he has the right to divorce his wife, and if it is repulsive in the woman's eyes she can make use of the right of *Khula'*. However, if both the parties are unhappy their object is gained through *Mubarāt*. In each of the three cases there exist some orders, conditions and special pre-requisities in the absence of which separation cannot be accomplished.

In view of the fact that Islam is a gregarious religion and is based on unity and concord and its greatest object is the establishment of love in the hearts of the people and it considers difference and discord to be the most abominable thing, it, therefore, represses divorce as far as possible. In many traditions divorce has been inhibited and declared to be abominable. One such tradition is, "No permissible act is more detestable in the eyes of Allah than divorce".

Thus on the one hand, divorce has been permitted for making matters easy for the people and for preventing corruption which sometimes takes place as a consequence of permanency of marriage. On the other hand, the divine wisdom and blessing necessitates that they should desist from divorce as far as possible and analyse the possible consequences of their actions politely. This is because they are usually unaware of the results of their actions and like things which are not beneficial for them and dislike those which are in their interest. Often it so happens that they take immediate and hasty decisions under the influence of different factors without taking recourse to proper study and thinking. For the aforesaid reasons, Islam has imposed many conditions on divorce which in practice become the cause of reduction in the number of divorces, for it has been said: "Everything to which stipulations are attached becomes rarer".

From the Shi'ah point of view one of the most important conditions is the presence of two righteous men as witnesses at the time of pronouncing divorce as laid down by the Holy Qur'an: *Let two men of integrity from among you be the witnesses.* (Surah al-Talaq, 65:2).[1]

Hence if a divorce takes place without the presence of two such persons it is void from our view-point and this condition in itself is the best means of achieving reconciliation between the two spouses and removing the causes of differences and discord. This is so because it is evident that such righteous and pious persons, besides possessing an effective say in the matter, would consider it their duty to bring the parties to reconciliation and advise the man and woman not to disrupt the peace of their family life. Even if their advice does not cut much ice it is possible that it may have at least some influence and may diminish the spiritual crisis which takes birth in man and woman on account of various factors.

Unfortunately, the Sunni brethren have deprived themselves of this great benefit because their scholars and ulema do not consider the presence of two righteous witnesses to be a necessary condition of divorce. It is for this reason that the number of divorces among them is exessive and in the present times this great social calamity is spreading in their society in a very alarming proportion. Incidentally, many among us and in them are negligent of the philosophy underlying the sublime orders of Islam and their real purpose although if we had paid heed and acted according to them, we would have acquired blessings in all

[1] It is not yet clear to us why the Sunni scholars have ignored this verse which gives a clear direction that two righteous witnesses should be present at the time of divorce and why they do not consider the fulfilment of this condition to be necessary and treat it to be of the nature of a recommendation only or as related to *Ruju'* (resumption of conjugal relations) although the difficulties involved in adopting both the views are well-known.

fields and would not have indulged ourselves in life of sadness and hardship mixed with all sorts of adversities. If we had done so the foundation of our family life would not have trembled as it does at present and the normalcy of married life would not have become subjected to such incompatibility and disturbance.

Another most important condition of divorce is that the husband should not have resorted to this action on account of compulsion or coercion or in a state of anger or annoyance when he may have lost his intellectual equilibrium. In the same manner the woman should have got through her monthly course and the man should not have had sexual intercourse with her thereafter. As is evident, these preconditions also play a part in the reduction of the number of divorces.

REGARDING THE THREE DIVORCES

The Shi'ah scholars believe that three divorces (three divorces pronounced at a time in one sitting) are tantamount to one divorce only and do not make the woman unlawful for man. On the other hand he can re-establish conjugal relations with her and does not also need *Muhallil* (the woman when divorced has to marry another person and after getting divorce from him can marry her former husband). However, if three divorces take place in three sittings in this manner that the man pronounces divorce and thereafter resumes conjugal relations and pronounces divorce again and thereafter resumes conjugal relations once again and for the third time they will become unlawful for each other and will not be entitled to a renewal of marriage except that the woman may marry another man and then obtain divorce from him. Only in that event will it be possible for her to remarry the first husband.

In case this action is repeated i.e. the man divorces the woman for the fourth time and so on till he divorces her for the ninth time they become permanently unlawful for each other and do not retain any right of re-marriage.

However, many Sunni ulema differ with us in this matter. They consider three divorces (in one sitting) to be lawful. Hence if a man tells his wife: "You stand divorced thrice" the woman, according to their belief, becomes unlawful for him and they cannot remarry without going through the formality of *Muhallil*. They hold this view, although according to the authentic narrations (whose authenticity they themselves admit) three divorces in one sitting are treated to be tantamount to one divorce only.[1]

Bukhari narrates from Ibn Abbas: "During the period of the Holy Prophet and Caliph Abu Bakr and even during the first two years of the Caliphate of Umar three divorces at one sitting were counted as one but Caliph Umar said: "Men on matters where they have a right to dilate make haste to do it so what this delay would really mean to them. Thus he (Umar) gave permission that three divorces can be pronounced in one sitting".

This was done notwithstanding the fact that if we study carefully the verses of the Holy Qur'an relating to divorce it becomes clear that it is not possible to give effect to three divorces pronounced in one sitting. Allah says in the Holy Qur'an: *A divorce is only permissible twice: after that, the parties should either hold together on equitable terms, or separate with kindness. So if a husband divorces his wife irrevocably (for the third time), he cannot, remarry her until she has married another husband and he has divorced her.* (Surah al-Baqarah, 2:229 – 230)[2]

---

[1]It was perhaps for this reason that the respected scholar Shaykh Mahmud Shaltut, the former Grand Mufti of Sunni, recently gave reference to the Shi'ah view regarding invalidity of three divorces in one sitting and passed verdicts accordingly.

[2]To explain the matter further it may be stated that the first verse clearly tells that the divorce which make the resumption of conjugal rights possible are two divorce *(at-talāq marratān)*. After each of these divorces it is up to each spouse whether to resume the conjugal relations or not. And the second verse tells that in the case of the third divorce resumption of conjugal relations is not permissible. Hence when the two verses are read in conjunction with each other the propriety of pronouncement of three divorces in three sittings can very well be realized.

This was the gist of the device of separation of man and woman from each other. Further discussions may be pursued in detailed books.

However, besides the different types of divorces referred to above there are also other factors which may bring about separation between man and woman. To this category belong the defects which may possibly appear in them and entitle the other party to demand annulment of marriage. For example if the following defects are found in the man the wife has a right to terminate the marriage: Complete sexual impotence, insanity, leprosy etc.[1] In case the woman possesses the following defects, the man has a right to bring the marriage contract to an end: The vagina of the woman being extremely narrow or bone being congealed in the vulva so that sexual intercourse is not possible, etc.[2]

Furthermore, *Zibār*[3] and *Ila'*[4] can also be the causes of separation of man and woman which have been explained fully in books on Jurisprudence. Similarly detailed discussions are contained in the said books regarding *Iddah* which a woman must observe after separation from her husband as well as about the kinds thereof viz. *Iddah* for divorce, *Iddah* for death, *Iddah* for *Wati bish Shubha* etc. It may, however, be stated briefly that according to the

[1]There are five defects in man which make dissolution of marriage permissible viz. insanity, leprosy, impotence, being an eunuch and the male organ being cut off.

[2]There are nine things which are considered to be defects in a woman making dissolution of marriage permissible. Their details are containedd in books on Jurisprudence.

[3]Zihār is tantamount to a man saying to his wife, "Your back seems to me like the back of my mother". During the Age of Ignorance (before the advent of Islam) Arabs used to say these words to their wives and considered it to be a permanent and irrevocable divorce. Islam declared this custom to be void and prescribed expiation in its stead.

[4]*Ila'* is tantamount to a person swearing that he will never have conjugal relations with his wife. This too carries expiation and some special orders apply to it.

Shi'ah a woman has to observe *Iddah* after the death of her husband in all circumstances, even if she is too old for conception or too young (less than nine years of age) or the husband had not had sexual intercourse with her. Nevertheless, the *Iddah* which is to be observed after divorce is compulsory except in the aforesaid three cases. *Iddah* is also compulsory for *Wati bish Shubha* except in the case of a too old or too young woman as mentioned above. However, there is no *Iddah* in the case of adultery, because an unlawful deed is not entitled to any respect.

Iddah for death in the case of a woman who is not pregnant is four months and ten days. However, if she is pregnant the following orders will apply to her:

If she gives birth to a child earlier than the expiry of the said period of four months and ten days her *Iddah* will be limited to that period only. If, however, delivery does not take place within that period her *Iddah* will come to an end only after the birth of the child.

Iddah for divorce in the case of women who do not have monthly course (although according to their age they should have it) is three complete months. As regards those who have the monthly course, it is necessary that they should have it thrice and then be purified of it.

Iddah for divorce for a pregnant woman is up to the date of delivery (whether it takes more time or less).

The Shi'ah believe that if the divorce is neither the third one nor a *Khula'* divorce, the husband has a right to resume conjugal relations throughout the period of *Iddah* and if he does so the divorce becomes ineffective and they revert to the former position of conjugal relations. If, however, he does not resume such relations till the expiry of the period of *Iddah* he has no further right left to do so. In case, they are inclined to renew their marital relations at this stage a new marriage will have to be performed with the agreement of the parties on other conditions.

The Shi'ah do not consider necessary the presence of two righteous persons as witnesses for resumption of conjugal relations as it is in the case of divorce, although their presence is recommended.[1]

Similarly use of no special words is necessary in this case. On the other hand every word, action or even hint which indicates the inclination of the husband to continue the marriage is considered to be sufficient and occasions their reversion to the former position.

TWO INTERESTING LETTERS

The respected author has reproduced in the footnote the text of two letters exchanged between him and an Egyptian scholar relating to the discussion regarding the presence of two witnesses for the purpose of resumption of conjugal relations not being essential. However, on account of these letters being very lengthy, we have placed them in the text of the book under the discussion regarding divorce. He says: During this year the erudite scholar Professor Ahmad Muhammad Shākir (Religious Magistrate of Egypt) sent me his fine book entitled **Nizamut Talaq fil Islam**. This book fascinated me much. I found it to be one of the epoch-making books and on receipt thereof I wrote a letter to the respected author, who published it in the 157th issue of the valuable Magazine *Risala* with the following introduction:

"One of the best and most excellent communications which I have received was the valuable letter written by my respectable friend and magnanimous teacher, the Chief of the Shi'ah Mujtahids in Najaf Ashraf, Allama Shaykh Muhammad Husayn Kāshiful Ghita. He has discussed and commented upon one of my views expressed in the discourses contained in the book on the subject of the condition of evidence for the correctness of the resumption of conjugal relations by a husband with his divorced wife.

I believe that the presence of two righteous witnesses is necessary at the time of the pronouncement of divorce and if it takes place without the presence of two such

---

[1]Presence of two righteous witnesses being not necessary in th case of reunion, is a sort of facility for cementing the conjugal relations as will be explained soon in the words of late Kāshiful Ghita.

witnesses it is void. Although this statement is opposed to the four well-known schools of thought of Sunni, still it is supported by the religious arguments available with us and also conforms to the religion of the members of the Holy Prophet's Progeny and the Shi'ah.

Furthermore, I believe that in the matter of reconciliation of a husband with his divorced wife also two righteous witnesses are necessary. This belief accords with one of the two decrees of Imam Shafi'i but is at variance with the school of Ahlul Bayt, the progeny of Holy Prophet and the Shi'ah.

I pondered over the Shi'ah belief in this regard and could not appreciate how they had differentiated between divorce and reconciliation when the same reasoning is applicable in both the cases. The Allama (Kāshiful Ghita) has, therefore, condescended to explain the difference between the two cases from the Shi'ah point of view and has written about it in his letter.

The letter is reproduced below:

From: Najaf Ashraf
8th Safar 1355 A.H.

In the name of Allah, the most Kind, the most Merciful, to whom belongs all praise and honour.

The Magnanimous Allama
Shaykh Ahmad Muhammad Shākir,

Peace be on you! I have received your valuable gift viz. the book **Nizamut Talāq fil Islam** and have studied it twice with great admiration. The deep insight and intellectual freedom employed and the correct views expressed therein deserve full attention. In this book you have extracted the very spirit of the meaning of tradition, torn the veil of superstitions from the sacred face of religion, disconnected the claim of following the old trend of thought and broken the idols of stagnation with logical arguments. Praise be to you and to your enlightened intellect and extensive knowledge!

The basic questions which you have discussed in this

treatise are three: (i) Three divorces (pronounced at one time in one sitting) (ii) Oath for divorce and freeing (of slave or slave-girl), and (iii) Evidence regarding divorce.[1]

In each of these cases you have done justice to the matter under consideration and opened the door of *Ijtihad* according to the principles of this branch of knowledge and of deduction of authentic evidence from the Holy Book and Sunnah. This firm basis and correct method has led you to the facts of the propositions, the spirit of Divine commands, and the sacred laws of Islam. Your firm opinions in these matters conform with the unanimous decrees of Shi'ah ulema and scholars and have been treated to be a part of the essential and indisputable articles of their faith from the early days of Islam to the present day. There is, however, one exception viz. that the Shi'ah ulema are unanimous in the case of reconciliation (resumption of conjugal relations) the presence of two righteous witnesses is not necessary, notwithstanding the fact that they consider such witnesses to be essential for purpose of divorce, failing which it is treated by them to be void. However, you have preferred the view of those who consider the presence of two witnesses to be essential in both the cases and have said, "The Shi'ah consider presence of witnesses to be necessary in the event of divorce and believe it to be one of the main elements of divorce as stated in the book **Shara'iul Islam**. However, they do not consider it (presence of two witnesses) to be necessary in the matter of reconciliation. Differentiation between these two is strange and is not supported by proof". I have an objection to this

---

[1]The meaning of Three Divorces and evidence regarding divorce (presence of two righteous witnesses) is quite clear. As regards oath for divorce and freedom, it means that a person may swear that if he does a particular thing his wife would stand divorced and his slaves would become free. Many Sunni consider this type of oath to be effective and sufficient, in the event of differences, for the separation of wife and freedom of slaves and in such a case the ceremonies regarding pronouncement of divorce are not necessary. However, according to the Shi'ah such an oath is ineffective.

statement and would seek your permission to mention it. It is strange that you have sought proof from a person who is the denier as this does not conform to the principles and rules which we have in hand. For a denier it should suffice that his statement conforms to the basis (basis of non-existence). It is for the claimant to furnish proof.

It is possible that you may say that apparently the Qur'anic verse: *When their waiting period (Iddah) is about to end, either keep them or separate from them lawfully. Let two just persons witness the divorce and let them witness for the sake of Allah.* (Surah al-Talaq, 65:2), testifies to your statement, as you have said: "On the face of it the context of the two verses is such that the phrase "two witnesses" applies to divorce as well as to reconciliation and on this account the presence of two witnesses is necessary in both the cases". However, it appears that you have not pondered deeply over these verses. If you had thought over this matter as you have done in others, the reality of the proposition would not have remained unknown to a person like yourself. The reason for my saying this is that this sacred verse is concerned with orders relating to divorce and it is because of this that the relevant surah has been named Surah al-Talaq. In this surah the subject matter commences with the verse: *O Prophet! (Say to the believers) that when you do divorce women, divorce them at their prescribed periods, and count (accurately) their prescribed periods and fear Allah your Lord, and turn them not out of their houses, nor shall they (themselves) leave, except in case they are guilty of some indecency. These are limits set by Allah and anyone who transgresses the limits of Allah does injustice to his (own) soul. You never know, perhaps Allah will bring about some new situation.* (Surah al-Talaq: 65:1) and then regarding necessity of enforcement of divorce in the beginning of *Iddah* is introduced i.e. divorce should take place neither during the monthly course of the woman nor at the time of ceremonial purity of the woman during which sexual intercourse has taken place (on the other hand it should take place after ceremonial purity and before sexual intercourse is resorted to). Thereafter, the necessity of observance of the prescribed period of *Iddah* by the women and about their not being turned out of the house during the period is mentioned. Then a reference has been made to the proposition of resumption of conjugal relations. However, this reference is certainly not a part of the real purport of the verses but only incidental to the discussion of divorce. The statement is dragged into the question of reconciliation where it is said: *When their waiting period (Iddah), is about to end, either keep them or separate from them lawfully (by means of resumption of conjugal relations) or part with them on equitable terms (wait till the period of mensturation comes to an end).*

Thereafter discussion about divorce is pursued and it is said, *"Take two just (ʿĀdil) men as witnesses"* i.e. in the matter of divorce which is the real subject under discussion and not in the matter of reconciliation because application of this condition to reconciliation which has been mentioned only incidentally, would appear to be disagreeable and inappropriate from the point of view of context. For example, if a person tells the other: "When a learned man comes to see you, receive him with due respect, whether he comes alone or accompanied by a servant or a companion, and take care to accompany and escort him properly at the time of departure". In that event it is probable that the question of escort should have reference to the servant and companion of the learned man, besides himself, notwithstanding the fact that 'and take care to accompany and escort' has occurred immediately after the mention of the servant and companion. In any case I feel that this matter is quite clear from the point of view of Arabic grammar and literary taste and is not a thing which should remain concealed from a scholar of Arabic literature like yourself except on account of lack of care. However, it is not very surprising because at times a learned man and research scholar also falls a prey to lack of care.[1]

---

[1]Another point which confirms the Shiʿah view-point in this behalf

Continued...

207

So much was with regard to the wordings of the verse, proof and the context of the sacred verse. However, there is another more subtle and interesting point also regarding the philosophy which Islam observes in various matters. There is no doubt about the fact that divorce is one of the 'most abominable of the things which are permissible and Islam, as we know, is a perfect social law and is not at all inclined to permit any kind of differences and discord in Islamic society, especially in a family and still more particularly in the matter of marriage. It is on this account that the law-giver of Islam makes persistent efforts that divorces and separations should be reduced as much as possible To achieve this object he has made the requisites and conditions of divorce very difficult so that divorces may become very few in accordance with the well-known maxim that the larger the number of conditions attached to a thing the more scarce will it become.

Besides other conditions the presence of two just witnesses has been considered necessary so that firstly this very fact (procurement of two righteous witnesses) may cause delay in the matter of divorce and secondly it may become possible that on account of the presence of two righteous witnesses and as a consequence of their advice the man and wife, or anyone of them may regret his/her decision to separate and the relationship of union and the tie of friendship and love may once again be cemented between them, as has been said in the Holy Qur'an: *You never know perhaps Allah will bring about some new situation.* (Surah al-Talaq, 65:1)

This is one of the benefits of the necessity of two

is this: Suppose we concentrate on the first part of the verse and ignore the analogies put forward by the learned author even then it will be necessary to consider the condition of two righteous witnesses as applicable to divorce only because this verse occurs immediately after the phrase "part them" and according to rules this condition refers to the recent phrase except when there is proof against it. For this reason the condition of two witnesses is confined to separation which is the same thing as divorce just witnesses in the matter of divorce which Islam had definitely in view while giving this order. It is, however, clear that the position is quite different in the matter of reconciliation, because Islam desires that the conjugal relations should become strong as early as possible and without any avoidable delay. This is so, because often it so happens that misfortunes and obstacles crop up due to delay! Hence there is no condition or pre-requisite in the matter of reconciliation. According to Shi'ah resumption of conjugal relations becomes effective by mere word, action or hint and does not necessitate special formalities. This is so because Allah, the Merciful wishes to provide all facilities to establish love and sincerity and to prevent separation and discord. Why should it not be so? And why should a hint which shows the husband's inclination for continuance of marriage or touching the woman's body with the intention of reconciliation not suffice? Why should it not be so when according to the belief of Shi'ah such a woman (a woman who is observing *Iddah* of a revocable divorce), although divorced, does not cease to be a spouse? Hence if one of the parties dies in these circumstances (i.e. before the expiry of *Iddah*) the other inherits from him/her. They also continue to be close relatives *(Mehram)* even after death and one of them can wash the dead body of the other. So long as the woman observes *Iddah* she is also entitled to subsistence. The man cannot marry her sister and if he has already three wives he is not entitled to select the fourth one because the woman in question (who is observing *Iddah*) continues to enjoy the position of his fourth wife.

In any case can all these arguments convince you of the correctness of the Shi'ah belief regarding the presence of two witnesses being essential at the time of divorce, but unnecessary at the time of reconciliation? If our arguments on the point at issue meet your acceptance and approval we shall thank Allah and shall also be grateful to you. Otherwise we shall be whole-heartedly ready to study your views in this regard. Our object is to understand the reality and follow the truth wherever it may be found and to cast away blind imitation and prejudice. May Allah protect us and you from such things and save us from going astray while traversing the path of truth.

We pray to Almighty Allah to enable you to leave behind such similar monumental works. *Deeds which continually produce virtue, one can obtain better rewards from Allah and are the best assets of human hope.* (Surah al-Kahf, 18:46)

It may also be pointed out that one of the matters which you have discussed very thoroughly is the question of divorcing a woman who is having her monthly course. You have screened the traditions of Abdullah bin Umar very properly.[1]

This is also one of the issues on which all the Shi'ah ulema are unanimous and consider divorcing of a woman having monthly course to be void except in a few exceptional cases.[2]

Muhammad Husayn Kāshiful Ghita

After reproducing this letter the said scholar makes the following addition:

"This is a copy of the letter of Allama Kāshiful Ghita, a great personality of Islam which has been reproduced word for word. I have deleted only one sentence which was not relevant to the subject under discussion and that related to the gift of some books which he sent to me".

Then he adds further, "I shall soon pronounce my views on the contents of this letter in the next issue of the

---

[1] The reference is to a tradition quoted from Abdullah bin Umar to the effect that once the Holy Prophet divorced one of his wives who was having monthly course. From our point of view this tradition is not authentic.

[2] Divorcing a woman having monthly course has been considered permissible in three cases: (i) If she is pregnant (because it is possible that pregnancy may be linked with monthly course). (ii) When the woman is absent. (iii) When sexual intercourse has not taken place.

magazine and shall mention, according to my capacity, the objections which I have in my view to what has been said by him.

Qazı Ahmad Muhammad Shākir Shar'i

This was the entire discussion which the respectable *Qazi* published in the magazine. Later he pursued the discussion in two comparatively more detailed articles published in the 159th and 160th issues which speak of the vastness of his knowledge. In these two articles he endeavoured to put forward different arguments to justify his former view-point. We also replied thereto point by point As, however, it is our intention, that this book should be brief and laconic we ignore the remaining objections and replies thereto. Those interested in studying them may refer to the said copies of the magazine. In all these discussions many useful points and rules which are important in Jurisprudence have been dealt with. In any case our real object is to throw light on the truth

KHUL'A AND MUBARĀT

There is no doubt that the reason for divorce and termination of conjugal relations is hatred and lack of inclination of the two parties for each other or lack of inclination of anyone of them for the other.

If lack of inclination is only on the part of the husband, he has the remedy of divorce in his hand and can achieve his object by resorting to it. In case, however, noninclination is on the part of the wife, she can get divorce from her husband and become free by paying him a sum equal to or exceeding her dower. This type of divorce is called *Khul'a* and is enforced in the following manner· *Fulanatun Taliqun 'alā mā bazalat fahiya Mukhtala'h* (For *fulanatun* the name of the woman is inserted).

In this type of divorce, all the conditions of ordinary divorce is necessary and there is one additional condition also viz. the woman should possess hatred, rather severe hatred for the husband in her mind, as the Holy Qur'an says: *If you (judges) do indeed fear that they (the two*

211

spouses) would be unable to keep the limits ordained by Allah, there is no blame on either of them if the woman gives something (ransom) for her freedom. These are the limits ordained by Allah; so do not trangress them. (Surah al-Baqarah, 2:299).

While commenting on this verse it has been said in the tradition and narrations of the members of the Holy Prophet's progeny that this payment of ransom and separation takes place in this manner that the woman says to her husband: "I do not give effect to your oath and am not prepared to enforce Divine limitations and regulations in your case and also am not ready to wash ceremonially for your sake. I am not going to share your bed and shall bring into your house people whom you hate".

Evidently it is not meant that all these words should be uttered. What is meant is that the woman should have severe abhorrence for her husband and there should be no possibility of their conciliation.

In case both the parties hate each other the consequent divorce is called *Talāqul Mubarāt.* This type of divorce is also governed by all the conditions necessary in the case of an ordinary divorce. However, the man is not entitled to claim from the woman any sum exceeding the dower which he has given her. While pronouncing divorce he says: *Bāra'toki 'ala kaza fa anti Tāliqun* (I divorce you in lieu of . . . .). And for the word *Kaza* he should mention the amount which the woman has given him.

In *Khul'a* and *Mubarāt* divorces there is no possibility of *Ruju'* (restoration of conjugal relations) and it is, therefore, called *Bā'in* divorce (because it occasions separation of husband and wife from each other). However, if the woman insists on the return of something given by her the man also acquires the right of resumption of conjugal relations, provided the period of *Iddah* has not expired.

Zihar, Ila' and Li'ān: According to Shi'ah Faith these three are also the concise causes of the separation of man and woman and consequently become unlawful for each other. The details of this subject and the relevant conditions may be studied in the books on Jurisprudence. As these matters arise very seldom we have decided to ignore their discussion here.

* * * * * *

Inheritance

Inheritance consists of transfer of property or right to another at the time of the owner's death, on account of their consanguinity or casual relationship. The person alive is called the heir, the deceased person the legator, and the property or right involved is termed as legacy (or inheritance). Consanguinity means the same blood or same ancestor, that is one person being the child of the other (like son and father) or both of them being the children of a third person (like two brothers). Casual relationship means relationship occasioned by marriage.

If the share of a heir has been specified in the Holy Qur'an it is said that his inheritance is *Bil Farz*[1] (by obligation) otherwise the inheritance is called *Bilqarābat* i.e. by affinity.

The *Farā'iz* which have been clearly mentioned in the Holy Qur'an, are divided into six portions:

(i) **Half:** There are three parties who inherit one half of the total property of the deceased viz. husband from his wife when there is no child, a daughter provided there is no other child and a sister if she is the solitary one.

(ii) **One Fourth:** Husband's share from the inheritance in the presence of children and similarly wife's share from husband's inheritance when there is no child.

[1]*Farz* 'or *fariza* is something which Allah has specified in the Qur'an.

(iii) **One Eighth:** Share of wife when there are children too.

(iv) **One Third:** Share of mother when there is no child and share of two sisters and a brother or more (however, the sister and brother should be from mother's side).

(v) **Two Third:** Share of two or more daughters when the deceased has not left any male child and in the same manner the share of two paternal or real sisters when there is no brother like them.

(vi) **One Sixth:** Share of father and mother each in spite of the presence of children and the special share of mother in spite of the presence of *Hājib* (i.e. brothers of the deceased) and the share of one maternal brother or one maternal sister.

These are the persons whose shares are *Bil farz* (i.e. by obligation). Others inherit by way of affinity and the general rule about them is that keeping in view the formula of class of inheritance the property of the deceased is divided among them in such a manner that the male gets twice the share of a female.

On the whole the class of inheritance of property consist of three categories and in the presence of people belonging to an upper category those confined to the lower categories do not inherit anything.

First Category: Father, mother and children of the deceased as well as his children's children and to the extent of latter's children in descending order.

Second Category: Paternal grandfather, maternal grandfather, their respective grandfathers and paternal grandfather, maternal grandmother and their respective mothers.

Third Category: Paternal uncles and paternal aunts (father's sisters) and maternal uncles and maternal aunts (mother's sisters). None belonging to this category has a prescribed *Farz* (i.e. share fixed by the Holy Qur'an).

THE ONLY POINT OF DIFFERENCE

'Awl and *Ta'sib:* If the total of the shares of those who are entitled to shares mentioned before (whose shares

have been specified in the Holy Qur'an by way of *farz*) is equal to the total property (like father and mother coupled with two daughters, in that case father and mother get one-sixth each and the two daughters get two third, thereby summing up the total of their shares to a unity i.e. equal to the total property) the manner in which the property is to be divided is abundantly clear. At times, however, the total shares exceed the total property e.g. when the deceased leaves behind father, mother, two daughters and a husband (in that case the share of father and mother is one-sixth each, that of two daughters is one-third and that of husband is one-fourth. Thus the total of the shares comes to 5/4 which exceeds the property by 1/4). At other times however, the position is the reverse of this i.e. the total of the shares is lesser than the total property e.g. when the deceased leaves behind a sister and a widow (in that event the share of the sister and widow being 1/2 and 1/4 respectively total thereof would be 3/4 which is lesser than the total property by 1/4). The position when shares exceed property is called the principle of *'Awl* and when shares fall short of property it is called *Ta'sib*. Orders relating to both of them are explained hereunder.

With the exception of these two (*'Awl* and *Ta'sib*) there is no appreciable difference between Shi'ah and other sects of Muslims in matters of inheritance.

In accordance with repeated narrations quoted from the Imams of the Holy Prophet's progeny, the Shi'ah believe that *'Awl* and *Ta'sib* are baseless viz. the real shares of the heirs are neither more nor less than the total property. And for the determination of real shares of everyone of the heirs in the above cited and other similar cases, action should be taken, as will be explained hereunder, so that the total of the shares will neither exceed nor fall short of total property. A number of distinguished companions of the Holy Prophet concurred with this belief and one of them was Ibn Abbas whose following remarks are well-known: "Allah , who is aware of the number of particles of sand heaped up in the desert, also knows that the shares in inheritance ought not to exceed the total property".

Hence, if something is in excess (i.e. the total of the shares is lesser than the property) the balance should be divided among those who inherit by *Farz* in the ratio of their shares and those who are *'Usabah* should get nothing (*'Usabah* means persons related to the deceased from the side of his/her father and son). For example, a deceased person may have left behind one daughter and parents and his brother and paternal uncle may also be alive (of course the daughter and parents who fall in the first category will be his heirs and the brother and paternal uncle who fall in the second and third categories respectively will be treated as *'Usabah*). In that event, according to Shi'ah belief the daughter, father and mother will get 1/2, 1/6, and 1/6 of the property respectively and the balance will be divided among them in the same ratio. Thus the brother and the paternal uncle will get nothing. However, other ulema consider the remaining 1/6 to be the right of the brother and the paternal uncle.

It should, however, be kept in mind that according to our belief the husband and wife always get their fixed share viz. they neither get anything lesser than their share in the event of shortage of property nor anything more than their share in case the property be in excess. However, if the total property falls short of total shares (as mentioned in previous examples) a reduction will be made in the share of one, two or more sisters, but no change will take place in the shares of husband and wife.

The general rule is that in all cases in which Allah has prescribed the upper and lower limits of the shares of heirs (like husband and wife who get 1/2 and 1/4 respectively if there is no child and 1/4 and 1/8 respectively if there is a child) no subtraction or addition will take place in the shares to be inherited. However, in cases in which only one limit for inheritance has been prescribed shortage will affect that share in the same manner in which excess, if any, will be allocated to it. However, there is difference of opinion as to whether shortage will affect the share of a father as well.

These are the views which have been expressed by

217

Shi'ah ulema in conformity with the teachings of the members of the Holy Prophet's progeny in the matter of total property exceeding total shares. However the Sunni jurists believe that in such cases shortage should be pinned to entire inheritance.

The Shi'ah ulema have advanced numerous arguments based on the Holy Qur'an and Sunnah regarding the futility of 'Awl and Ta'sib which are contained in detailed books written on the subject.

One of the other beliefs regarding inheritance particular to Shi'ah is that according to them the garment, the copy of Holy Qur'an and the ring belonging to the deceased is the right of the eldest son and other heirs have no claim on it. This is called *Habwah* and it carries conditions and details which are contained in relevant books on Jurisprudence. Furthermore, one of the questions particular to Shi'ah is the question of inheritance by the widow of an owner of agricultural property. The Shi'ah believe that the widow does not at all inherit land (or its price). She cannot also inherit the trees or buildings but does inherit their price. This decree is based on traditions reported from the Holy Imams who have quoted them from the Holy Prophet himself. These are the basic points on which differences exist among Shi'ah scholars themselves as well as with Sunni scholars.

* * * * *

Endowments, Gifts and Alms

There are certain methods by which a person can dispense with his property rights over his belongings:

(i) **Fakk-u Milk** (Termination of Ownership): It not only brings to an end one's own proprietary rights over the property but sets it free from encumbrances and ownership so that none can be considered to be its owner in any manner. This is called **Tehrir** (freeing) or setting the property free like setting slaves free or endowing a house or land for a masjid. This sort of endowment is not ownership but termination of ownership. It is evident that such property cannot revert to the ownership of anyone although all sorts of accidents may happen to it.

(ii) Transfer of property to another person against consideration with the consent of the parties by way of verbal contract or something similar to it. This kind of transfer is called **Bay'** and **Sulh** etc.

(iii) Transfer of property to someone else without consideration with the object of spiritual reward in future life and pleasing Almighty Allah. This is called **Sadaqa** (Alms).

Sadaqa is also of two kinds:

(i) Endowment: It is a property which is managed by a trust. It can utilize its income for appropriate uses but cannot transfer the ownership of such an endowment.

(ii) **Sadaqa**: In its special sense **Sadaqa** consists of property which a person transfers to another without any consideration but only to please Allah. In this case the latter person can utilize the property in any manner he likes.

(iv) Transfer of ownership to another person without consideration and without the intention of pleasing Allah (e.g. when a person gives something to another as a token of friendship or on account of attachment with him). This is called *Hibah* (Gift).

Hibah too is of two kinds. Firstly, gift for consideration, which is like one telling the other, "I give you this dress provided you give me that book", and the other person also agrees. Gift of this type is an obligatory contract which cannot be cancelled except with the consent of both the parties. Secondly, gift as an award which carries no consideration

Delivery is necessary for all sorts of gifts without which they are not deemed to be in order. Gift in the shape of award can be revoked even after delivery i.e. the owner of the property can take it back except when the other party consists of kinsmen, husband or wife, and when the original property is destroyed, in which case revocation is not possible.

Sadaqa (Alms) of any kind is not, however, revocable and delivery is also its necessary condition. Hence, when a settler *(Wāqif)* pronounces the formula of endowment and, for example says: "I have settled this house on such and such person for the sake of Allah" and later delivers it to the *Mutawalli* (Custodian or Administrator) or *Mawquf Alayhim* (Beneficiaries) or in the event of his being the *Mutawalli* himself commences to hold it by treating it as an endowment contrary to the previous position becomes impossible and the property in question cannot be purchased, sold, mortgaged, divided etc. For this purpose it makes no difference whether it is a special endowment (e.g. endowment for children) or general endowment (e.g. endowment for schools, caravansaries etc.

Sale of endowed property is permissible only in exceptional circumstances occasioned by extreme necessity. The general rule in this regard is that the endowed property itself can be sold out in two cases:

(i) When the endowed property is impaired in such a manner that it does not carry any appreciable profit or its condition is such tht there is a danger of its being so impaired. (ii) When serious differences arise among the beneficiaries and it is apprehended that these differences will result in assault and loss of life and property.

Notwithstanding this, however, the resale of the endowed property or its division among the beneficiaries is not permissible wihout giving prior intimation to the Magistrate dealing with religious matters and without obtaining his permission. Unfortunately people display great carelessness in these days in the matter of endowments. They undertake their sale very informally and ignore the regulations and the religious procedure on the subject. However, Allah is well aware of the intentions of all.

These are the general beliefs of Shi'ah ulema in the matter of endowments. We have some other comments also on this subject which it is not possible to discuss here.

* * * * * *

Administration of Justice

The authority to adjudicate and to enforce the law for the settlement of various disputes among the people enjoys a very eminent and honourable position in human society. From the Shi'ah view-point adjudication is one of the most fruitful trees of the garden of Prophethood and one of the stages of public administration and vicegerency of Allah on earth as He says: *O Daud! We have appointed you Our Vicegerent on Earth. Therefore judge rightly between the people on the basis of justice"*. (Surah Sād, 38:26) And also the Holy Qur'an says: *But by your Lord, they will not believe (in truth) until they make you judge of what is in dispute between them and find within themselves no dislike of that which you decide, and submit with full submission.* (Surah al-Nisa, 4:65)

Why is the status of the Judge so lofty and honourable? It is because he is the Trustee of Allah on earth for three sacred things viz. the life, property and the honour of the people. However, just as the status of the judge is high, his perils and blunders are also great and irreparable. Expressions regarding the perils of adjudication can be observed in the traditions of the Holy Prophet and the members of his progeny which make one tremble, for example: "The judge sits at the edge of Hell and his tongue is between the two flames of Fire".

It has been reported in a tradition that the Holy Prophet said to Shurayh, the judge "O Shurayh, you are sitting at a place where none other than a Prophet or the Successor of a Prophet or a tyrant sits".

In another tradition it has been reported that the Holy Prophet said: "The head of a person appointed to the office of a judge is cut off without the use of a knife".

Specimens of such traditions are numerous. A point necessary to mention here is: When the orders extracted and inferred by a jurist or a *Mujtahid* by means of reasoning related to a topic they are generally called *Fatwa* (decree) e.g. when, it is said, 'No one has a right to utilize possession of another's property' or 'it is lawful to have sexual intercourse with one's wife but it is unlawful to have such an intercourse with a stranger woman.

However, if the order relates to a personal or particular matter it is called *Qazawat* and *Hukumat* (Judgement and Decision) as for example when it is decided, "This woman is the wife of such and such person and that one is a stranger or this property belongs to such and such person". Both of them are the functions of a righteous *Mujtahid* who possesses the office of a general representative entrusted to him by the Imam.

However, this fact should not be ignored that a Judgement which in fact consists of assessment of matters, whether or not it is linked with dispute and litigation (for example decision about a place being endowed or about the parentage of a person) carries much severer conditions as compared with *Fatwa* and deducing decrees. The reason for this is that correct adjudication is not possible without special aptitude, enormous intelligence, strong insight and quickness of communication. Harm from those persons who occupy this office without possessing the said intellectual merits will be greater than the benefit to be derived from them and the number of their mistakes will be larger than their correct judgement.

Now if a person other than a righteous *Mujtahid* holds charge of this sensitive office, this would, in the opinion of Shi'ah, be one of the major sins and will even border on infidelity. Hence we have always seen that the distinguished Shi'ah ulema and teachers have, as far as possible, desisted from giving decisions and pronouncing judgements and have usually endeavoured to settle by compromise matters involving disputes and litigation. We, too follow this admirable practice of our pious predecessors.

Another thing necessary to mention here is that the main evidence on which a judge should base his judgement has three factors, namely confession, oath and *Bayyinah* i.e. two righteous witnesses. Very extensive discussions have been made by Shi'ah ulema as to whose evidence be given preference if two or more witnesses are opposed to one another (i.e. two persons testify something and another two give evidence to the contrary). Some hold the view that the internal witness should be preferred to the external one.[1]

Others, however, believe that extra preferences should be resorted to. Fortunately a large number of our jurists have written independent and detailed books particularly on the subject of adjudication. Furthermore, all the scholars who have reviewed Shi'ah Jurisprudence have made discussions under the heading *Kitabul Qaza* which covers this field. It is not possible for us to mention here the names of even a few of those books.

We have cited some important portions of discussions relating to adjudication in the fourth volume of *Tehrirul Majallah*. Those interested in the subject may refer to it.

The last point which we consider necessary to mention in connection with this discussion is that if a judge or a ruler who fulfills all the conditions, gives a decision, nobody has a right to oppose it or to find fault with it, and rejection of his decision is in fact rejection of Allah's decision so much so that even another *Mujtahid* does not have the right to interfere in the matter when the aforesaid decision has been given. It is only the chief ruler who has a right to review his own decision and to reverse it if he finds that there has been some error in arriving at it.

---

[1] If something is in the possession of a person and another person claims its ownership each one of them might produce *Bayyinah*. In that case *Bayyinah* of the first party will be **internal** and that of the second party will be the **external** one. There is a difference of opinion among our scholars as to which of them should be given preference.

Hunting and Slaughtering of Animals

The animals, the meat of which is allowed to be eaten, such as sheep, goat, cow, camel, deer, domestic fowl etc. have to be slaughtered in the prescribed manner. Otherwise if they die their natural death or are killed by beating, wounding or in any way other than the prescribed one their flesh is not lawful.

There are two kinds of animals. Firstly, those which are unclean in themselves and cannot be purified by any means such as dog and pig. Secondly, those animals which are clean in themselves. (All animals, except dog and pig, are clean in themselves.)

Since, the first kind of animals are not clean it is not lawful to eat their meat. They cannot become clean and lawful under any circumstances.

In case the second kind of animals die they will be unclean and their meat will also be unlawful unless religious purification takes place.[1]

The religious purification of animals takes place in two ways.

(i) **Hunting:** Hunting is lawful in two circumstances only. Firstly by means of hunting dogs who are duly

---

[1] It means that the prescribed ceremonies and conditions of slaughtering should be observed. In case, however, such purification does take place they remain clean in the same manner in which they were while alive but their meat will be lawful only in case they are not wild beasts and carnivorous animals.

trained and do not have the habit of eating their animals of prey. A person who sends a dog for hunting should, besides being a Muslim, say *Bismillah* (In the Name of Allah) while sending it and should also not lose its sight. An animal of prey which such a dog catches fulfilling all these conditions is lawful.

The second method is hunting with weapons such as arrow, sword, spear and even the bullets of a rifle if they rend the body.

The meat of the lawful wild animals and birds killed with hunting weapons is legally edible provided the following five conditions are observed.

(i)   The weapon must be incisive or sharp, and must not be of the nature of a net, a stick or a stone.

(ii) The hunter must be a Muslim.

(iii) He should utter the Name of Allah at the time of using his weapon.

(iv) The weapon must be used with the intention of killing the game. If it is killed accidentally, its flesh is not lawful.

(v)   When the hunter reaches the game, it should be already dead. If it is caught alive and there is sufficient time to slaughter, it must be slaughtered.

Hunting in circumstances other than the two mentioned above is unlawful whether the animal is hunted with a snare or the like or with the help of animals other than hunting dogs. In case, however, an animal is caught alive by these means and then slaughtered it is lawful.

(ii) **Slaughtering:** The animals, the meat of which is allowed to be eaten, have to be slaughtered in the prescribed manner. If they die in any way other than the prescribed one their flesh is not lawful.

An act of slaughter to be legal must satisfy the following five conditions:

(i)   The person who slaughters must be a Muslim.

(ii) The animal while being slaughtered should be facing the *Qiblah*.

(iii) He must utter the Name of Allah when slaughtering.

(iv) He must cut the throat of the animal with a sharp implement made of iron in a way that the jugular artery,

226

jugular vein, oesophagus canal and trachea are cut. (If, however, an iron-made instrument is not available it should suffice if the animal is slaughtered with some other incisive implement).

(v) It must move after having been slaughtered.

In the case of a camel the only prescribed method of its slaughter is *Nahr*, which means thrusting a knife or any other sharp implement into the cavity between its neck and chest. Other conditions are the same in this case also.

If for some reason it is not possible to slaughter an animal (e.g. when it falls down into a well or is unruly) it can be made to submit by means of a sword or the like. It is lawful if it is killed with those strokes but should be slaughtered in case it remains alive.

Animals whose blood does not gushes out are usually unlawful except the fish with scales. If the fish having scales is caught alive and dies after having been taken out of water, it is lawful. But if it dies inside the water it is unlawful. The fish having no scales is unlawful, even if it is caught alive and dies out of water.

An interesting story: Muhammad bin Nu'mān Ahwal alias Mumin Tāq (who was one of the learned and witty disciples of Imam Ja'far Sadiq) relates thus: One day I went to see Abu Hanifah. I saw that he had a large number of books before him so much so that the books screened him from my sight. Then the following conversation took place:

Abu Hanifah: Do you see these books?

Mumin Tāq: Yes.

Abu Hanifah: They all relate to orders regarding "Divorce".

Mumin Tāq: Allah has made us independent of all these books of your by means of one verse in the Holy Qur'an wherein He says: *Prophet and believers, if you want to divorce your wives, you should divorce them at a time after which they can start their waiting period. Let them keep an account of the number of the days in the waiting period. Have fear of Allah, your Lord.* (Surah al-Talāq, 65:1)

Abu Hanifah: Have you ever enquired from your friend (Imam Sadiq) regarding this problem as to whether the meat of a cow which comes out of the river is lawful or not?

Mumin Tāq: Yes. He has told me that it is lawful to eat any animal which has scales, whether it be a camel or a cow and the one which does not have scales is unlawful. And the purification of a fish is that it should die while out of water.[1]

* * * * * *

[1]It appears that by assuming this strange problem Abu Hanifah wanted to render Mumin Tāq speechless who used to say, "We have acquired general rules from the Holy Qur'an and the traditions of Ahlul Bayt which provide replies to all secondary problems which may arise". However, he (Mumin Tāq) immediately stated the general rule about aquatic animals which he had heard from Imam Sadiq and thus gave him (Abu Hanifah) an appropriate reply.

Foods and Beverages

According to the Shi'ah Faith the eating and drinking of all foul things such as carrion, blood etc. and every food and beverage polluted by such things is forbidden. Similarly, all dirty and obnoxious things such as clay, mud, polluted water and putrid and rotten food are also forbidden.

As has already been mentioned the aquatic animals are usually unlawful with the exception of fish having scales. The eggs of these animals are also governed by the same rule i.e. if their meat is lawful their eggs are also lawful and if their meat is unlawful their eggs are also unlawful.

As regards land animals, the meat of the following few is lawful, viz. sheep, goat, cow, camel, deer, mountain ram, wild cow and wild ass. The meat of horse, mule and donkey is, however, abominable.

If a lawful animal eats human excrement it becomes unlawful and is called *Jallāl* animal. In order to make it clean and lawful it is necessary that it should be given exclusively pure food for some time (the period differs from animal to animal) as explained in the book Articles of Islamic Acts, ISP 1982.

The meat of all predatory animals like lion, wolf, bear, jackal etc. is unlawful. Similar is the case with hare, fox, lizard, field-mouse and other wild animals as well as invertebrate animals like snakes, scorpion, wasp, worms and the like. Some other animals such as elephant, rat, monkey, frog and tortoise are also forbidden.

The meat of the birds which possess hooked beaks and talons and are treated to be predatory birds like eagle, hawk, falcon etc. is unlawful. As regards others if anyone of the following three signs (each of which is related to one condition of the bird) is available in it, it is lawful and otherwise unlawful:

(i)   If at the time of flying, it flaps the wings more than keeping them straight, it is lawful, otherwise unlawful.

(ii)   If, while the bird is sitting on the ground, we see that it possesses *Sisa* (spur which grows on the hind part of the feet of some birds) it is lawful, otherwise unlawful.

(iii) When a bird has been slaughtered and any of the above-mentioned two signs cannot be traced in it, it is lawful if it possesses a crop.

For these reasons bat, peacock, different kinds of bees and the like are usually unlawful. The meat of crows too is unlawful if they are carrion-eaters and lawful if they are grass-eaters.

Urine is the worst liquids but alcoholic beverages are even worse than that. As a general rule everything intoxicant or narcotic which is definitely injurious for human health comes under this category.

Shi'ah are very strict in the matter of alcoholic beverages so much so that by this they are distinguished from other Muslims.

Such unusually shocking and extremely alarming narrations have been quoted from the Ahlul Bayt about alcoholic beverages that they make even the reckless sinners tremble. They have repeatedly cursed all those persons who, in any way, assist in drinking of wine, collect and brew grapes and sell or drink wine. It should suffice to point out that in our religion it is called the mother of evils so much so that from some of the traditions of the Ahlul Bayt it can be learnt that sitting by a dinner table on which wine is also served is unlawful. And possibly the point involved in this severity is to ensure protection from fumes which occasionally rise from wine and have an impact on various foods laid on the dinner table or from some of its contaminated articles which might enter the throats and noses of the people sitting round the table.

Experience and medical research have proved that alcoholic beverages and narcotic drugs are injurious to health and undermine physical and mental fitness. From moral and social point of view also they are the source of many evils. A drunken man loses the control of his senses and is liable to foolish action and undignified behaviour. Such a person may even commit crimes. These poisonous stuffs have ruined many a family. People get addicted to them just to seek momentary exhilaration and false satisfaction. These things not only do not resolve the worries of their life, but also make them further complicated. Instead of making life happy they cause infatuation and frustration.

How sublime, exact and complete is the Law of Islam and how much misfortune and destitute are the Muslims who have abandoned it and have consequently lost themselves. I hope this state of affairs will not continue and Allah will bring about in future a change in our thoughts and behaviours.

This was a short account of the lawful and unlawful foods and beverages. However, there are a large number of problems related to this topic but it is not possible to deal with in this brief treatise.

* * * * * *

Punishments

In Islam penalties and punishments for felonies and other crimes have been prescribed which should be awarded under the supervision of the Islamic Government. Their object is to ensure security of social order and to uproot mischief from human society.

These punishments are called *Hudud* and according to the Shi'ah Faith they are as under:

(i) Punishment for Adultery and Fornication

When a sane person commits an immoral act knowingly and wilfully with a stranger woman in a manner opposed to chastity, it is obligatory for the Islamic Government to administer him one hundred lashes. In case he is married he should also be stoned *(Rajm)*. However, if that be not the case, one hundred lashes should suffice. Thereafter, his head should be shaved and he should be banished from his town for a period of one year.

If the woman also gives in to this act willingly she should be subjected to punishments like man.

In case this offence has taken place with relations of the same blood or foster relations, or father's wife, or if a *Zimmi* (i.e. a non-Muslim living under the protection of an Islamic Government) commits this offence with a Muslim woman or this act is committed with a woman under coercion or violence (i.e. rape) the penalty is death.

Adultery can be proved either by making confession four times or by the evidence of four just male witnesses or by the evidence of three just males and two just females.

If only two just men and four just women testify, the only punishment of one hundred lashes will be awarded and the offender will not be stoned.

Adultery cannot be proved by any testimony lesser than those mentioned above. In case only three or two persons give evidence regarding adultery, not only will their evidence carry any weight, but they themselves may also be awarded punishment for accusing others of adultery *(Qazf)* as will be explained later.

In the case of evidence regarding adultery it is necessary that the testimony of the witnesses should be correct beyond doubt and all of them should be eye witnesses.

If a person admits having committed adultery *(Zina al-Muhsina)* but later denies, he shall not be stoned.

If a person admits having committed adultery and later repents, the Islamic Ruler may decide to forgive or punish him in the manner he deems expedient. In case, however, the offender repents, after the witnesses have deposed, his repentance will be ineffectual and he shall be awarded punishment.

If a person is found guilty of adultery twice and is awarded punishment each time and commits this offence for the third time, he should be executed.

Punishment cannot be enforced against a pregnant woman before delivery or against a sick person before recovery.

(ii) Punishment for Sodomy and Lesbianism

Punishment for none of the major offences is equal to that which is prescribed for this dirty act so much so that the punishment of burning alive has not been fixed in Islam for any offence other than this.

The Islamic Ruler has the discretion to punish the culprit either by killing or stoning, or burning alive or hurling down from such height that his bones should break.

As regards the person who has been the object of sodomy he may be sentenced to death in case he is sane, adult and free in his actions. If, however, he is a minor the ruler should subject him to *Ta'zir*.[1]

The manner of proving sodomy is the same as prescribed for adultery

Lesbianism can also be proved in the same aforesaid ways and the punishment prescribed for it is one hundred lashes for both the sinners. It is also probable that if the women are married the punishment of stoning may be fixed for them.

Punishment for a person who acts as a pimp is twenty five lashes. Thereafter, his head is shaved and he is banished from the town. The method of proving such an act is evidence by two just witnesses or confession made twice.

(iii) Punishment for False Accusation

Whosoever accuses a Muslim, and is of full age and a free person, of an offence which carries punishment (e.g. adultery, fornication, sodomy, lesbianism, or drinking wine) but cannot prove it, should be administered eighty lashes. However, if he proves it by means of just witnesses or the person concerned confirms it himself the punishment ceases to be valid in his case.

To prove that a person has attributed such an offence to another (without justification) it is necessary that there should be two just witnesses or the person concerned should make a confession in this behalf twice.

If a person attributes something discomforting to another in his face that does not exist in the latter (e.g. says, "O libertine! O debauchee! O leper!") he should be subjected to *Ta'zir*. Whoever claims to be a prophet or says something abusive or unbecoming about the Holy Prophet or Holy Imam should be executed.

---

[1]*Ta'zir* carries the meaning of admonition. It covers all the corporal punishments which are not prescribed in law and decision about their extent depends on the circumstances, persons, conditions and discretion of the ruler. In most of the cases their extent has been fixed at twenty five lashes.

(iv) **Punishment for Drinking Alcoholic Beverages**

Punishment prescribed for a person who is of age and who drinks knowingly and intentionally wine, beer, grape water (before two thirds of it is evaporated by boiling) or any kind of alcoholic beverage, whether new or old, is eighty lashes on his bare back. In case he repeats this action and is again awarded punishment but even then does not desist and again repeats this action, his punishment, when he is found guilty for the fourth time, is that he should be execu.ed This would be the position if he considers these beverages to be unlawful. In case, however, he denies their being unlawful and drinks them he is an apostate and should be awarded capital punishment in the very first instance.

Those who undertake sale of wine should, in the first instance, be advised to repent. If they repent and abandon this business they would not be subjected to any punishment. However, if they insist on continuing this business, they should be executed.

(v) **Punishment for Theft**

If a sane person who is also of age, commits theft and steals from a secured place (i.e. secured with lock, chain, chest etc) property worth about 1/4th of a *mithqāl* (4.5 grain) of pure gold or more, a reference should be made to the Islamic Ruler. In case the offence is proved by *bayyinah* or the thief himself makes a confession four fingers of his right hand should be cut off. If he commits this offence for the second time, a part of his left foot should be cut off. In case he commits this offence for the third time he should be awarded life-imprisonment. And if he repeats this offence even then, he should be awarded capital punihsment.

If before being awarded punishment a person has committed theft a number of times he should be subjected to only one punishment.

In case a minor or an insane person commits theft he can be awarded punishment in the shape of *Ta'zir* under the orders of the ruler.

235

In case the stolen property is destroyed, it is necessary that the thief should pay compensation for it. Compensation can be ordered if the person committing theft makes admission once or a just witness testifies it on oath.

If a father steals something from the property of his child (son or daughter) the punishment (cutting of fingers) is not enforced against him. However, if the child (son or daughter) steals from the property of his/her father he/she is awarded punishment subject to the conditions mentioned above.

(vi) Punishment for Violence and Corruption

If anyone takes weapons in hand (whether in the land, sea or air) and threatens people with the object of looting their property it is the duty of the Islamic Government to award him one of these punishments which have been mentioned in the Holy Qur'an: *The only punishment for those who fight against Allah and His Messenger and try to spread corruption in the land is that they shall be killed, crucified, or their hands and feet shall be cut off from the opposite side or they shall be banished.* (Surah al-Ma'ida, 5:33).

And whenever the ruler orders the banishment of that person, he (the ruler) should write to the people of that town (to which he is banished) that they should refrain from sharing their victuals with him, or associating with him or having any dealings with him until he repents.

In case a person attacks the houses of the people, and is killed in the process, his blood carries no value like the blood of a person who violates the honour of a woman or a girl. In such an event the inmates of the house have a right to defend themselves by whatever means they can and if the attacker is killed in the meantime his blood has no value.

As regards persons who are guilty of embezzlement, fraud and forgery or giving false evidence, it is for the Islamic Ruler to award them such punishment as should serve as a deterrent for them and a lesson for others.

(vii) Other Miscellaneous Punishments

If a person commits an unnatural offence with a quadruped he should be punished in the shape of *Ta'zir*. If he commits this offence time and again and does not desist from it in spite of being subjected to *Ta'zir* every time, he should be executed.

If the animal belongs to the category of those animals whose meat is lawful, the same will become unlawful after the perpetration of this act. Similarly the flesh of its future off-spring would be unlawful. Such an animal should be slaughtered in the first instance and thereafter its corpse should be burnt and destroyed. The person guilty of this act, is required to pay the price of the animal to its owner. In case the particular animal gets mixed up with other animals, one animal should be selected by casting a lot.

In case, however, the animal belongs to the category of those whose flesh is not usually eaten (e.g. horse and the like) it should be taken to another town and sold there. The proceeds of the sale should be given away as alms in the path of Allah and the person who has been guilty of the act in question should pay the price of the animal to the owner. There are two ways of proving the perpetration of the act in question, viz. testimony of two just witnesses or confession by the offender twice.

When a person commits adultery with the dead body of a stranger woman, maximum punishment which would have been applicable in the event of her being alive, would be enforced in a severer manner. In case, however, a man commits sexual intercourse with the dead body of his spouse or slave-girl he should be subjected to *Ta'zir*.

As in the case of adultery while alive, as well as in the case of sodomy, the method of proving this act (i.e. sexual intercourse with a dead body) is the evidence of four just witnesses.

Everyone has a right to defend his life, property and honour by all means available to him. However, as far as possible, he should resort to easier means but if such easier means do not bear fruit he can gradually resort to more effective means so as to ward off the invader by undoing his action.

237

As and when a person peeps into the house of some-one from above the wall and does not desist from this act in spite of being warned, the inmates of the house have a right to drive him away by stoning him or by any other means. Even if his blood is shed in this process nobody will be held responsible for it.

* * * * *

Retaliation and Compensation

Killing of an innocent person is one of the serious crimes in Islam. It is this very murder which has been referred to in the Holy Qur'an as the mischief and corruption in the land. The Holy Book also says, *Whoever kills a believer intentionally, his recompense shall be Hell, wherein he shall abide for ever.* (Surah al-Nisa, 4:93) Similarly amputation or rendering useless any part of human body is also a great crime.

In any case a felony (whether it be murder or rendering the limbs useless) does not fall beyond one of the following three categories, viz: (i) Intentional (ii) Resembling an intentional one (iii) By mistake.

The meaning of intentional felony is quite clear. As regards felony resembling an intentional one, it means that though that act was committed by the person concerned intentionally he did not mean to kill the other. For example one person may strike the other by way of chastisement and the means used for it may also not be such as usually culminate in death. However, by sheer chance and without the former having intended or thought of it, the other person is killed This will be called "resembling an intentional murder".

As regards felony comitted by mistake, it means that the persons concerned should have intended neither manslaughter nor the basic action which has led to it. For example, one may intend hunting a bird but may suddenly hit a man. Or that he may raise the rifle or revolver and a

239

bullet may be fired from it accidentally, killing another.

One of the clear examples of felony commited by mistake is that committed by one during sleep or due to error, without having had any prethought about it. Actions emanating from an insane person or from a child not possessing power of discrimination or even from a child possessing such power are also tantamount to a mistake, because even an intentional act of a minor is treated to be a mistake.

If a person wishes to kill another without justification, but accidentally hits a third person whose blood too demands security and respect, he will be treated to have committed an intentional felony. In case, however, he wishes to kill a man whose killing is justified, but accidentally hits another person, his action will be treated to be a felony resembling an intentional one

It may also be mentioned that in the cases stated above there is no difference between *Mubāshirat* (Directly) or *Tasbib* (Indirectly) i.e. it is immaterial whether the person concerned commits felony with his own hands or provides means which culminate in its being committed by someone else (of course, in case the providing of means is such that the action should be attributed to the person who has provided them). Similarly there is no difference between individual action and joint action. i.e. a felony is unlawful whether committed by an individual alone or by a number of persons jointly and the person or persons concerned should be awarded punishment.

According to law, punishment by way of retaliation *(Qisās)* can be awarded in the case of intentional felony alone and only compensation or blood-money *(Diyat)* is admissible for felony by mistake. Furthermore, retaliation is admissible in case the person who has committed felony is sane and adolescent. Hence, retaliation cannot be applied to a minor even of ten years old, whether he has committed felony with regard to a minor or otherwise. The same is the case with an insane person when he commits a felony in the state of insanity (whether his insanity be permanent or periodical). It is also immaterial whether or not the other person is insane like him, for retatiation is not admissible in either case. The reason for it is that his intentional act is also tantamount to error which invites only compensation. The compensation in his case should also be paid by his near relations from his father's side like brothers, paternal uncles and paternal cousins.

These are the conditions of retaliation as far as the felon is concerned. As regards the person on whom felony is committed, it is necessary that he, too, should be sane and of age. In case, therefore, a minor is subjected to felony, compensation and not retaliation would be admissible (although some scholars believe that retaliation is admissible in such cases as well). The same is the case with an insane person. Another condition of retaliation is that the felony should not have been committed under compulsion. This condition is, however, attached only to cases other than murder and compulsion is immaterial in this case. In other words a person is not permitted to kill an innocent person on the ground that he has been forced to do so or because his own life is in danger or he apprehends some other harm. The reason for it is that there can be no *Taqayyah* (Dissimulation) in the matter of murder. He should be subjected to retaliation and execution. As regards the person who compelled him to commit murder he should be imprisoned for life. Another condition is that the person who has been subjected to felony should be innocent and his blood should be worthy of respect. In case he is one who must be punished by death, the question of his killer being subjected to retaliation does not arise.

If the felon is the father or grandfather of the person subjected to felony (whether the grandfather be proximate or not) he is liable to pay compensation which should be distributed among the heirs of the victim but he himself (i.e. the felon) should not take any share out of it. Moreover, a Muslim is subjected to retaliation for having committed felony only against another Muslim, and similarly a free man vis-a-vis a free man or a free woman vis-a-vis a free woman. However, if a free man is murdered on account of his having committed felony upon a free

241

woman it is the duty of the guardian of the woman to pay to the kinsmen of that man compensation equivalent to half the prescribed amount because compensation paid in such a case is treated to be equal to twice as much as ordinary compensation.

However, when the position is reverse of that mentioned above i.e. if a free woman is subjected to retaliation for having killed a free man and is consequently executed it is not necessary that any compensation should be paid to the kinsmen of the murdered person because a felon cannot be subjected to any penalty over and above the capital punishment.

Amount of Compensation: Compensation for the murder of a free Muslim is one hundred camels or two hundred cows or one thousand sheep or two hundred suits of dress, everyone of which should consist of two sets, or one thousand dinars. Every one of these is a sufficient compensation.

As has been pointed out the kinsmen of a murdered person are entitled to claim retaliation. In case, however, they agree to accept compensation, retaliation would lapse. It is also necessary that the said compensation should be paid to them within the maximum period of one year.

In the case of murder resembling an intentional one, however, only compensation is allowed and the maximum period for its payment is two years. Similarly in the case of murder committed by mistake, compensation is allowed but the maximum period for its payment is upto three years and at least one third of it should be paid every year.

Now as regards felonies which result in the parts of the body being rendered useless e.g. amputation of hand or foot or blinding the eye and the like. In such cases, if the felony is committed intentionally the felon may be subjected to retaliation viz. an eye for an eye, an ear for an ear, a tooth for a tooth etc. as has been mentioned in the Holy Qur'an

In case. however any part of the body is rendered useless as result of mistake or something resembling it, there is a special compensation for that part. Some of these compensations are about as much as the total compensation for a human life, while others are half of it and still others are even lesser than half. Generally the compensation for those part which are single (e.g. nose or male organ) is equal to one full compensation. However, as regards parts which are more than one (like eyes, ears, hands, feet etc.), compensation equal to one half of full compensation is payable if one of them is destroyed, but in the event of both of them being destroyed full compensation becomes due.

Compensation for intentional felonies or those resembling intentional felonies is the responsibility of the felon, but in the case of felony by mistake, it is payable by felon's kinsmen from father's side like brothers, paternal uncles and paternal cousins.

The above is a brief description of Shi'ah beliefs relating to retaliation and compensation. Further information in this behalf may be obtained from detailed books written on the subject.

Our intention has been only to point out some of the Shi'ah beliefs relating to different items of Jurisprudence. As such we have not at all mentioned a large number of topics and branches of Jurisprudence like time-bargains, sale of consumer goods, sale of fruits on trees, sale of animals and similarly, monopoly, mortgage, loans, deposits, tenancy, competition, surety, assignment, guarantee, promises, atonements, etc. although all these subjects have been discussed in detail in Ja'frite Jurisprudence.

O Scholars of Islam! Have you observed anything in these propositions which we have put forward regarding Shi'ah Faith which may destroy the foundation of Islam?[1]

Has any of these things been copied from Judaism, Christianity or Zoroastrianism? Can anything be observed in these discussions which may be opposed to the principles and commands of Islam or beyond the span of the Holy Qur'an and the Sunnah.

[1]This is with reference to the attacks made on Shi'ite Islam by Ahmad Amin in his book **Fajrul Islam.**

And has not the time now arrived that just and knowledgeable persons should give a clear verdict in this behalf and the ignorant people should desist from falsehood and calumny after becoming acquainted with these facts?

It is possible that Almighty Allah may, under the auspices of these discussions, change this dispersion into unity and alliance and the fear which Muslims entertain in their hearts against one another may disappear so that all Muslim brethren should come together under the standard of the Holy Qur'an and regain their former greatness and leadership of the world. It should, however, be remembered that unless the Muslims forsake unjustified religious bigotry and racial fanaticism, this great wish will not be fulfilled and they will not regain their honour and real life. I have always reiterated these words that we should treat all Islamic Schools of Thought to be respectable and consider ourselves above all these differences. The Muslim brothers should sincerely exchange love and friendship with each other and should share their profits in the manner that they should work for their benefit by themselves. They should not deal with one another in a manner which should damage their authority and supremacy. They should, in the real sense of the word like the same thing for their religious brethren which they like for themselves. However, it is possible that with all the differences which exist generally among the Muslims today some persons may consider the establishment of such friendly relations and acquisition of sublime attributes to be only a dream and wishful thinking. Nevertheless, we have not lost hope in Divine Mercy and do not consider it beyond the Grace of Allah that He may infuse fresh spirit into the lifeless frame of this despairing nation and favour it with a new life so that the eyes of Muslims may acquire sight and they may, with Allah's Grace, recover from this stupor.

* * * * * *

THE END

ISLAMIC BROTHERHOOD

Though the Sunni Muslims differ with us (Shi'ah Muslims) on the question of caliphate and succession to the Holy Prophet, We consider them to be our brethren and co-religionists.

Our Allah is the same; and our Ka'bah is the same. We consider their honour and progress; their success and victory to be our honour and progress; their success and victory to be our success and victory, and their disgrace and defeat to be our disgrace and defeat. We share with them both in happiness and grief.

In this respect we have been inspired by our great leader, Imam Ali ibn Abi Talib. Had he wanted, he could have defended his right to caliphate, but in the larger interest of Islam, he not only abstained form fighting the caliphs, but also rendered help to them on critical occasions. He never hesitated to take any action in the interests of the Muslim Ummah.

We believe that the only way for the Muslim world to live as a strong nation, regain its past glory and get rid of foreign domination, is to keep the Muslim away from dissension and discord, and to let them concentrate their energies on the achievement of their goals, so that they may take collective step in the way in the glory of Islam, thus ensuring progress and prosperity for the Muslims.

Obey Allah and His Messenger. Do not quarrel with each other lest you fail or lose honour. (Al-Anfal, 8:46)

Hold fast all of you together to Allah's bond (Islam) an do not be divided (among yourself). (Ale Imran, 3:103)

ISLAMIC SEMINARY PUBLICATIONS

(English Section)

1. ARTICLES OF ISLAMIC ACTS
    By Ayatullah al-Uzma Sistani

2. ISLAM AND SCHOOLS OF ECONOMICS
    ISLAMIC POLITICAL SYSTEM
    HE, HIS MESSENGER AND HIS MESSAGE
    A SHORT HISTORY OF ILMUL USUL
    TRENDS OF HISTORY IN QUR'AN
    By Ayatullah Muhammad Baqir al-Sadr

3. THE MARTYR
    MAN AND HIS DESTINY
    (On Qaza and Qadr)
    MASTER AND MASTERSHIP
    (On Walayat in Islam)
    WOMEN AND HER RIGHTS (H/B)
    MAN AND UNIVERSE (H/B)
    By Allama Murtaza Mutahhari

4. UNIVERSALITY OF ISLAM
    SHI'ITE ISLAM
    By Allama Muhammad Husayn Tabatabai

5. LESSONS FROM ISLAM
    STORIES FROM QUR'AN
    (On the Lives of the Prophets) H/B
    By Muhammad Suhufi

6. PHILOSOPHY OF ISLAM (H/B)
    By Dr. Husayni Behishti &
    Dr. Jawad Bahonar

7. THE MESSAGE (H/B)
    (On the life of the Holy Prophet)
    By Ja'far Subhani

246

8. PEAK OF ELOQUENCE (H/B)
   (Nahjul Balagha)
   Translation by Askari Ja'fari

9. THE VOICE OF HUMAN JUSTICE (H/B)
   (On the life of Imam Ali)
   By George Jordac

10. MANNERS & ETIQUETTES
    By Allamah Majlisi-I

11. A PROBE INTO THE HISTORY OF ASHURA
    By Dr. Muhammad Ibrahim Ayati

12. A PROBE INTO THE HISTORY OF HADITH
    By Allamah Murtaza al-Askari

13. THE BELIEFS OF THE SHI'ITE SCHOOL
    By Allamah Muhammad Riza Muzaffar

14. THE SHI'AH - ORIGIN AND FAITH
    By Allama Muhammad Husayn Kashif al-Ghita

15. THE DESPOTIC RULERS
    By Allamah Muhammad Jawad Mughniyah

16. THE EARLY HISTORY OF ISLAM
    By Sayyid Safdar Husayn

17. A TEXT BOOK OF ETHICS
    By Allamah Muhammad Naraqi

18. AMMAR YASIR - the companion of the Holy Prophet
    By Sadruddin Sharafuddin

19. IT REMOVES THE MISCONCEPTION
    ABOUT CALIPHS' CALIPHATE .
    By M. A. A. Sattar

20. LESSONS FROM QUR'AN (H/B)
    By Mohsin Qaraiti

21. BILAL OF AFRICA
    By Husayn Malika Ashtiyani